Advanced Robotic Vehicles Programming

An Ardupilot and Pixhawk Approach

Julio Alberto Mendoza-Mendoza
Victor Gonzalez-Villela
Gabriel Sepulveda-Cervantes
Mauricio Mendez-Martinez
Humberto Sossa-Azuela

Apress®

Advanced Robotic Vehicles Programming: An Ardupilot and Pixhawk Approach

Julio Alberto Mendoza-Mendoza
FI UNAM, Ciudad de Mexico, Mexico

Victor Gonzalez-Villela
FI UNAM, Ciudad de Mexico, Mexico

Gabriel Sepulveda-Cervantes
CIDETEC IPN, Ciudad de Mexico, Mexico

Mauricio Mendez-Martinez
UPIITA IPN, Ciudad de México, Mexico

Humberto Sossa-Azuela
CIC IPN, Ciudad de México, Mexico

ISBN-13 (pbk): 978-1-4842-5530-8
https://doi.org/10.1007/978-1-4842-5531-5

ISBN-13 (electronic): 978-1-4842-5531-5

Managing Director, Apress Media LLC: Welmoed Spahr
Acquisitions Editor: Natalie Pao
Development Editor: James Markham
Coordinating Editor: Jessica Vakili

Distributed to the book trade worldwide by Springer Science+Business Media New York, 233 Spring Street, 6th Floor, New York, NY 10013. Phone 1-800-SPRINGER, fax (201) 348-4505, e-mail orders-ny@springer-sbm.com, or visit www.springeronline.com. Apress Media, LLC is a California LLC and the sole member (owner) is Springer Science + Business Media Finance Inc (SSBM Finance Inc). SSBM Finance Inc is a **Delaware** corporation.

For information on translations, please e-mail rights@apress.com, or visit www.apress.com/rights-permissions.

Apress titles may be purchased in bulk for academic, corporate, or promotional use. eBook versions and licenses are also available for most titles. For more information, reference our Print and eBook Bulk Sales web page at www.apress.com/bulk-sales.

Any source code or other supplementary material referenced by the author in this book is available to readers on GitHub via the book's product page, located at www.apress.com/978-1-4842-5530-8. For more detailed information, please visit www.apress.com/source-code.

Printed on acid-free paper

To my grandma, girlfriend, teachers, students, friends,
co-workers, and family.
Julio Alberto Mendoza-Mendoza, 2019
Xijtemiki, ximonekilli, xichiua.
Dream it, wish it, do it.

Table of Contents

About the Authors

Julio Alberto Mendoza-Mendoza earned his computing doctoral degree at CIC IPN in 2016, where he specialized in underactuated robotics, UAS, and intelligent and nonlinear control. He also earned his advanced-technologies master's degree and mechatronics-engineering bachelor at UPIITA IPN in 2011 and 2008, respectively. Currently, Julio is working on five patents related to his research field and developing his flying serial-robot manipulator theory at FI UNAM through his postdoctoral 2017 DGAPA grant.

Victor Gonzalez-Villela acknowledges the financial support of the DGAPA postdoctoral fellowship, UNAM, given to the first author and above mentioned, the partial financial support of the "Support Program for Research and Technological Innovation Projects" (PAPIIT), UNAM, and the CONACYT for its support given via its "National Researchers System" (SNI file 57520). He wants to thank all of those who contributed in making this book a reality and the members of the Mechatronics Research Group at UNAM for their unconditional support and friendship (https://mechatronicsrg.wixsite.com/home).

Gabriel Sepulveda-Cervantes wants to thank to God and his family for the life and opportunity to grow and for the support received in all his projects. He also wants to thank his hobbies and jobs, the research in animation, virtual reality, haptics, and videogame programming. If you want to play videogame tournaments or work with him, maybe you can challenge him on UMVC3 where he can be found as TA Wero or through his workgroups at https://edissa.com.mx/ and CIDETEC IPN. He also thanks the IPN project under grant number SIP 20190245.

ABOUT THE AUTHORS

Mauricio Mendez-Martinez acknowledges his family and his students, teachers, and colleagues at UPIITA IPN.

Humberto Sossa-Azuela would like to acknowledge first of all his wife, Rocio, for her kindness, patience, and unconditional support. Secondly, he would like to thank his colleagues for their professional work to complete this book. To end up, he would like to express his deepest acknowledgment to the National Polytechnic Institute (IPN) and CONACYT for the always timely economical support to finish this project under grant numbers SIP 20190007 and 65 (Frontiers of Science), respectively.

Acknowledgments

Julio Alberto Mendoza-Mendoza and Victor Gonzalez-Villela are with the Advanced Engineering Center (CIA), Faculty of Engineering, UNAM. Gabriel Sepulveda is with the CIDETEC of the IPN. Mauricio Mendez is with the Interdisciplinary Professional Unit of Engineering and Advanced Technologies (UPIITA), IPN. Humberto Sossa-Azuela is with the Computer Research Center (CIC), IPN.

This book is a result of the Quetzalcoatl, Ehecatl, Papalotl, and Kukulkan projects for the design and operation of robotic flying arms, with five patent procedures in Mexico and with the invaluable collaboration of

- The National Autonomous University of Mexico (UNAM), through its DGAPA "Program of Postdoctoral Scholarships at UNAM" given to the first author, who is a postdoctoral researcher, since 2018, at the Advanced Engineering Centre, Division of Mechanical and Industrial Engineering, Faculty of Engineering, UNAM

- The National Polytechnic Institute (IPN), which also partially sponsored these works with SIP project 20164905

The first author wants to express appreciation for the access and use of laboratories and facilities and the participation of researchers from ESCOM, CMPL, UPP, Cinvestav, and CIDETEC, Dr. Carlos Aguilar Ibañez, Miguel Santiago Suarez Castañon, Ramon Silva Ortigoza, Ricardo Barron, Erik Zamora, Jesus Chimal, Rogelio Lozano-Leal, Eduardo Steed, Filiberto Muñoz, Leonardo Fonseca Ruiz, Jose Antonio Aquino, and Ignacio Garcia. Special mentions go to Orlando Garcia Perez and Manuel Jesus Rodriguez

ACKNOWLEDGMENTS

from UAEH and UPIITA because without them this book would not exist, the first as our ArduPilot sensei and the second as a great friend and coach.

Gratitude to Aidronix, with broadcast and support of Pedro Matabuena, Tornillos Irator, TDRG and Marco Hugo Reyes Larios with the book-logo design support, Juan Jesus Gonzalez and Hazur Socconini with diffusion and patenting processes, Proyectil MX and projects INADEM 2.4 of the Mexican Secretary of Economy, and Francisco Arteaga and Jesus Castillo for our Quetzalcoatl aerial manipulator logo design (www.behance.net/jcmd).

Julio also thanks to the people of Mexico for their capacity to generate valuable results and the endurance and tenacity to always overcome the worst situations.

Clause of Responsibilities

Neither the publisher, nor the authors, nor the development community of ArduPilot or Pixhawk projects are responsible in any way for the use that the reader could make of any vehicle or robot designed, programmed, or operated by them.

It is the responsibility of each reader to do the following:

1. Read and properly understand the entire text of this book.

2. Have the proper permissions and security measures for their personal projects.

3. Use appropriate materials and equipment for their project.

Neither the publisher, nor the authors, nor the development community of ArduPilot or the Pixhawk projects will answer questions or observations related to the personal projects of each reader, no matter how important or urgent they may be. Understand that this book contains enough detailed material and in very specific cases, there exist online forums:

- http://discuss.px4.io/

- https://discuss.ardupilot.org/

- http://ardupilot.org/dev/docs/apmcopter-programming-libraries.html at Community section

CLAUSE OF RESPONSIBILITIES

Neither the publisher, nor the authors, nor the development community of ArduPilot or the Pixhawk projects are responsible for the damage that the reader could cause to their computer equipment or embedded systems during or after the installation process. It is the responsibility of each reader to follow the provided instructions.

Neither the publisher nor the authors are responsible for variations of code and syntax made by the ArduPilot development communities or the Pixhawk projects. This is understood since the software and hardware evolve, so this book should be interpreted as a base template to understand future modifications.

Foreword

Although the purpose of this book is to teach the capabilities of the ArduPilot libraries in conjunction with the Pixhawk autopilot exemplified with a quadcopter generic multi-rotor, it also provides guidelines for extending the knowledge acquired in other types of custom-designed aircraft (see the appendix on omnidirectionality) or terrestrial or aquatic vehicles, as well as other autopilots compatible with the aforementioned libraries.

This book is composed of an introductory section where the characteristics of the autopilot and the libraries are presented, a section of sequential programming focused on a didactic understanding of the most important parts of the ArduPilot libraries, where each main component of the code is described, and a final section of advanced character where the acquired knowledge is expanded to real-time applications.

Each section has a detailed description of the code and its components, its application and interaction, and of course, a bibliography suggested by the authors for those who want to deepen the exposed topics.

It should be mentioned that the use of the ArduPilot libraries is not exclusive to the Pixhawk autopilot and can be extended to many other platforms. However, this combination was adopted by the authors' preference, as well as by its performance capacities. This implies that reading this book offers training in these libraries and allows the end user to adapt their work to a wide range of autopilots and test platforms.

Warning

The use of aircraft and in general all types of vehicles in certain areas and countries are restricted by taxes, laws, and, of course, penalties, due the fact that equipment, buildings, living beings, and people can be damaged.

Even if the user has all the legal permissions to operate their vehicles, this book has the purpose of teaching to develop prototypes, so user tests must be carried out in closed spaces under adequate safety conditions or in open non-public spaces designed for those experiments.

The readers must avoid public places or restricted areas. The readers, and nobody else, are responsible for their tests. Avoid infringements and accidents.

Pay particular attention to LIPO mobile batteries. These batteries can be incendiary and explosive, which is an additional risk.

Finally, the cost of an aerial vehicle and its components can become expensive if you do not have the required care and design and this is therefore the responsibility of the reader.

Under no circumstances will the authors reply to private or public projects, regardless of the urgency. Instead, the reader is recommended to do additional research on forums.

Prior Knowledge

This book is aimed to anyone with a level of education equivalent at least to the last year of high school or a technical baccalaureate, since you must be familiar with the following concepts.

Mandatory Knowledge

Programming: Knowing how to use an Arduino is the necessary starting point.

Financial intelligence: The world of unmanned vehicles represents a moderate to high cost in the purchase of various components. You are responsible and solvent for the acquisition or assembly of your own vehicle and corresponding spare parts.

English: Frequently, it will be necessary to access forums, stores, and videos to resolve certain concerns. Given that the topics addressed here do not have such extensive information in local languages, it is necessary to have a moderate level of English.

Desirable but Not Essential

Mathematics: You should know basic derivation and elementary operations of vectors and matrices.

Physics and control: You should understand the concept of damped harmonic oscillator and PD control, the concept of force and torque, the use of coordinate systems, and how to obtain the components of movement and force.

Expected Results

With this book you will learn

- To program in an advanced way the Pixhawk, which is an open autopilot created by the ETH and widely used in the world of research and development of autonomous vehicles

- To use the ArduPilot libraries, one of the software development interfaces for unmanned vehicles research and development with most users around the world

- To model and implement elementary semiautomatic controls in any unmanned vehicle of the aerial, terrestrial, and aquatic type and in a very specific way in a quadcopter

- To link theory with practice in the development of unmanned vehicles

- To select hardware and software components during the design process of an unmanned vehicle

- To use other hardware and software development packages compatible with those described here

- The most employed scientific and technical nomenclature in the field

- To become familiar with the most relevant articles and books in the field

EXPECTED RESULTS

- To scale the knowledge applied with the quadcopter to three-dimensional vehicles through the basic theory of omnidirectional vehicles (those that can achieve "any" position with "any orientation")

- To identify the most relevant complexities and processes for the operation of an unmanned vehicle if you plan to build your own autopilot (by programming microcontrollers, DSPs, FPGAs, embedded cards, or any other method that you prefer)

Licenses

ArduPilot libraries and Mission Planner software are GPLv3 license-free software. They can be redistributed and/or modified under GNU GPLv3 terms and restrictions as described by the Free Software Foundation (www.fsf.org/).

The code and programs are distributed with the hope of being useful but without any guarantee, even without the implied warranty of merchantability or capacity for a particular purpose. See the General Public License section of the GNU project for more details.

- ArduPilot libraries can be downloaded from http://ardupilot.org/dev/docs/apmcopter-programming-libraries.html.

- Mission Planner software can be downloaded from http://ardupilot.org/planner/.

- Pixhawk autopilot has a CC-BY-SA 3.0 license (https://creativecommons.org/licenses/by-sa/3.0/deed.es) which belongs to Lorenz Meier.

- Its official documentation is at https://dev.px4.io/en/contribute/licenses.html.

- PX4 libraries have a BSD 3-clause license (https://opensource.org/licenses/BSD-3-Clause).

Almost any terminal is public domain software. We recommend terminal.exe, putty, or any other equivalent.

LICENSES

The Java SE Development Kit 8u111 update with the executable named `jdk-8u111-windows-i586.exe` belongs to Oracle and, only if needed for the correct execution of the Eclipse version included with the libraries, can be downloaded from `www.oracle.com/technetwork/java/javase/downloads/java-archive-javase8-2177648.html`.

PART I

Introduction

CHAPTER 1

Hardware and Software Description

In this chapter, we will show you what an autopilot is. We'll also introduce the characteristics and history of the hardware and software used throughout this book, which are the ArduPilot libraries and the Pixhawk autopilot. You will learn the difference between a GUI and an SDK, and how many types of SDKs there are for programming autopilots. Additionally, we will discuss other compatible projects and you will learn to distinguish between clone and original versions.

Autopilot

An autopilot is an embedded card designed to perform on-board operations during the unmanned tasks of a vehicle, such as the flight of an aircraft, the journey of an autonomous car, the immersion of a submarine robot, or any other type of mobile robot.

Unlike a development card, the autopilot usually has a greater capacity for processing and data transfer. This is because

1. Orientation and position sensors are read.

2. Signals are read from the remote control.

3. Other sensors coupled to the system are read, either through analog ports or digital or serial transmission protocols.

© Julio Alberto Mendoza-Mendoza, Victor Gonzalez-Villela 2020
J. A. Mendoza-Mendoza et al., *Advanced Robotic Vehicles Programming*,
https://doi.org/10.1007/978-1-4842-5531-5_1

4. Flight data is stored for later statistical or graphical use.

5. The unmanned vehicle is intercommunicated with other vehicles or a base on the ground, using wireless networks.

6. The battery is measured.

7. Visual and sound alerts are sent.

8. The control is processed.

9. The data obtained is filtered.

10. The control is written to the motors.

11. Selected processes are executed in real-time modules.

12. Demanding mathematical operations are performed in very short times, such as multiplication of large dimension matrices, calculation of trajectories, and estimation of speeds and accelerations.

With the demand for resources, a development card tends to collapse or simply can't achieve such performance. For example, the Arduino development board, in its mega model, cannot operate more than a brushless motor at 490hz since in principle its clock barely manages 300hz for a single motor, compromising the operation of the rest of the ports and systems.

Now, if we compare it against another type of development cards or even more sophisticated and specialized processors such as a Raspberry Pi or an FPGA, the autopilot only contains the minimum equipment necessary and is only optimized for the teleoperation of a vehicle; that is, writing to an adequate number of motors (from 4 to 12, for example), writing to auxiliary motors (servos, for example), reading of positioning and orientation data, data feedback and control by the remote user, storage of flight data, and additional reading of on-board equipment (distance sensors, GPS redundant modules, etc.). Therefore, space, weight, and power consumption are optimized for the task of driving a vehicle.

Among the best known autopilots are the Pixhawk, the Naza, the ArduPilot, the Crazyflie, and the CC3D.

Kinds of Autopilot: SDK vs. GUI

There are two types of autopilots, as shown in Figure 1-1.

- **Closed or semi-closed architecture programming**: In this case, a GUI (graphical user interface) is usually available. It is known as semi-closed programming because the user only has the ability to modify the parameters of predefined functions through a highly visual and interactive interface that does not imply knowing a specific programming language, where you can, for example, configure the path to be completed by the drone, but you cannot program each motor independently with a controller designed by the user. A GUI example is Mission Planner; it's used throughout this book but only as a way for graphic visualization, matching of telemetry communicators, loading designed programs to the autopilot, and extracting flight memory data.

- **Open architecture programming**: This case makes use of an SDK (software development kit). Here the programming is open because the users can modify flight parameters and also perform by themselves the whole algorithm of flight execution. This goes from the reading and filtering of the sensors, the incorporation of its own sensors, the choice of the data to be stored, up to the individual writing of each engine. This way requires the knowledge of a specific programming language.

GUI

SDK

Figure 1-1. *GUI vs. SDK interfaces*

Kinds of SDKs

For vehicles and especially drones there are three types of SDKs, as shown in Figure 1-2.

- **Cartesian command mode with yaw rotation**: In this case, the vehicle can only be "controlled" as a mass moving in X, Y, and Z directions and capable of turning on its vertical axis. In this case, the SDK only accepts position and rotation references, and it is not possible to command each component at a low level (motors, sensors, main control, etc.). As an example, see the appendix on dronekit.

- **Altitude command mode and attitude**: Here the vehicle can only be commanded as a mass moving in Z direction and capable of spinning on its three axes of movement. It's a moderately powerful development interface because although it allows the vehicle to have a command closer to what is necessary for experts in control, robotics, and artificial vision (among other areas), it still does not allow the most basic level of control and design: the motor level control. This is the case of the most recent SDK versions of the Ardrone multicopters.

- **Command mode on each motor**: This SDK allows you to control each engine. The flight of the unit is the responsibility of the designer. This is the case of the Pixhawk and the ArduPilot libraries and although it is risky if you do not read an extensive manual or this book, it provides the designer with greater control over all the components and behaviors of the aircraft or vehicle (remember that "with great power comes great responsibility").

It is also a very powerful modality because it not only allows you to control standard vehicles but also allows you to customize your own designs or make vehicles that do not exist (see the appendix with an introduction to omnidirectionality).

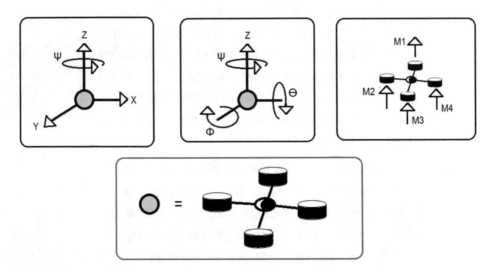

Figure 1-2. *Kinds of SDKs. In order from left to right, top row: cartesian command mode with yaw rotation, altitude command mode and attitude, and command mode on each motor. Bottom row: A quadcopter point mass representation*

Pixhawk Autopilot (Hardware)

The Pixhawk dates back to 2008. It was initially developed as a student project in the ETH of Switzerland by Lorenz Meier, and it was marketed in mid-2012 by the company 3DR. Throughout this text, you will see that the ETH is an important part of the history of drone design.

The Pixhawk has in its FMUv2 version (which will be used for this text) the following features (note that they change a little bit between manufacturers and clones):

- **Processor**:

  - 32-bit STM32F427

  - 168Mhz RAM 256Kb

  - 2MB flash memory

- **Integrated Sensors**:

  - 3-axis gyro with 16-bit resolution ST Micro L3GD20

  - Acelerometer with 3-axis magnetometer and 14 bits of resolution ST Micro LSM303D

  - Acelerometer with redundant 3-axis gyroscope Invensense MPU 6000

  - Barometer MS5611

  - Some versions have GPS

- **Weigh and dimensions**:

  - 33-40 grams depending on the model and manufacturer

  - 80x45x15mm approximately

- **Power consumption**:

  - From 7.5 to 37V (cells 2-10s)

- **Communication ports**:

  - I2C

  - Analog inputs 3.3V and 6V

- SPI

- MicroUSB

- Futaba and Spektrum radio ports

- Power port

- CAN

- 5 UART

- PPM port

- microSD

Throughout this text, we will use Pixhawk version 1 or its clones 2.4.8 or 2.4.6 (note that they are only names, since the real version 2 of the autopilot dates from 2017). However, the use of the libraries is extensible to other autopilots of the Pixhawk family and even other families of autopilots and drones. The compatibility chart is available at `http://ardupilot. org/dev/docs/building-the-code.html`.

As mentioned, although version 1 or its clones contain more ports, the most used throughout this book are as follows (and as shown in Figure 1-3):

- **Serial communication port (wired)**: With this port, it's possible to connect an Arduino or any other development card with the intention of external processing of data and receiving only simplified information. For example, one use is image processing with the Raspberry Pi to identify positions of objects and send these positions to the Pixhawk by standard serial protocol. See FRONT 3 in Figure 1-3.

- **Serial communication ports (wireless)**: With this port, it's possible to connect an intercom in order to transfer data wirelessly between autopilots (altitudes, angles, sequences of operation). This shouldn't be confused with the radio control port; this interface operates at 915Hz, except in Europe and countries with the European standards. See FRONT 2 in Figure 1-3.

- **Analog interface ports**: With these ports, it's possible to connect analog sensors such as potentiometers, ultrasonic position sensors, temperature sensors, or pressure sensors. The Pixhawk has three analog ports; one at 6.6V and two shared at 3.3V. See FRONT 13 and FRONT 14 in Figure 1-3.

- **Ports of digital interface**: It is possible to use these ports as GPIO ports (generic digital input and output ports). With them it's possible to use push buttons, LEDs, or any other device that works with binary logic (on and off). They are shared with the Auxiliary PWM ports. See AUXILIARY SLOTS PWM in Figure 1-3.

- **Fast PWM ports for brushless motors**: These ports are used to connect the main motors of the system and operate at 419hz. See MAIN SLOTS PWM in Figure 1-3.

- **PWM ports of slow writing or auxiliary ports**: These ports are for servos and motors aimed at secondary operation of the system (fins, robotic arms of support, stabilizers of cameras, etc.). They operate at 50hz. See AUXILIARY SLOTS PWM in Figure 1-3.

- **Radio interface ports**: The most commonly used is the PPM port, not to be confused with the serial ports of wireless communication. They work in a way that allows the user to have manual control of the vehicle. This can serve as an emergency stop or to activate a sequence of operations in a semi-automatic way (takeoff, trajectory following, rotation and anchoring, descent). This interface works at 3Mhz, except in countries with European standards. See RC Input Port in Figure 1-3.

- **LED signaling**: This is a Toshiba device incorporated in order to indicate visual alerts. See FRONT 15 in Figure 1-3.

- **SD memory port**: This stores the flight data to use later for statistics or graphics. See SIDES 2 in Figure 1-3.

- **Emergency or auxiliary buzzer**: Used to activate a variety of sound alerts. See FRONT 8 in Figure 1-3.

- **Security switch**: If it is not activated, the motors simply will not turn. The security switch is a button to avoid cutting or injuring anyone with propellers or motors due to unwanted behavior. See FRONT 7 in Figure 1-3.

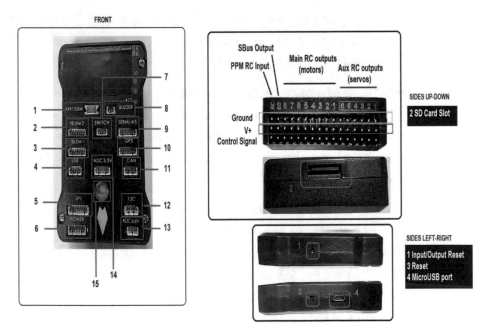

Figure 1-3. *Pixhawk ports*

Clones vs. Originals

The advantages of the original version of the Pixhawk, with respect to its clones, are mainly reported in the performance of the sensors and in the response of the motors. However, for prototyping purposes, both the clone version and the original one are acceptable.

The advantages of the clones are: price, existence in the market (getting an original Pixhawk in its version 1 is somewhat difficult), and medium to high degree of compatibility with the original version.

The disadvantages of the clones are: some batches are totally defective, and some units have bad finishing so it is necessary to make some adaptations (cuts and perforations) to be able to use the ports.

Although the clones are labeled with numbers 2.4.8, 2.4.6 etc, it should be remembered that these are only their brand names and the numbers correspond to the original version of the Pixhawk officially called FMUv2. This is confusing because currently there is an original version 2.0 of the Pixhawk which corresponds to the FMUv3. When dealing with original or cloned versions, it's enough to know what version of FMU hardware they have (interestingly, there is currently a commercial FMUv5 with commercial name Pixhawk4). The FMU nomenclature means Flight Management Unit. The FMUv1 version corresponds to the base hardware project called PX4, which is currently extinct.

It is very important to know which FMU version has a cloned or original card, since the code compilation of the programming libraries you'll use depends on that.

We recommend also reading `https://docs.px4.io/en/flight_controller/pixhawk_series.html`.

Commercial Autopilot vs. Your Own Design

As noted, the Pixhawk started as the result of hardware development for ETH prototypes and over time became a relatively standardized commercial option. Designing a stable autopilot takes months to years and, as already emphasized, it is not enough to know how to use development cards. It involves low-level software development and a deep level of knowledge of programmable devices such as microcontrollers, FPGAs, DSPs, microprocessors, etc., as well as assembly language or other machine languages necessary for the execution of interruptions, generation of pwm signals, generation of processes in real time, development of wireless transmitters, and management and development of data transmission protocols in communication buses among other desirable characteristics.

For a user with such knowledge, the development of a homemade autopilot is feasible. It also takes time to do, which is why the Pixhawk, both hardware and software, as well as its extensive documentation and thousands of worldwide users for almost a decade, are simple and functional alternatives for a fast, professional, and economic implementation.

Said another way, by using the concept of lumped abstraction of Anant Agarwal, a professor at MIT on the edx platform: The Pixhawk and other autopilots, together with their programming libraries, have reached a level in which coding a task of advanced level does not require the user to know how to design an autopilot by itself, but just to know how to use at an intermediate level a programming language.

This allows developers to focus on high-level programming (C++, Java, Python, etc.) and control theory.

However, for the reader interested in the development of these platforms, it is recommended to take a look at the bibliography of this section.

ArduPilot Libraries (Software)

Although the Pixhawk is compatible with the GUI, Mission Planer, it also supports SDKs called ArduPilot and PX4. This book will address the first SDK given its relative easiness of use, fast implementation, and compatibility with Arduino coding. In fact, the ArduPilot libraries owe their name to the project: ARDUPILOT MEGA.

Interestingly, the name of the ArduPilot libraries (see Figure 1-4) is based on the hardware project parallel to the Pixhawk, called the ArduPilot navigation card, developed by the company 3DR. Once the developers realized the limitations of the Arduino-based hardware and the advantages of its software, they chose to preserve the software and migrated to the Pixhawk base autopilot, all during approximately 2012.

Finally, knowing how to use these libraries does not restrict the autopilot, as they can be used with other projects (navIO, ErleBrain, etc).

Figure 1-4. *ArduPilot logo*

Compatibilities and Similar Projects

The Pixhawk autopilot is hardware-compatible with the ArduPilot, PX4, Dronekit, Mavros libraries, and even with Parrot Bebop drone. On the other hand, the ArduPilot libraries are compatible with the Pixhawk autopilot, the APM, Snapdragon, ErleBrain NAVio, and Parrot Bebop drone. The complete lists of compatibilities as well as versions currently not supported are on their respective web pages.

Similar SDK projects are

- PX4

- Paparazzi

- Crazyflie

- Dronekit

Confusion Between Hardware and Software?

As mentioned, the software and hardware share names and this is a little confusing. For this reason, you should consult Table 1-1.

Table 1-1. *Nomenclature of ArduPilot and Pixhawk Projects*

Project name	PX4 (Pixhawk)	ArduPilot
Compatible hardware (autopilots and embedded cards)	Pixhawk family, Snapdragon, etc.	Pixhawk family, ArduPilot board, Erlebrains, PxBerry, etc.
Software	PX4 libraries	ArduPilot libraries

Chapter Summary

In this chapter you learned the following:

- What an autopilot is and information about its design

- The history and general information about Pixhawk and ArduPilot projects

- The difference between SDKs and GUIs, and the different kinds of available SDKs based on the level of vehicle control

- Related projects and compatibilities

- How to distinguish between clones and original autopilots and their corresponding advantages and disadvantages

In the next chapter, you will learn about the generalities concerning the working environment of the ArduPilot libraries and certain particular characteristics of importance for those who chose to use the version of the libraries included with this book.

CHAPTER 2

ArduPilot Working Environment

In this chapter, you will learn about the file types and some specific types of variables that are usually employed with the ArduPilot libraries. You will learn the programming flow we recommend using for the development of projects. You'll also see how to create projects and identify errors using the example of the Eclipse interface development environment (IDE) that comes preloaded with the version of the libraries included with this book. Finally, you'll explore the use of the ArduPilot libraries in conjunction with development boards.

File Types Related to ArduPilot Libraries

There are basically two important file extensions:

- `*.pde`: Although the name may seem very rugged, it is simply an extension associated with source code in C/C++. In fact, as you will see in the corresponding section, you must adjust this extension so that it is recognized in the editor and compiler with this type of files. Note that source code editing files are in the C++ language.

© Julio Alberto Mendoza-Mendoza, Victor Gonzalez-Villela 2020
J. A. Mendoza-Mendoza et al., *Advanced Robotic Vehicles Programming*,
https://doi.org/10.1007/978-1-4842-5531-5_2

- *.px4: In this case, it is the executable file generated once the *.pde file has been compiled. This file must be loaded to the corresponding autopilot (the Pixhawk in this case) and has the purpose of activating the functions previously encoded on the navigation board. As you can see, they are execution files for the Pixhawk processor.

Specific Data Types

Because the Pixhawk is an embedded unit for piloting a vehicle in a semi-autonomous way, its memory has a limit depending on the time of operation, so you must use special caution in the types of data used. This means that in this case, it's not enough to just declare variables INT, FLOAT, CHAR, etc., but also their variants. For example, if you want to store the flight time, you can use the standard variable: int_16 t.

In this case, you're committing two errors. The first is that the variable int_16 can only store 64000 signed numbers. Furthermore, you're going to waste half, because the variable int stores data from -32000 to 32000, and since you won't measure negative time (as it always starts at zero), the negative 32000 numbers can't be used.

The second error is that if you want to save time in units of milliseconds, you can only save 32000 milliseconds, which is only 32 seconds of flight.

The question then arises, how can you extend these ranges? The answer is to use subtypes. For example, uint_32t only stores positive integers (u is unsigned, and therefore is only positive) in a range of 0 to 4,300,000,000, which equals 71,600 flight minutes!

Let's go over one more example, this time for motors. Motors only accept "operation percentages." These percentages go from zero, indicating "totally off," to a positive number, indicating the maximum speed value or "totally on." Standard motors vary from 1000 to 2000, so it is enough to use a uint_16t, and therefore you can use up to a value of 65536. Note that an u_int8t variable only covers values from 0 to 255.

A further example is in the standard serial transmission that only accepts 8-bit numbers from 0 to 255. In this case, it is convenient to use the uint_8t.

Implementation Tip: PPM, PWM, 1000, or 2000?

Without going into too much detail, both PWM and PPM are ways to digitize a signal for its encoding and transmission. This enables you to then reinterpret the numbers to a language of easy understanding and send them for machine communication (binary, 0-1, logical, true-false, on-off, etc).

Throughout this book, and in extension to the autopilot documentation, we use the term PWM. However, it should be noted that the Pixhawk does not use the usual PWM for machinery operation based on the percentage of operation of an actuator (duty cycle), but one based on timing, which is very common in servo motors, radio controls, and brushless motors. In fact, it is known as PWM of servo controls. In this way, the numbers 1000 to 2000 indicate the length of "on time" measured in microseconds, where 1000 is the minimum value and 2000 is the maximum, since 1000 microseconds equal one millisecond. According to various sources, this standard comes from old-school radio-controlled aviation.

Later you will see that if you want to use this PWM with equipment different than servo motors or ESCs (i.e. directly to DC motors), you need to make a reconversion to the duty cycle mode.

On the other hand, you will also occasionally find the term PPM, and although it is another type of modulation, it is basically used for the encapsulation and multiplexing of PWM signals. This means that it is the combination of two or more signals and transmits them in a single channel, which reduces the number of physical cables needed to communicate a radio. For example, the autopilot ArduPilot did not have a PPM receiver, so it was necessary to use a large number of cables to communicate with the remote control.

The Pixhawk uses servo-type PWM signals to receive radio control data and send data to brushless motors or auxiliary servo motors. In the case of reception, it uses the combined encapsulation method PPM.

For more information, consult these websites:

- `https://discuss.ardupilot.org/t/understanding-ppm-vs-pwm/8197`

- `https://oscarliang.com/pwm-ppm-difference-conversion/`

Description and Flow of the Programs Used

The design and implementation of the code through the ArduPilot libraries consists of the parts shown in Figure 2-1.

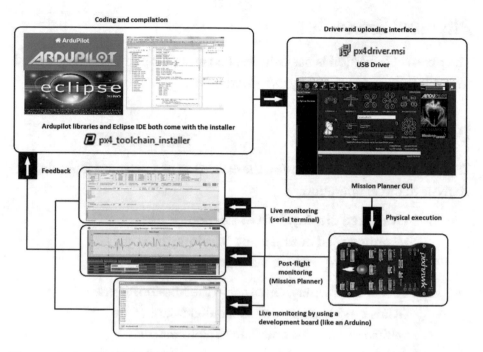

Figure 2-1. *Program flow*

Coding and Compiling

In this case, the necessary software is divided into two components. The first is the set of ArduPilot libraries that allow you to program the necessary commands within the development and the second is the compilation interface, which for the purposes of this book is a version of Eclipse preinstalled together with the ArduPilot libraries using the installer named px4_toolchain_installer (see on the corresponding Appendix).

Connection and Loading Interface

The interface is also divided into two components. The first is a driver that allows you to link the USB ports of the computer so it can be used with the Pixhawk autopilot. The second is the GUI for loading custom files called Mission Planner.

Physical Execution

The physical execution is basically the Pixhawk autopilot, properly loaded with the software encoded by the programmer.

Display

There are three ways to supervise the execution of a program flight data analysis or direct operation:

1. **Live wired display**: This wired mode is not recommended during flight. It is done through generic serial terminal software.

2. **Post-flight display**: Once again the MissionPlanner GUI is used to either download flight data of the vehicle to a text file and then to a plotter (Excel, Scilab, Python, etc.) or to graph the data extracted from the SD card.

3. **Live wireless display**: Here you can watch live flight data by writing to an auxiliary development card like an Arduino, Raspberry Pi, Beagle Bone, etc. (such as using the Arduino and its serial monitor).

Feedback

Based on data monitoring or simply the actions carried out by the autopilot, the codification and compilation stages again developed are fed back and retaken by the user who modifies the program.

Uploading Custom Code to the Autopilot

This section is crucial for the proper implementation of the code included in the rest of the book. Therefore, it's necessary to carefully read the following steps:

1. Open Mission Planner and check the Pixhawk port. The port is assigned when connecting the Pixhawk to the computer. It is advisable to display the corresponding tab and make sure that it says PX4 FMU (COM #). The same COM number is available in the Windows device manager. That port will not change while the Pixhawk is connected. Never press the connect button; see Figure 2-2. If you do this, the Mission Planner GUI will take control of your autopilot and you will not be able to use it to load your custom code.

Figure 2-2. *Mission Planner Pixhawk port*

2. In Mission Planner, go to the initial setup and install the firmware. You should see a graphic interface, as shown in Figure 2-3. Look for an option called "Load custom firmware" in the lower area and click it.

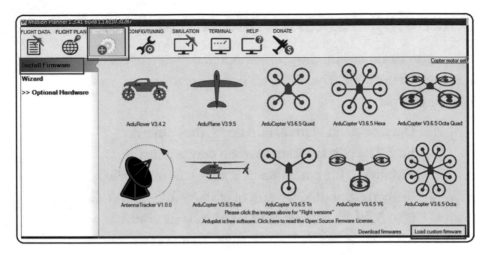

Figure 2-3. *Mission Planner loading custom firmware*

3. When clicked, a navigation box will appear, as
    shown in Figure 2-4. Search for the .px4 file that
    you want to upload to the Pixhawk. Remember
    that .px4 is the extension of executable files, which
    are obtained after the compilation of the editable
    file with extension .pde, as you will see in the
    compilation section.

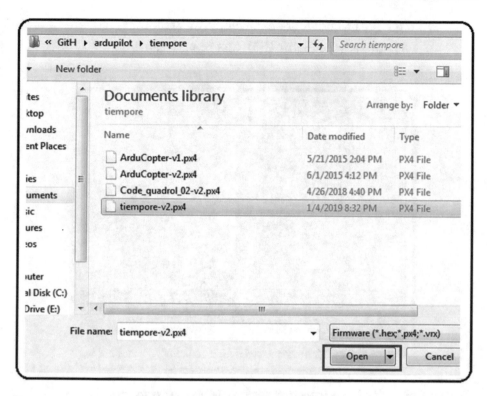

Figure 2-4. *Mission Planner uploading px4 files*

4. Follow the uploading procedure. The screen will ask
    you to disconnect the autopilot. Press the OK button
    and reconnect it. See Figure 2-5.

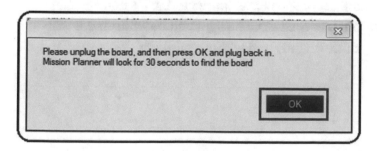

Figure 2-5. *Mission Planner uploading indication*

5. If the file has not loaded correctly, an error message will appear (see Figure 2-6). Just repeat step 4.

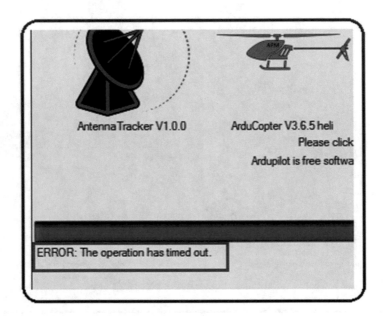

Figure 2-6. *Mission Planner's uploading error message*

6. If the firmware upload was successful, the system will alert you with a message indicating that you must wait for the sound of the Pixhawk to press OK (see Figure 2-7). You'll hear the sound as long as a buzzer or speaker is connected. If it's not, you can observe the LED. The light will be white and it will shine brightly and without blinking.

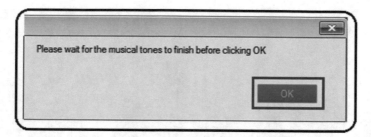

Figure 2-7. Mission Planner's successful uploading message

Implementation Tip   The key of this section is to make sure that
Mission Planner, once the autopilot is connected, has enabled the
Load custom firmware button. If this does not happen, you must look
for previous or superior versions of Mission Planner until you find one
that allows for the installation of the custom firmware.

Making New Projects by Using Eclipse

This section is also imperative because it indicates how to work with
the files you've designed, as well as how to compile them. However, you
should be careful because this is a method only for the Windows installer
with the included Eclipse IDE, which is the mode in which we develop our
code. Therefore, what we'll cover here can differ considerably with respect
to other ArduPilot installations.

1.   Copy a preexisting project. Here we show the
     process with a random project but in the case you
     don't have one, we've provided the hellodrone
     folder; see Figure 2-8. Notice that our hellodrone
     folder is based on an arducopter folder project.

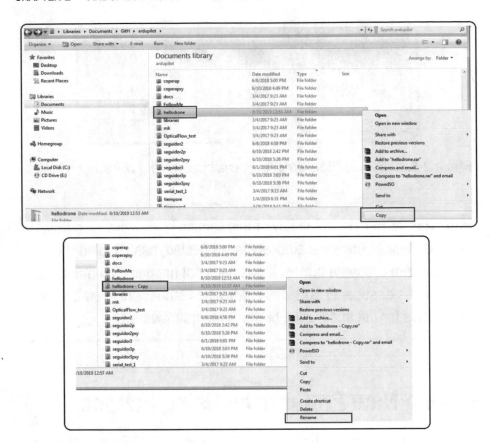

Figure 2-8. *Making a new project, step 1*

2. Change the name of the copied folder. In this
    example, we've renamed it as newtry. Inside this
    folder you'll find the previous main file (the main
    file is the one with the same name as the previous
    folder) which you'll also rename so that the file
    shares the same name as the folder: newtry.pde.
    See Figure 2-9.

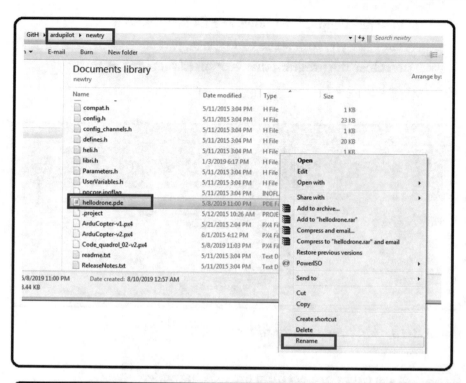

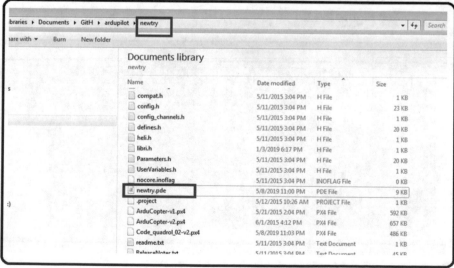

Figure 2-9. *Making a new project, step 2*

3.   Open px4 Eclipse (Windows ➤ PX4 Eclipse, so if a
     dialog ask you to select a workspace, just click OK)
     and close the program that is open (if there is one).
     See Figure 2-10.

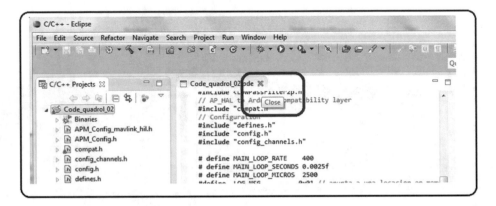

Figure 2-10. *Making a new project, step 3*

4.   Make a new project from the existing code.
     See Figure 2-11.

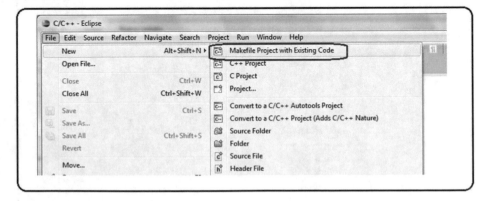

Figure 2-11. *Making a new project, step 4*

5. In the pop-up screen, verify that the C, C ++, Cross
    GCC language is selected, and then click the search
    option. In the auxiliary window, find the folder you
    need (for this example, you're looking for the newtry
    folder) and press the accept option. If everything
    was correct, the name of the main project will
    automatically appear as newtry. Then click the
    Finish button. See Figure 2-12.

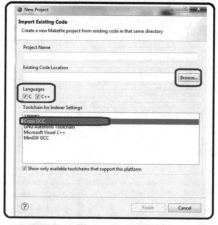

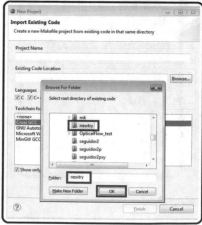
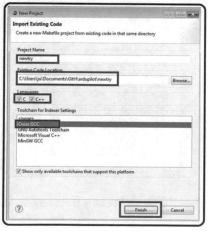

Figure 2-12. *Making a new project, step 5*

6. The new project will appear in the drop-down menu. Open the main program (`newtry.pde`). The compilable option will appear on the right side. Press it and if `px4-v2` appears, right-click and delete it. Next, generate a new one also by right-clicking. You do this so the new compiler avoids inheriting data from the copied folder. See Figure 2-13.

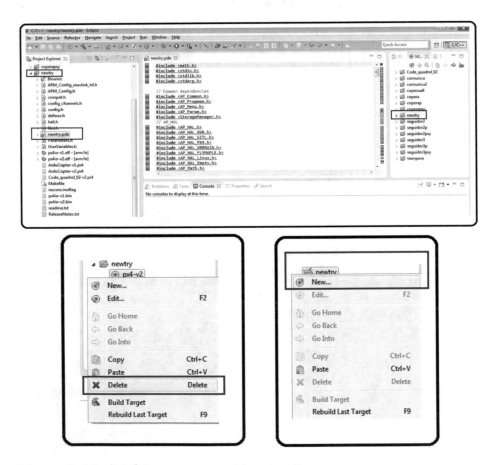

Figure 2-13. *Making a new project, step 6*

7.   Click the New button, type px4-v2, and then press
     OK. Now if you click the drop-down folder, the
     new compiler will appear. Right-click it and press
     the Build Target button (or simply execute it with a
     standard click). See Figure 2-14.

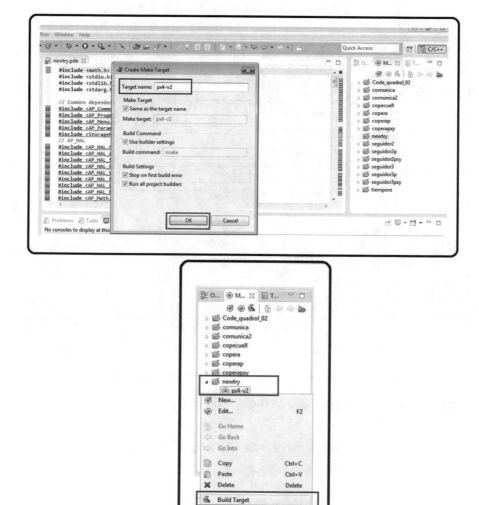

Figure 2-14. *Making a new project, step 7*

8. If no code error occurs, the compilation was successful. You can also verify this by checking the folder to see if the .px4 file shares the same time stamp as the time displayed in the console. You might need to be patient. The first time you compile a new project, it can be very slow. See Figure 2-15.

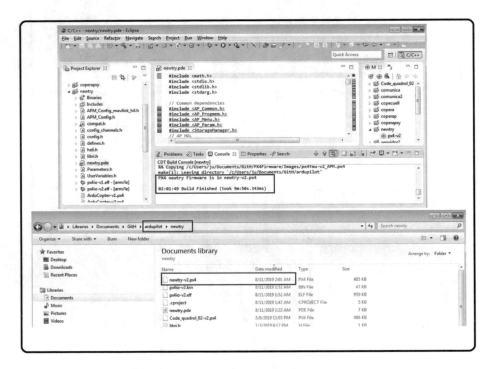

Figure 2-15. *Making a new project, step 8*

9. Now it is possible to rewrite the main file or its secondary files and recompile.

Error Checking

Once the compilation process is complete, errors might either incur or the compilation might be satisfactorily completed. If the latter, the terminal will indicate that a file with a .px4 extension with the same name as the main file was generated, as well as its date of creation. This is the file that you'll load to the drone. If you cannot find the file in the main folder or the date of creation doesn't match the compiled file, then there are programming errors.

NOTE: Do not confuse the command or syntax errors with those of ArduPilot programming. Although the errors from command syntaxes are highlighted before the code compilation, the ArduPilot libraries commands are not standard in C ++, so you should not be concerned about them. Instead, you should focus on errors after the compilation.

For the process of error verification you must always have the Console tab active. Remember that this checking process is valid for the Eclipse editor. If another editor is installed with the px4 libraries, it may be necessary to follow another sequence of error identification.

The process for compiling code is the following: Normally the compilation process is slow. So if instead of several minutes, it takes seconds or very little time to do it, there is a problem. In Figure 2-16, for example, it takes approximately 9 minutes and 50 seconds.

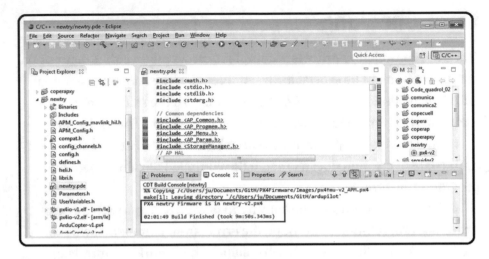

Figure 2-16. *Usual compilation (slow process)*

A successful compilation shows a message indicating that the firmware with the .px4 extension was created and also the time stamp. This means that you can check the folder where the .px4 file lives and see if the timestamps match. See Figure 2-17.

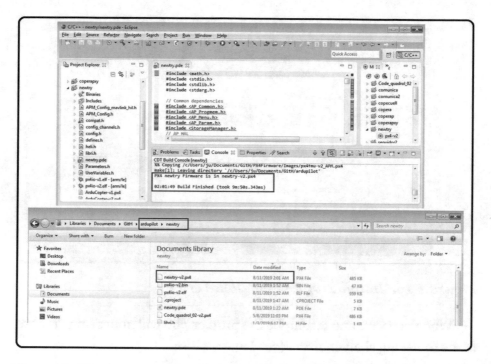

Figure 2-17. *A succesul compilation comparison between file and console properties*

Now let's introduce a typical error and see how to identify it. In this example, remove a semicolon (;) from the code in line 210. See Figure 2-18 (you can do this with any line number you prefer).

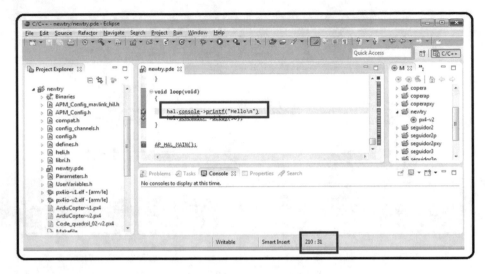

Figure 2-18. *Introducing an intentional error*

When you save and recompile the project, you will notice one or more of the following characteristics (see Figure 2-19):

1. A very fast compilation (56 seconds in this example)

2. A compilation not showing that a file with .px4 extension was generated

3. One or more error messages before the finished build line

Figure 2-19. *An unsuccessful compilation after the intentional error*

At this point, use the scroll bar to look for the line that generated the error. This information should show right above the error messages itself. See Figure 2-20.

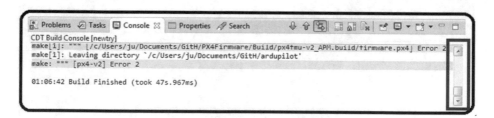

Figure 2-20. *Scroll bar for searching code errors*

In this example, notice that the interface indicates an error in line 211 of the code. See Figure 2-21.

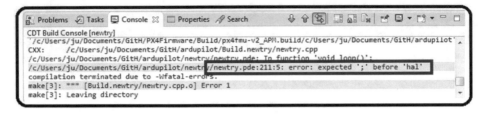

Figure 2-21.   *Explicit error message*

When you go to line 211, take a look at the lines before and after (lines 210 and 212). You will see that the error is triggered by the absence of the semicolon in line 210. See Figure 2-22. Correct the error and recompile the file again. This time you should see a successful compilation. You'll notice a longer compilation time and finally the creation of a .px4 file with the same timestamp into the folder.

Figure 2-22.   *Locating the error line*

Note   If the main file has dependencies of secondary files (we will talk about this next) and there is an error in those secondary files, the console will also displays the name of the file and the line where the error occurs in that file.

Let's see another example. In the project folder called comunica, there is a main file called comunica.pde and some auxiliary .pde files; one of them is called Envio_datos.pde. See Figure 2-23.

Figure 2-23. *A project with secondary files*

In the Envio_datos.pde file, line 10 introduces "a variable not previously defined" error when you save and try to compile the file. See Figure 2-24.

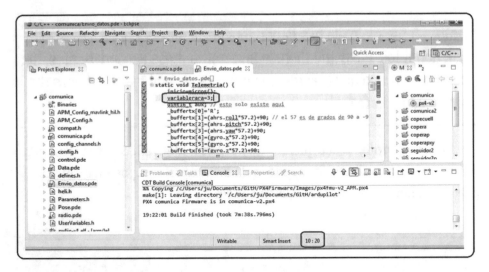

Figure 2-24. *Introducing an error in the secondary file*

Now repeat the search procedure. As expected, an error was reported in line 10 of the Envio_datos.pde file (see Figure 2-25). Correct the error, in this example, by deleting that line or defining the variable. Again, save, recompile, and verify the file with the .px4 extension.

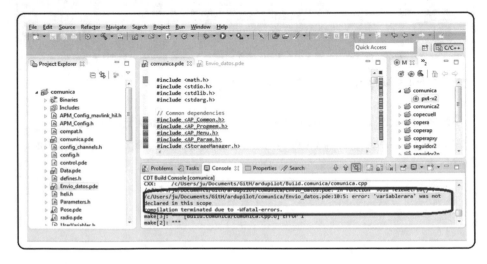

Figure 2-25. *The error message highlighting the secondary file*

Warning   There is a special case, as you will see later, on writing SD memories where, despite introducing an error in the syntax, it will not be displayed and the entire code will be compiled correctly. This is because an auxiliary compiler other than C ++ is used for writing to the SD memory. In this case, you must take special care when programming this kind of procedures.

Is It Feasible to Use Arduino Directly with ArduPilot Libraries?

Yes and no. In fact, the predecessor of the Pixhawk autopilot was the so-called ArduPilot autopilot (ArduPilot Mega), as the name suggests, based on Arduino development boards. In fact, this is why the ArduPilot libraries share the same name.

The ArduPilot libraries were designed to be similar to the use of the Arduino commands. However, using an autopilot based on this development board entails risky system situations, where it was possible to fly a four-engine drone, but in the moment of data transmission or storage, or controlling the interaction of high mathematical processing plus filtering of signals, the system simply collapsed. So, while the hardware was forced to evolve, leading to the Pixhawk based on ARM processors, the libraries were preserved. In this case, it was a better idea to update the hardware than the software.

One of the main problems of using Arduino on its own to operate a multicopter is its deficiency in generating several simultaneous PWM signals to operate several brushless motors, each one independently at 490 Hz.

Therefore, it's recommended to use the Arduino or any other development board or processor as an assistant or a hardware translator. An example is an assistant for some kind of visual detection of objects, or to interpret a PWM RC native Pixhawk format to a PWM-type duty cycle format compatible with a standard direct current motor. It can also be used as a Wi-Fi reader and then broadcasted to the Pixhawk.

Chapter Summary

In this chapter, you learned

- About common file types related to the ArduPilot libraries

- A hint for choosing certain kinds of specific data types

- Our recommended programming workflow and an overview of the required software

- How to create projects and identify errors with the preloaded Eclipse IDE just in case you want to use our libraries

- How you can interact with development boards like the Arduino

In the next chapter, you will build the groundwork for the rest of the book. This includes learning the main parts of ArduPilot code, a brief on common robotic components employed with the Pixhawk autopilot, and some elementary concepts about motion.

CHAPTER 3

Concepts and Definitions

This chapter will refresh your knowledge about certain concepts that will be useful throughout the rest of the book. First, you will learn about common robotic components employed with the autopilot, such as spatial pose, getter and setter concepts, variables, functions, modules, objects, coding and installation differences, and computational efficiency. Concerning the ArduPilot libraries, you will learn the usual parts of ArduPilot code and the archetypes of programming.

Auxiliary Components

The following sections review the auxiliary robotics components commonly used with the autopilot.

Brushless Motors

As shown in Figure 3-1, brushless motors are the components that give rotation to the propellers. With the Pixhawk, it is common to use brushless motors. It is necessary to describe them briefly since most of the projects of robotic vehicles use standard DC motors, also known as brushed motors.

© Julio Alberto Mendoza-Mendoza, Victor Gonzalez-Villela 2020
J. A. Mendoza-Mendoza et al., *Advanced Robotic Vehicles Programming*,
https://doi.org/10.1007/978-1-4842-5531-5_3

Although it is also possible to use brushed motors with the Pixhawk, they require certain adjustments because they are used indirectly (we'll go into this in more detail later in the book).

Returning to the point of this section, the brushless motors used by the Pixhawk are motors fed by direct current but operated with a kind of three-phase alternating current, for which they have three cables. They must be operated by a transformation element to those three phases, called a variator or electronic speed controller (ESC).

As an interesting fact, brushless motors can be used directly underwater, so they are ideal for aquatic applications as long as the connection wiring and the rest of the components (autopilot and GPS, for example) are carefully sealed.

Parameters to consider   kv, weight and dimensions, maximum current and voltage, maximum thrust

Component keywords   BLDC motor, brushless motor drone, BLDC kv, thrust motor

---

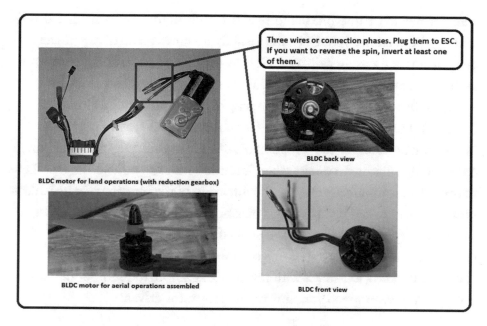

Three wires or connection phases. Plug them to ESC. If you want to reverse the spin, invert at least one of them.

BLDC back view

BLDC motor for land operations (with reduction gearbox)

BLDC motor for aerial operations assembled

BLDC front view

Figure 3-1. *Brushless motor overview for aerial/aquatic or land operations*

ESC

The batteries that feed the brushless motors are single-phase direct current; however, this must be transformed to three phases and a type of digital alternating current needs to be able to operate the brushless motors. This is where the electronic speed controllers appear. They internally have all of the preprogrammed algorithms necessary to perform this transformation at both the software and electronic level. This consists of three sections of cables: the first is to take the power they need to the battery with two cables, the positive and the ground; the second consists of the three output cables to supply the brushless motors; and the last section is the control signal to vary the motor speed by PWM (remember that is a PWM signal specialized for servos). This PWM signal is the one that is transformed to a three-phase mode in the body of the ESC (see Figure 3-2). Finally, the section of control wires usually includes an auxiliary power cable from a subcircuit called a BEC (battery eliminator circuit), or simply an "eliminator." With this, it is possible to supply some input module of PWM as the radio receiver without using an additional battery.

In addition to the above, the ESC according to the way they are connected determines the direction of rotation of each engine which, once connected, will remain unalterable. Attention must be paid to the fact that in order to automatically change the direction of the rotation of a brushless motor, as is required by the wheels of robots, for example, it is not enough to electrically alternate the cables. So if you want a motor capable of changing its direction of rotation, you must buy specialized ESCs that allow it, also known as ESCs with reversible rotation. Remember that ESCs are also known as speed variators or simply motor drives.

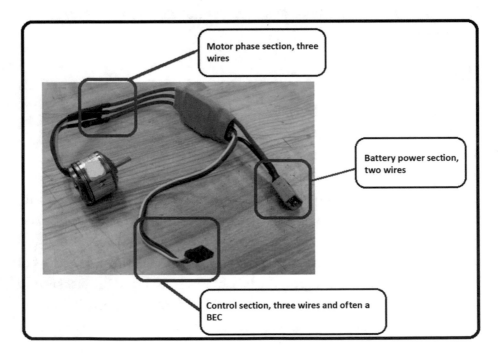

Figure 3-2. *ESC overview*

Parameters to consider   Maximum size, weight, current and voltage, reversibility, BEC or optocoupling

Component Keywords   ESC, BEC, reversible ESC, opto ESC

Propellers

The trilogy to determine the performance of a drone (by land, air, or water) consists of engines, propellers (**or wheels**), and batteries. In this way the propellers (or "props") are obviously essential for the operation of an aerial vehicle or an aquatic one. They consist of at least two blades whose most important parameters are the radius and the step. For a vehicle, it is common to use half of the propellers turning in one direction and the other half in the opposite direction. This is achieved simply by swapping the connections of the ESCs with the motors. See Figure 3-3.

Parameters to consider   Pitch, diameter, edge, number of blades, flexibility, hardness, direction

Component keywords   Propeller, propeller blade, flexible propeller, props

Figure 3-3. *A propeller*

Frame

For the body of the drone, in this case and unlike many other components, the frame (Figure 3-4) can be purchased or manufactured freely by the user. The standard criteria for designing is focused on materials and very specifically in its hardness, size, and lightness. Also, certain distances must respect some aerodynamic criteria to avoid interference between the propellers, the floor, or other objects.

Parameters to consider   Material, hardness, lightness, holes, levels, accessories, size and weight, landing gear, anti-shock systems, folding, electromagnetic shielding

Component keywords   Frame, landing gear, waterproof

Figure 3-4. *A quadcopter frame*

Special Connectors

To avoid having undesirable welding effects such as electrical unbalance, to achieve easy replacement, and also to avoid accidentally disconnecting cables by simple movements, the autopilots are connected to the ESCs, the battery, and the sensors, as well as the engines to the ESCs, through special connectors. Although there are many versions, here is a list of the most common:

- **Motors to ESCs by using bullet connectors**: Here the consideration is the diameter. They are available in different sizes and the choice depends on the thickness of the cables and the maximum current supported. See Figure 3-5.

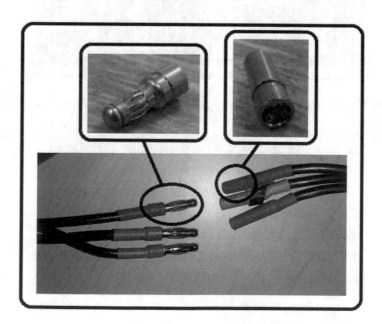

Figure 3-5. *A special connector for joining motors to ESCs*

- **Autopilot to ESCs through connectors of three outputs (one PWM, one earth, and one for the power supply of the BEC):** Although there are many types, the most common is the JR. See Figure 3-6.

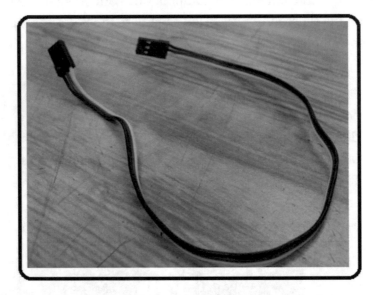

Figure 3-6. *A special connector for joining the autopilot to ESCs*

- **Batteries to distributor or distributor to ESCs:** In this case, there are many types, but one of the most used is the XT (XT60, XT90, etc.) which also has the characteristic of irreversibility, which means that it is specifically designed in order to not be connected in the opposite direction and generate a short circuit or other electrical problems. See Figure 3-7.

Figure 3-7. *A special connector for joining batteries to ESCs or distributors*

- **Sensors to autopilot**: Here are many versions too, particularly the Chinese Pixhawk clone called 2.4.8, which uses a so-called picoblade molex 1.25 while the original uses the df13. In any case, it is worth mentioning that there are several pins and sizes so it is advisable to consult forums about which to use in a specific autopilot model. See Figure 3-8. Also see www.lambdrive.com/depot/Robotics/Controller/ PixhawkFamily/Connector/.

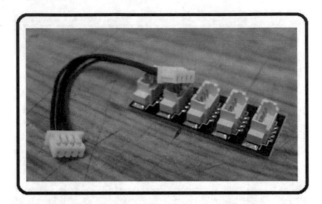

Figure 3-8. *A special connector for joining different devices to the Pixhawk autopilot*

Parameters to consider   Size, current and operating voltages, accessories required for their use, number of pins, compatibility, special or regular versions, sealed or not, special operating conditions such as explosive atmospheres, low or high temperatures, electromagnetic shielding

Component keywords   Drone connectors, bullet connectors, shield connectors, twisted drone connector, EMI noise

---

Telemetry Module (Wireless Serial Communication)

If you want to send or receive wireless data from and to the vehicle other than the remote control signals, you will need telemetry modules (see Figure 3-9). They are wireless serial communicators. The most common are those of 915Mhz, but you must be careful and check which standard is allowed. There are also 433Mhz modules.

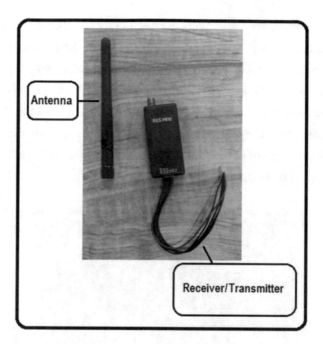

Figure 3-9. *An overview of a telemetry module*

Parameters to consider   Size, current and operating voltages, accessories required for its use, compatibility with connectors, maximum distance reached, legality of operation frequencies

Component keywords   Telemetry module, wireless serial transmission, range, connectivity

---

LIPO Battery

The battery determines how long the vehicle will move. In general, LIPO batteries are used for wireless flights but have durability problems (15 to 30 minutes in most vehicles), so if long operation times are desired, a more durable choice is a wired connection (a specialized electric extension or tethered drone or a non-specialized but limited in performance option like a battery from a car or a computer power supply, for example).

If the option for the desired application is a LIPO battery (Figure 3-10), it should have specialized chargers and protection covers for storage and transportation since they are also highly flammable and explosive. They usually have two sets of cables: one that is used with both the charger and the monitor, and the other to feed the vehicle.

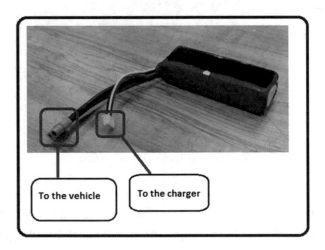

Figure 3-10. *A LIPO battery*

Parameters to consider   Size, weight, amp hours, operating voltages, number of cells, C or discharge rate, connectors, accessories required for their use

Component keywords   LIPO battery, discharge rate, LIPO cells, LIPO connectors, LIPO charger, LIPO handling

---

Battery Tester or Battery Monitor

If the vehicle tests are carried out wirelessly (with no tether), it is advisable to frequently know the status of the LIPO battery. In those cases, it is convenient to buy one of the modules shown in Figure 3-11, which is nothing but a specialized voltmeter reduced in volume and weight. This module usually incorporates visual and sound alerts to indicate the integrity or low charge of a battery.

Figure 3-11. *A battery tester or monitor*

Parameters to consider   Portable or external (on-board or not), maximum number of cells, light, and/or sound indicators

Component keywords   LIPO tester, LIPO monitor

GPS Module

A GPS module (Figure 3-12) is the way vehicles know their planar position and height with respect to the planet. The drawback is that it only operates properly outdoors when there is no satellite signal interference from buildings or wooded areas.

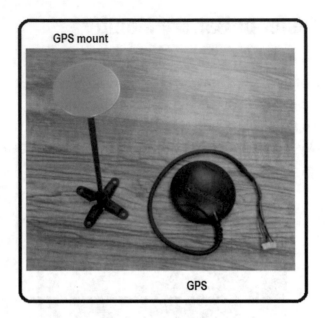

Figure 3-12. *A GPS module*

Parameters to consider   Multiple modules or only one, type of connector, pedestal, signal amplifier, resolution and precision, electromagnetic noise protection

Component keywords   EMI noise, redundant GPS, GPS accuracy, drone GPS mount

Distributor

Distributors are the way that more than one ESC can connect simultaneously to the main battery. They can be of an integrated circuit type or a simple current divider (a harness like an octopus connector). See Figure 3-13.

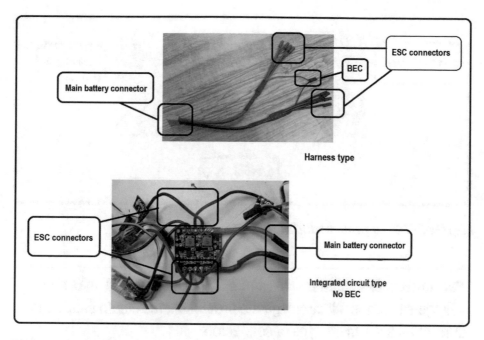

Figure 3-13. *Two kinds of power distributors*

Parameters to consider   Maximum current supported, maximum voltage supported, number of motors to be powered, BEC, size, weight, type, electromagnetic protection

Component keywords   Drone power distribution board, wiring harness drone

---

Power Module

A power module is the way the autopilot is connected to the main battery; see Figure 3-14. It has two outputs: one for the distributor and one for the autopilot. Always remember to verify your own battery input and distributor output.

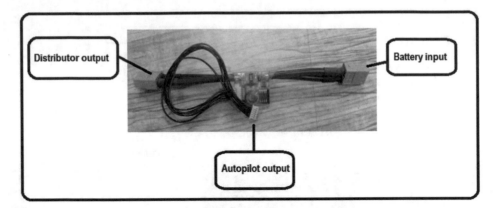

Figure 3-14. *A power module overview*

Parameters to consider   Maximum current supported, maximum voltage supported, electromagnetic protection, maximum support for current measurement, type of connectors

Component keywords   Drone power module

Silicon Wire

The cable used to power the electronics and electricity of devices, like brushless motors, usually has special characteristics due to the high current circulation. Therefore it must also be resistant to heating and of course aggressive movements. That is why silicon AWG is preferred. See Figure 3-15.

Figure 3-15. *Silicon wire*

Parameters to consider   Current and voltage to be dissipated, operating temperature, cable size, color code, rigidity or mobility

Component keywords   Silicone wire

Thermofit

It is useful to cover the exposed joints with a Thermofit (Figure 3-16) to avoid a short circuit between them.

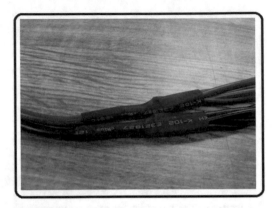

Figure 3-16. *Thermofit*

Parameters to consider   Current and voltage to be dissipated, operating temperature, cable size

Component keywords   Thermofit

Fasteners

Fasteners can be tapes, belts, glue, flanges, clamps, or any other light material whose function is to link in a reversible or permanent way different devices such as sensors and drone batteries. It is recommended that components that are consistently replaced, such as batteries, have reusable fasteners.

Parameters to consider   Replacement frequency, degree of subjection

Component keywords   Zip tie, releasable zip tie, rubber band, hose clamp, tube clamp, hook and loop fastener

---

Passive Antivibration Modules

All motion sensors are affected by the vehicle's own vibrations, so it is convenient to use passive damping modules between the sensors, the autopilot, and the vehicle's frame. See Figure 3-17. These modules are called passive because they are not motorized; they are simply absorbent rubbers. They are for specific components such as motors, cameras, GPS, and other sensors, or exclusively for autopilots.

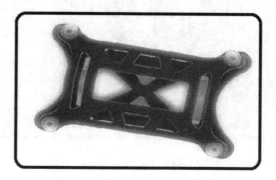

Figure 3-17. *Antivibration mount*

Parameters to consider   Size, compatibility, mobility

Component keywords   Vibration damping drone, antivibration mount drone, vibration isolator drone

---

Remote Control

A remote control (Figure 3-18) is the manual control of the vehicle. It should not be confused with the telemetry modules to operate a quadcopter-type flying drone. They must have at least four channels, while a land drone vehicle only needs at least two channels. However, it is

65

always recommended to have at least other two auxiliary channels, and it is also worth considering whether the frequency of operation of the remote control is legal in the area of operation.

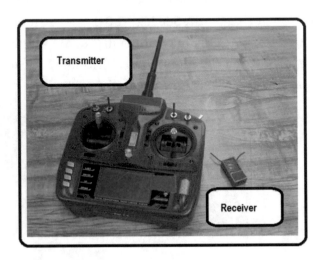

Figure 3-18. *Remote control components*

Parameters to consider   Maximum distance, support for LIPO batteries, legality of operation frequencies, number of channels, binding mode, type of auxiliary channels (knobs, two or more positions, sticks, push buttons, etc.), sensitivity, transmission modes, screen or not, presence or not of PPM channel in the receiver

Component keywords   RC transmitter, RC receiver, binding, ppm, ppm encoder, six-channel transmitter and receiver

---

Embedded On-Board Computer

Most of the time a task can be done exclusively with the capabilities of the autopilot, while other tasks require a more demanding processes, such as the use of vision or artificial intelligence, or the cooperation of multiple vehicles. So it is convenient to have a central unit to do these activities and send feedback to the autopilot with processed data, for example, a Raspberry Pi. It should also be mentioned that some devices already incorporate an all-in-one card, both the command computer and the autopilot, like the navIO or the Erle Brain. Also, some recent modules of the Internet of things (IoT) can do all the activities by themselves (such as the Sony Spresense).

Special Pixhawk Components

There are three special Pixhawk components, as shown in Figure 3-19. They are usually included with the autopilot. These components include the motor on/off button, the alarm, and the microSD card. The importance of the motor on/off button is that while this is not pressed, all the operations with the motors will not be performed. In a way, it is a type of security button. The alarm is a sound indicator complement of the onboard LEDs, and finally, the SD card, in addition to storing flight data, is important because without it the entire device will not work.

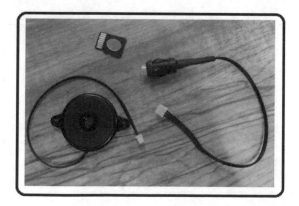

Figure 3-19. *Special Pixhawk components*

Parameters to consider   Cable resistance, twisted wire, flexibility, use of an adapter to connect the microSD card to the computer

Component keywords   Pixhawk arming switch, Pixhawk buzzer, microSD

Computational Efficiency Against Mathematical Equality

Because computational calculations are done on-board a vehicle, the mobile processing devices, as autopilots and development cards, must be efficient in their processing capabilities. In the same way, during codification you must be careful with the following statement: "Mathematical equality is not computational equality."

For example, for mathematics it is true that

$$e^{i\pi} + 1 = 0$$

Note that the simplest side to assimilate in the equation is the right side, because everyone knows the number 0.

It is also true that

$$\frac{1}{2}(6) = 0.5 * 6 = 3$$

In this way, you must be careful with which representation you prefer. In the second example, the first expression has two mathematical operations, the second expression has only one, and the last has one operation. However, this entails truncation errors, such as

$$\frac{1}{3} \approx 0.33 \approx 0.33333$$

Hence, during the design of your program and before coding it, you must be aware of the degree of precision or the errors with which you want to work. Also remember that the more precision you desire, the more resources will be necessary to process the number of decimals required.

In particular, when coding you should prefer simplified expressions because they represent less operations, although they are mathematically equal to more complex terms. However, you should always take into account a degree of precision for irrational operations (1/3, Pi, etc.). Therefore, it is your responsibility to simplify your equations when programming them.

Working with Variables, Functions, Modules, and Objects

Although there are more entities than those mentioned here, given that they are the most usual concepts for the use of ArduPilot libraries, the following are described in the next sections.

Variable

A variable is a computational object capable of receiving a single value. It contains two arguments: the value and the type of variable. See Listing 3-1.

Listing 3-1. Variable Examples

```
float a=5.5
int i=3
char c='X'
bool logic=True
```

In Listing 3-1, four variables are shown: one is a floating type (associated with decimal numbers), one is an int type for integer numbers, one is used with characters, and one is a boolean type to handle logical states (on/off).

As you will notice later, it is necessary to use subtypes. For example, the ArduPilot libraries can use the subtypes shown in Listing 3-2.

Listing 3-2. Example Subtyptes for the ArduPilot Library

```
uint16_t motor
uint8_t serial
```

Subtypes are useful to economize the use of resources. In this case, as the exemplified variables (`motor` and `serial`) can only receive positive values and the number zero, the prefix unsigned is used. Postfixes are also used (`16_t` and `8_t`) because they represent the maximum extension in bits that the variable can read. For example, the values of the radio are usually between 0 and 2000. When you specify the `16_t` you are indicating that the variable cannot exceed the range [0, 65535]. This means that the previous postfix has enough space for the value 2000. On the other hand, when working with the serial port, only a value of [0 255] is allowed. So the 8 bits of `8_t` are exactly enough for that task.

Structure

A structure is a collection of variables of different types. Or, in other words, it is a variable of variables. See Listing 3-3.

Listing 3-3. Example of a Structure

```
struct product {
  int soldunits;
  double price;
  char mallsection:
} ;
```

As you can see in this example, a variable called product is in this case a collection of different variables, containing a price, a hall, and a number of sold units.

Function

A function is a segment of code accessed from different sections of a program. It is used to avoid excessive repetition and to maintain a readable format. For example, Listing 3-4 shows the Arduino map function. First, note that there is code (in this case, the main one) where the function is used or invoked.

Listing 3-4. Example of a Function

```
void loop()
{
  int val = analogRead(0);
  val = map(val, 0, 1023, 0, 255);
  analogWrite(9, val);
}
```

In Listing 3-5, there is a section of code where the function is defined.

Listing 3-5. Map Function

```
long map(long x, long in_min, long in_max, long out_min,
long out_max)
{
  return (x - in_min) * (out_max - out_min) / (in_max - in_min)
  + out_min;
}
```

Module

A module is a segment of internal code (written in the main program) or external code (written in an auxiliary file) that contains one or more functions. See Figure 3-20.

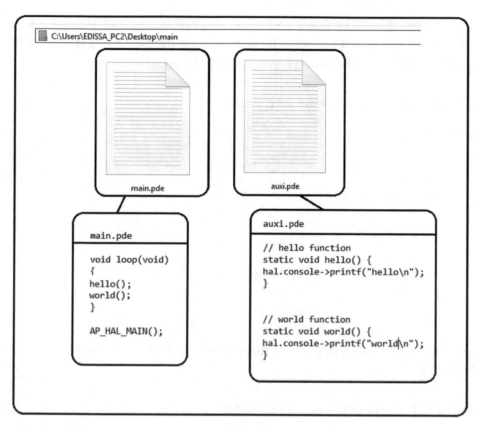

Figure 3-20. *Main code with external modules*

- **Class**: A class is simply a structure that contains methods or functions in addition to variables (it has many more characteristics than this, but in a simplified way and for the use that we are going to give it, this is the concept of a class).

- **Object**: An object is the invocation of the class (the invocation in programming technicalities is also called an "instance").

The example in Listing 3-6 shows optimization and standardization errors, but is used to exemplify the concept in a simplified way. Listing 3-6 shows the section of code where the class is defined.

Listing 3-6. A Class Definition Example

```
class Circle
{
    public:
    float radius;

    double Area()
    {
     return 3.14 * radius * radius;
    }
};
```

Listing 3-7 shows the section of code where the class is used or invoked.

Listing 3-7. A Class Invocation Example

```
int main() {
    Circle circle1;
    circle1.radius = 5;
    float area1=circle1.Area();
    return 0;
}
```

There are two different ways to access the methods and properties of a class. It depends on whether it is accessed from an instance or from a pointer. If it's from an instance operator, . is used; if it's from a pointer operator, -> is used. In order to declare the components, the operator : : is used, which means that when you see them, you are using an object corresponding to a predefined class.

Listing 3-7 uses the operator . in the following lines:

```
circle1.radius = 5;
float area1=circle1.Area();
```

This implies that you are invoking the variable called radius and the function called area for the instance called circle1 associated with the class Circle.

Henceforth, in order to use the ArduPilot libraries, you will be just a user of objects. You will not be a designer of objects. This means that you will not define the classes because they are already part of the libraries, so you will only invoke them. So it is enough to know that the indicated symbolism represents that type of invocation.

Listing 3-8 has more common example of code in the ArduPilot libraries that show that an object is being used. This is recognizable by the use of the symbols previously described to access methods using both instance and pointers. Note that the you don't create them because they already come as part of the ArduPilot libraries. You simply use them.

Listing 3-8. Sample Code Showing How ArduPilot Libraries Employ Objects

```
// instance or invocation
static AP_Baro barometer;
AP_HAL::AnalogSource* ch;

// use
barometer.init();
barometer.calibrate();
ch->set_pin(15);
```

Application Tip   if you have extra time or are more curious, in
addition to taking an object-oriented programming course (as is
already indicated in this book, it is only necessary to identify and
invoke them), you can read about the following operators:

:: Scope resolution operator

. Element selection by reference

-> Element selection through pointer

Getter and Setter Concepts

The programming of a device becomes a little more accessible if you
understand the concepts of getters and setters. The first is used to obtain
or read values (to read from sensors, for example) and the second is to
establish or write values (to write to motors, for example).

In this way, you will notice that the set of functions present in the
ArduPilot SDK consists of reading and writing methods of the RC signals,
the serial ports UART, the terminal, the GPIO ports, the SD card, etc.
Basically the instructions consist of programming the desired device with
the READ (getter or read mode) and WRITE (setter or write mode) suitable
extensions.

Once this concept is assimilated, understanding any other library, no
matter how complex, consists of locating its getter and setter modes. The
differences between each library lie in the device initialization modes
and the fact that other SDKs, such as PX4 libraries, should also contain
subscription functions. However, all have their corresponding writing-and-
reading-to-device methods.

Concepts of Orientation and Position

The position is the spatial place occupied by a body. Orientation is the spatial alignment of a body in a certain position (seeing to the north, the south, front, back, etc.). See Figure 3-21.

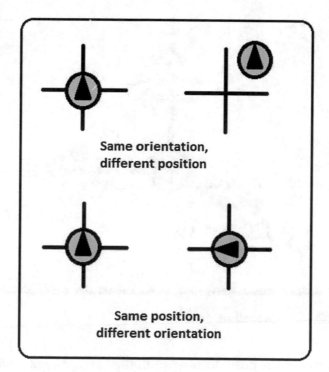

Figure 3-21. *Orientation and position*

Both integrate an entity called *pose*. In the plane or two-dimensional space, the pose of an object can have two components of position and one of orientation (this is where a wheeled robot works). These components are usually called coordinates X, Y, and body angle.

On the other hand, in three-dimensional space, there are three position components and three orientation components (this is where a multicopter works). They are usually called XYZ coordinates and roll, pitch, and yaw angles. Notice in Figure 3-22 how the happy face can move towards any of the three positions of space and at the same time look with any particular orientation.

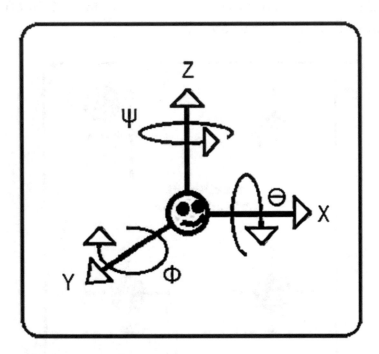

Figure 3-22. *3D Cartesian pose*

Note that both the position and orientation components can have a multitude basis. For example, for the position there are Cartesian, polar, ellipsoidal, triangular, spherical, cylindrical, toroidal, etc. For orientation, there are Euler angles, but also quaternions, rotation matrices, exponential representations, representations of complex numbers, etc.

Note   Throughout this text we will use the Cartesian base called XYZ and the Euler angles of the type roll, pitch, and yaw.

Both the position and the orientation can be measured in relative or absolute frames. It is said to be an absolute measurement if something has a common point of reference. It is said to be relative if something has as reference in a specific point of interest (which is used to facilitate calculations or have a guide, such as the center of gravity of an object). An example of its use can occur when we use a screwdriver. We unconsciously tend to reference our body with respect to the absolute frame of the earth's surface, but when using the screwdriver we do it with respect to the relative frame of our hand. See Figure 3-23.

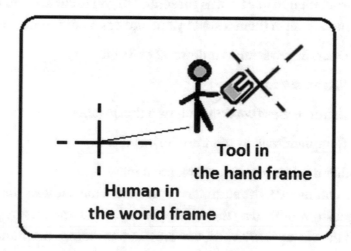

Figure 3-23. *Absolute and relative frames*

Attention: Difference Between Installation and Coding

There are two independent processes for the use of programming libraries:

1. The installation

2. The coding

This book deals with coding, which is relatively homogeneous, since the installation, besides the fact of being variable between different equipment, is subject to compatibilities and also has many variants (in Linux, in QT, in Eclipse, in Arduino IDE, in Mac or Windows, in 32 or 64 bits, in a Raspberry Pi, Erlebrain, Pixhawk, ArduPilot, etc).

The installation in this book is presented to you exclusively in the following modes, all of them tested by the authors on different computers:

-   Operating system: Windows 32 or 64 bits

-   Versions: 7 to 10

-   Editor: Eclipse version built into the installer

-   Compiler: Make, built into the installer

Any other mode is at your own responsibility.

On the coding side, the commands presented here, unless they have been drastically modified by the developers, are the same for any platform. To verify if the syntax is still valid, see the corresponding command directly on the webpage of the ArduPilot libraries. For example, to verify the validity of the command `hal.rcout-> write ()`, you should look for the associated library in the official and updated webpage (in January of 2019 it was `https://github.com/ArduPilot/ardupilot/blob/master/libraries/AP_HAL/RCOutput.h.`)

In this way, you will find the definition of the corresponding command (and its function overloads if they exist). In this case, it is `write (uint8_t chan, uint16_t period_us)`.

Here is a second example:

```
hal.rcin-> read ()
```

On the official webpage (`https://github.com/ArduPilot/ardupilot/ blob/master/libraries/AP_HAL/RCInput.h`), you can find the definition of the read RC command (and its function overloads if they exist). This case it is `uint16_t read (uint8_t ch)`.

Usual Parts of ArduPilot Code

The main parts of ArduPilot elementary code are illustrated and described in Figure 3-24 and Table 3-1.

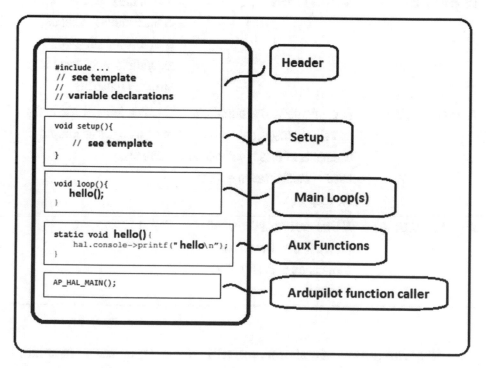

Figure 3-24. *Usual parts of ArduPilot code*

Table 3-1. *Description of the Parts of ArduPilot Code*

Name	Contents	Allowed actions
Header	Libraries and definitions	Use restricted to ArduPilot libraries; use and creation for the definitions of variables or classes (objects)
Setup	Initialization of ports or functions, only once executed	Use only for initialization methods
Loop or main loop	Main user code	Use of the classes defined in the ArduPilot libraries, creation of customized algorithms, and use of auxiliary functions
Auxiliary functions	Both internal and external, contain extensive code segments or those that will be used in multiple segments of the loop	Creation for later use in the main loop cycles (maybe setup also)
AP_HAL_MAIN ()	Allows the invocation of all the available classes and commands in the ArduPilot libraries	Use of them

Later, with the use of real time, you will see that it is possible to create new loops or main cycles, which are executed at different frequencies. However, this is the basic template of ArduPilot code.

Usual Models for Programming ArduPilot Code

Listed here, and shown in Figure 3-25, are the usual models for programming ArduPilot code:

- **Serial or sequential**: It is the principal; each code is executed line by line in successive order.

- **Modular**: It is an improvement of the previous model and contains internal functions or modules (external code with one or multiple functions), such that it simplifies code reading, code use, and also allows you to reuse repetitive or extensive code sequences.

- **Object-oriented**: Although the user is free to use or not use their own objects, the ArduPilot libraries and specifically their commands are invoked by means of instances to objects (all the lines of code that you see that are of the OOP type are identifiable by the use of operators ., : and ->, which are point, colon, and arrow).

- **Parallel**: In this mode, which is a very efficient pseudo-parallelization, the autopilot can perform "multiple lines of code" at the same time, which entails performance advantages over the sequential mode. In these cases, it uses its scheduler in real time.

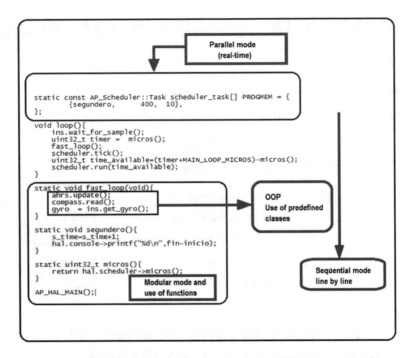

Figure 3-25. *Usual programming paradigms of an ArduPilot code*

Chapter Summary

Congratulations, you have passed the introductory part of the book. Next, you'll start coding, at least in the sequential way, which means one line of code at a time. In this chapter you learned the following:

- A description of the auxiliary robotic components commonly used with the autopilot

- To have efficient and not only mathematical thinking

- To work with variables, functions, modules, and objects

- The getter and setter concepts, present in almost any programming language

- That our main objective is not to teach you to install the ArduPilot libraries but to program them

- The usual parts of ArduPilot code

- The usual programming models of ArduPilot code

- The motion concepts of orientation, position, and pose

In the next chapter, you will start with basic input and output operations.

Part 1 References and Suggested Websites

Webpages that explain in detail the different autopilots and SDK programming libraries based on Pixhawk apm and compatible:
www.lambdrive.com/depot/Robotics/Controller/PixhawkFamily/
www.lambdrive.com/depot/Robotics/Controller/index.html

For the use and deepening of the ArduPilot libraries, including its installation on diverse platforms and hardware tips: http://ardupilot.org/dev/docs/apmcopter-programming-libraries.html

For the use and deepening of the Pixhawk autopilot: https://pixhawk.org/

History of the Pixhawk narrated by its creator, as well as of other usual standards in the world of drones: https://auterion.com/the-history-of-pixhawk/

Commercial advertisement of the Pixhawk by 3DR: https://diydrones.com/profiles/blogs/introducing-the-px4-autopilot-system

Alternative project of open programming libraries called PX4:
https://dev.px4.io/en/
https://github.com/PX4/Firmware/tree/master/src/examples
https://dev.px4.io/en/middleware/modules_communication.html

Interesting article that describes in detail the Pixhawk design (useful if you want to design your own autopilot): Lorenz Meier, Petri Tanskanen, Lionel Heng, Gim Hee Lee, Friedrich Fraundorfer, Marc Pollefeys.

"Pixhawk: A micro aerial vehicle design for autonomous flight using onboard computer vision," *Autonomous Robots 33* (2012), no. 1-2, 21–39.

Interesting article complementary to the previous one for those who like to make their own autopilot: J. Rogelio Guadarrama-Olvera, Jose J. Corona-Sanchez, Hugo Rodriguez-Cortes. "Hard realtime implementation of a nonlinear controller for the quadrotor helicopter," *Journal of Intelligent & Robotic Systems 73* (2014), no. 1-4, 81–97.

PART II

Sequential Operation Mode

If you are here, it means that you know all the introductory information and you just want to start coding. If you are not familiar with certain concepts, please read the previous chapters; they may contain a useful tip or keyword, or maybe it could help you to update your state of the art.

This part of the book is composed of code written in sequential or serial mode, where each line is executed immediately after the previous one; that is, each line of code respects its turn in the queue and there is no way of parallelizing the execution of tasks. Although this is not as efficient in execution as code that uses parallelization of tasks, it better demonstrate to you a didactic approach to programming. The biggest disadvantage is that the system does not perform important tasks like writing to engines until the entire process execution cycle is repeated. None of the processes is more or less important than the others; they are simply executed in the order of appearance.

CHAPTER 4

Basic Input and Output Operations

In this chapter, you will learn to code with the ArduPilot libraries. This chapter focuses on what we consider the most important basic input and output operations: terminal writing and reading, radio control reading, how to use analog and digital ports, how to read the battery, how to use the onboard main LED, and most importantly, how to read and filter position and orientation signals, which are essential in order to command a vehicle.

In the sequential programming mode, usually each command has four sections of code:

- **Declaration**: In this part, you declare the variables that are going to be used.

- **Initialization**: In this part, you execute the code related to the configuration and initialization of the physical ports and components only once, in order to later use these components in the main code. It is common to find it under the name of "SETUP." It is not standard in C++ code but it is usual to find an initialization section when using hardware like Arduino.

© Julio Alberto Mendoza-Mendoza, Victor Gonzalez-Villela 2020
J. A. Mendoza-Mendoza et al., *Advanced Robotic Vehicles Programming*,
https://doi.org/10.1007/978-1-4842-5531-5_4

- **Execution**: This is where you find the main code, that is, the code that runs indefinitely while the system has a battery or a power source. It is common to find it under the name "MAIN LOOP," in which the associated functions of each task are invoked.

- **Definition**: This is where each task that will be used within the execution block is defined, or more specifically, where the functions are defined.

Let's go over an example of a function used throughout this text to map values (Listing 4-1). This function is useful if you want a compatible range in the output, such as an angular meter that goes from 0 to 360 degrees, but the input has arbitrary dimensions like an encoder that displays values between -pi and pi radians. This function is based in linear interpolation. You will use it later.

Listing 4-1. Function for Mapping Values

```
///////////// DECLARATION ///////////////
float yaw, yawdeg;

///////////// USE ///////////////

void loop(void)
{
    yaw    = ahrs.yaw;
    yawdeg=maps(-3.14,3.14,0,360,yaw);
    hal.console->printf("%f\t\n",yawdeg);
}
```

```
///////////  DEFINITION  //////////
```

```
static float maps(float minent,float maxent,float minsal,float
maxsal,float entrada)
{
  return ((maxsal-minsal)/(maxent-minent))*(entrada-minent)
  +minsal;
}
```

Now, let's review an example of a function used throughout this text to saturate values (Listing 4-2). This function is useful if you want to establish safety limits for the operation of motors or for reading a sensor. It is based on the mathematical function of saturation, which you'll use it later.

Listing 4-2. Function for Saturating Values

```
///////////  DECLARATION  ///////////
float roll, pitch;
float yawdeg, pitdeg, rolldeg, pits, rolls;
```

```
///////////  USE  //////////
```

```
void loop(void)
{
    roll  = ahrs.roll;
    pitch = ahrs.pitch;
    pitdeg=maps(-1.57,1.57,-90,90,pitch);
    rolldeg=maps(-3.14,3.14,-180,180,roll);

    pits=sat(pitdeg,45,-45);
    rolls=sat(rolldeg,45,-45);

    hal.console->printf("%f\t %f\t\n",rolls,pits);

}
```

```
//////////// DEFINITION    //////////
static float sat (float a, float b, float c)
{
    if(a>=b) a=b;
        if(a<=c) a=c;

    return a;
}
```

About the Header

Before discussing the commands that are based on the `Ardupilot.pde` source code, let's first go over the header. If you prefer, you can simply save it in a `.txt` file and copy it to your main program. To use the code in this chapter, it is necessary to use the header included in the corresponding appendix, which was taken directly from the `Ardupilot.pde` code. This code also serves as the basis for the decomposition of important modules explained in upcoming chapters.

Broadly speaking, the libraries listed here are more commonly invoked. Only the most important ones are described here; however, as there is interdependence, it is recommended to leave the `.h` file intact or just add in ones that are necessary. Furthermore, you should review online libraries to understand how they were designed, the correct syntaxes, their overloads, or the variants of the commands explained in this book. They are as follows:

- `AP_Common`: It contains commonly used functions such as a high and low parts converter for serial communication, conversion between angular measurement systems (radians to degrees), and others.

- `AP_Param`: It contains functions for the conversion and interaction among the different types of variables. Although it is not common for end users to employ this library directly, the rest of the code needs it to function properly, so it is essential.

- `AC_AttitudeControl`: This library contains commands necessary to monitor and control the attitude (orientation) and position of a vehicle.

- `AP_Hal`: It is perhaps the most important library as it contains all the commands for reading radios, writing to motors, handling digital and analog ports, serial communication, scheduler for operations in real time, writing of data packages to SD memory, and others. This library also has variants for other types of hardware platform such as an AVR base, Linux base, etc.

- `AP_Math`: It contains specialized mathematical functions for matrix and vector operations, normalizations, transformations of unit types, etc.

- `AP_SerialManager`: It contains functions for serial communication commands.

- `AP_GPS`: It contains necessary functions for linking and using the GPS.

- `DataFlash`: It contains the necessary commands for writing to the SD card.

- `AP_Baro`: It contains functions for linking and using the barometer.

- `AP_Compass`: It contains functions for using and linking the magnetometer.

- AP_InertialSensor: It contains functions for using and linking the accelerometer and the gyroscope or the inertial measurement unit (IMU).

- AP_AHRS: It contains functions to determine orientations and angular velocities as data fusion among the compass, the gyroscope, and the accelerometer.

- AP_NavEKF: It contains commands for using the kalman filter, which is necessary for filtering noisy data in the sensors.

- RC_Channel: It contains the most basic functions for reading the radio control and writing to motors.

- AP_Scheduler: It contains the functions necessary for real-time operations and those of the task manager.

- AP_BoardConfig: It contains the necessary functions to set up an autopilot or its variants.

The header also contains internal definitions of the ArduPilot libraries' most used variables. They are mainly known as defines.h and config.h. The header is placed in the program as shown in Listing 4-3.

Listing 4-3. Header Code

```
// place here the header code //
// See appendix

// insert your program here //
// Here will be placed the code of each example along with
// its respective defined functions, the setup cycle,
// the loops and fast loop etc
```

Note Perhaps the advanced reader will want to create an auxiliary `.h` library. If this is your case, see how to do it in the related appendix.

About the Setup

Similar to the use of an Arduino, the code of a program that uses the ArduPilot libraries requires an initialization section called setup, where the instructions to declare a specific hardware functionality are executed only once, such as setting the boot and channel configuration of the motors, setting the start signal of the analog ports, setting the transfer speed of some serial ports and the serial channel to be used, among others. Also, as shown in the corresponding appendix, essential setup instructions are those related to the registration of the autopilot card by itself, and those related to the declaration of sensors, as well as the logging of the SD memory and the serial terminal interface necessary to visualize data and interact with the Pixhawk through a computer.

Writing to the Terminal

- **Components**: USB cable and serial terminal

- **Description**: This is one of the most useful commands because it allows you to visualize, in a test mode, if the required data and actions are being executed properly. Basically it consists of sending or receiving information to a serial terminal (a serial port monitor), which allows visualization of the input and output data in a computer screen.

In other words, its usefulness lies in the calibration of radios, sensors, and in the test of code routines of digital and analog sequences.

Some development cards already have an integrated serial monitor version (such as the Arduino). In the case of the Pixhawk autopilot, this is not available so you must use one of the software components described in the following paragraph.

- **Connection**: As mentioned, it has two components: the USB that is directly connected to the Pixhawk and communicates with the computer, and software called terminal, for which you could use several options (for example, TERATERM, PUTTY, TERMINAL, among others).

Although TERMINAL will be used generically in this text, the important parts of these programs are the following:

1. **Port selection**: For this, you must know in which port of the computer your autopilot was connected (Windows device manager).

2. **Selection of the communication speed**: This is measured in bps. When possible, it is suitable to select a high speed. However, two factors affect this selection. The first one is the equipment used, such as telemetry radios, which only operate at 57600 bps. The second is the capacity of the autopilot and the tasks that it executes. In this case, a very high speed will require the autopilot to demand greater processing which could be necessary in keeping a drone flying. In contrast, a very low speed will force a collapse if the autopilot should execute faster tasks.

Considering the previous points, the selection of the transmission speed is left to your criteria, so try suitable values according to your tasks. However, it is suggested to operate at 57600 bps at the beginning and as long as the performance allows it.

3. **Serial data storage**: In this case, if you want to save test data directly to the computer without saving it on the SD memory card of the autopilot (see the following sections), it is convenient for the terminal software to have a LOG mode, where it is enough to select the output file and a destination folder that will contain the operation data.

4. **Connection button**: It connects into the autopilot port and obtains or sends data via serial transmission protocols. Before connecting, make sure the system is well energized. Also, before unplugging the device, make sure to first disconnect the serial connection button.

IMPLEMENTATION TIP

Because data are stored consecutively, it is convenient to place tabs and spacers between in order to not to get lost into the information and use it easily with any other software for its corresponding analysis.

Before physically unplugging devices, do not forget to cancel serial reading. Otherwise, port disablement or even burning may occur.

You must remember that the use of the serial monitor interrupts the autopilot's proper operation by accelerating or slowing it down (because it requires coordination between two different systems: the autopilot and the computer where it is connected). Therefore, it is convenient to comment or delete all lines where the serial monitor reading or writing is invoked before executing important applications (such as a drone flight).

Some applications only allow the Pixhawk to be energized via the computer's USB port, so there is no need for a connection to a LIPO battery. Some of these applications are reading of internal sensors, reading of analog and digital ports, lighting of LEDs, etc. However, for applications with higher power demands such as starting of motors and servos or serial communication between other autopilots, it is highly convenient to also use the LIPO battery. For its correct operation, first energize the autopilot via LIPO and then connect the autopilot to the USB to the computer. Once this is done, connect the serial monitor.

Avoid floating electrical connections in the same power channel of the computer. In this case, the floating connection (for example, a cable that is placed on the same power line but disconnected from the corresponding equipment) can induce logical noise and cause the autopilot to detect fault at the logical levels and malfunctioning.

Listings 4-4 and 4-5 provide examples of writing to the terminal. Note the following:

- The syntax is `printf("text, spacers and variable references %f \n", data);`.

- The references are usually %d for integers, %f for floats, %c for characters, and so on.

- The spacers are usually \n for line breaks, \t for tabulation, and so on.

You can find more information at `http://ardupilot.org/dev/docs/learning-ardupilot-uarts-and-the-console.html`.

Listing 4-4. Example Code, TerminalWrite.pde

```
//////////////////////// DECLARATION ////////////////////////////
//                    Put the header here
//                       see the appendix

/////////////////// the code goes here ////////////////////////
```

```
// Here is placed the code of each example
// its respective defined functions, the setup cycle, the loops
// and fast loop before initializing, other variables or
// libraries must be defined
```

```
//////////////////////// INITIALIZATION ////////////////////////
```

```
//           Similar to arduino  setup
//              Copy from apendix
//////////////////////// EXECUTION ////////////////////////////
```

```
//              Main loop, similar to arduino coding
void loop(){
    hello();    // internal function hello
    world();    // external function world
}
```

```
//        auxiliar functions, includind Ardupilot libraries
//        hello internal function, which is defined in this file

static void hello(){
    hal.console->printf("HELLO\n"); // printf command
}

AP_HAL_MAIN(); // Ardupilot function call
```

Listing 4-5. Auxiliar Code, WorldFunction.pde

```
// External function world, which is in WorldFunction.pde file
static void world(){
    hal.console->printf("WORLD\n");
}
```

Implementation Tip   As you can see, the way to execute these files and the following code is by using functions. This can be done in a standard way within the main file or in an auxiliary external file.

This is called a module and although the use of modules is more complex outside the work environment of ArduPilot libraries, designers optimized it so that the only requirement to consider when compiling the main file is that its name coincides with the folder of the complete project. The use of modules facilitates information management, its flow and design, and is suitable with real-time sections. Likewise, the basic program predesigned by ArduPilot libraries, (ArduCopter.pde) is designed based on modules.

Terminal Reading

Some tests, such as determining the starting value of a motor, involve writing a series of values sequentially generated or manually introduced by keyboard. Although an Arduino or other development card can be used for said purpose, in this section you will learn how to do it from the SDK itself. For this, you will use the read terminal interface.

Listing 4-6 reads from the keyboard and displays the received character on the screen (note that this command returns characters).

Listing 4-6 provides an example of reading from the terminal. Note the following:

- The syntax is:

```
char read( );
```

You can find more information at: http://ardupilot.org/dev/docs/
learning-ardupilot-uarts-and-the-console.html

Listing 4-6. Example Code, TerminalRead.pde

```
///////////////////////// DECLARATION /////////////////////////
//                 Put the header here
//                    see the appendix

/////////////////////// the code goes here ///////////////////

char readd;

// Here is placed the code of each example
// its respective defined functions, the setup cycle, the loops
// and fast loop before initializing, other variables or
// libraries must be defined

/////////////////////// INITIALIZATION /////////////////////////

//           Similar to arduino   setup
//              Copy from appendix

///////////////////////// EXECUTION /////////////////////////

//              Main loop
void loop(){
    toread();    // toread function is called
}
```

```
//           toread function definition
static void toread(){
    readd= hal.console->read(); // read command
    hal.console->printf("hola %c\n",readd);
    hal.scheduler->delay(300); // without this delay you won't
                               // see nothing
}

AP_HAL_MAIN();// Ardupilot function call
```

Radio Reading

- **Components**: Radio transmitter, radio receiver and PPM modulator (if needed)

- **Description**: This device is a two-part system, the transmitter and the receiver, plus an additional device in case the receiver does not have the PPM data modulator.

- **Connection**: The Pixhawk requires a connection to the PPM type radio receiver: a single channel that contains a mix of all the radio channel signals. For this, you use receivers that contain the PPM output port or a third element called a PPM modulator.

- **Radio binding**: In general, the transmitter and the receiver of the radios are matched, which means that the receiver responds to the transmitter. If they were purchased separately, consult their binding procedure.

Radio tests without using the Pixhawk can be performed in two ways:

1. With a brushless motor. See Figure 4-1.

   a. Verify that the ESC is not optocoupled or the ESC has a BEC.

   b. Assemble them as shown in Figure 4-1 (connecting the motor with the ESC and the battery, and allowing the use of the speed modulation port), and check the electrical compatibility of the BEC with the radio receiver.

   c. Connect the speed modulation port of the ESC with one of the outputs of the remote receiver (not the PPM). For example, use the throttle port, the yaw port, etc.

   d. By doing this the receiver will be energized and able to receive the direct output sent by the radio receiver to the ESC.

   e. The throttle output must be activated with the throttle lever transmitter. The yaw lever output must be activated with the yaw lever transmitter, etc. The motor should begin to rotate according to the channel where it is connected.

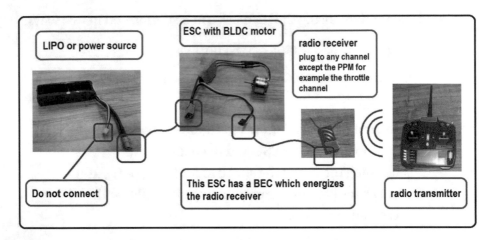

LIPO or power source

ESC with BLDC motor

radio receiver
plug to any channel
except the PPM for
example the throttle
channel

Do not connect

This ESC has a BEC which energizes the radio receiver

radio transmitter

Figure 4-1. *Testing a radio control with a BLDC and without a programmable device*

2. With a servomotor, see Figure 4-2.

   a. Verify that it is a small servomotor, specifically with low current and voltage consumption. If the servomotor is high voltage or current, it should not be connected directly as shown in Figure 4-2. It will require an intermediate power stage according to its requirements (basically an eliminator or electronic regulator, a 7805, for example). If the verification process is not complete, the receiver could be damaged. In order to avoid this, check the maximum voltage and current supported by both the receiver and the servomotor.

   b. Make the connection indicated in the figure, respecting the current and voltage values from step 1.

c. Move the lever of the radio transmitter that
corresponds to the receptor channel. This must
be done slowly in order to avoid damage to the
servomotor. Remember that the servomotor
imitates the lever and if the lever moves too fast, the
servomechanism will break or burn.

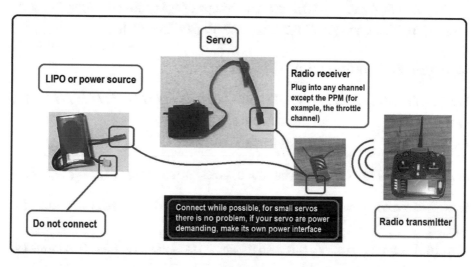

Figure 4-2. *Testing a radio control with a servo and without a
programmable device, as said in the blackbox, remember to see the
servo power details before connecting*

Caution   Although there are other types of radios that are
interconnected through other ports of the Pixhawk (see, for example,
TARANIS), this algorithm is used for those that are connected via
PPM. Please avoid using two types of radios at the same time.

Listing 4-7 provides the example code for reading the radio control signals.

Listing 4-7 provides an example of radio reading. Note the following:

- The syntax is:

```
uint16_t read(uint8_t channel);
```

You can find more information at: https://github.com/ArduPilot/ardupilot/blob/master/libraries/AP_HAL/RCInput.h

Listing 4-7. Reading Radio Control Signals

```
///////////////////////// DECLARATION /////////////////////////////
//                  Put the header here
//                  See the appendix

//////////////////////// the code goes here /////////////////////

int radio_roll, radio_pitch, radio_yaw, radio_throttle, aux_1,
aux_2;
uint16_t radio[6]; // the radio on this example has 6 channels

///////////////////////// INICIATIZATION /////////////////////////

//            Similar to Arduino setup
//            Copy from apendix

///////////////////////// EXECUTION /////////////////////////////

//              Main code

void loop(){
// step 1 read all the channels
for (uint8_t i = 0; i <6; i++)
      {radio[i] = hal.rcin->read(i);}
```

```
// step 2 assign the readings to variables and adapt them
// according to personal scales mode 2 of remote control are
// usually associated with multicopters

radio_roll  = (radio[0]-1500)/3;
radio_pitch = (radio[1]-1510)/3;
radio_throttle = radio[2];
radio_yaw = (radio[3]-1510)/2;
aux_1 = radio[4];
aux_2 = radio[5];

// Displaying data every 20 milliseconds by using pause or delay
hal.scheduler->delay(20);
hal.console->printf("%d\t %d\t %d\t\n",radio_roll,radio_
pitch,radio_yaw);

}

AP_HAL_MAIN();// Ardupilot function call
```

IMPLEMENTATION TIP: MAP FUNCTION

Radios have continuous values and vary according to each manufacturer. For the example shown in Listing 4-7, the radio used is one with values between 1000 and 2000. Therefore it is convenient to carry out a mapping of values on a range interpretable by the user. For example, if the value of yaw is intended to work between 0 and 360 degrees, a conversion via the map function is convenient.

```
float map (float value, float minin, float maxin, float minout,
float maxout)
{
  return (value - minin) * (maxout - minout) / (maxin - minin) +
  minout;
}
```

The map function assumes that the response of the equipment to be mapped is linear. In fact, it can be noticed since it follows the equation of the straight line that passes through two points. If the equipment to be mapped has another behavior (exponential or logarithmic, for example), it is convenient to use some other type of mapping. For this purpose, you should review the data sheets that manufacturers usually offer (for radio controls, sensors, motors, etc.), or do it empirically by means of graphing and applying the most convenient mapping function. If the graph looks like a straight line, you can use linear mapping. If it adopts another form, you can associate it with some other type of equation.

$$P(x_1,y_1) \quad Q(x_2,y_2)$$
$$y = \frac{y_2 - y_1}{x_2 - x_1}(x - x_1) + y_1$$

In this case,

$$P(\mathbf{minin},\mathbf{minout}) \quad x = \mathbf{value}$$
$$Q(\mathbf{maxin},\mathbf{maxout}) \quad y = \mathbf{map}$$

Note that both the function output and input must be associated with types of variables appropriate for the application to use. For example, in the case of Arduino (which is where this function has been taken from), the function uses integer types by definition. However, if you want better precision and count decimal digits, you can use floating or double types. Nevertheless, this reduces the processing power. In some cases, it may be more convenient to use integer data type (especially for low resolution sensors or inputs whose data are purely made of integers, like some remote controllers).

The example given in Listing 4-8 is simple: assuming that the remote control reads values between 1070 and 1920, this fact must be verified by you for each channel of your remote control.

Listing 4-8. Mapping of Radio Channels

```
/// minimum and maximum values of the yaw channel of the remote
/// control measured by the reader
float yawminrc=1070;
float yawmaxrc=1920;

/// initialization of the variable that contains the transformation
/// in degrees from 0 to 360

float yawgrados=0;

/// reading the yaw channel of the remote control,
/// assuming it is in mode 2
/// mode 2 is the one commonly used for multicopters and helicopters

float yawradio=hal.rcin->read(3);

/// mapping
yawgrados=map(yawradio,yawminrc,yawmaxrc,0,360)

/// this can also be used if a symmetric operating range is desired
/// yawgrados=map(yawradio,yawminrc,yawmaxrc,-180,180)
```

IMPLEMENTATION TIP: SATURATION FUNCTION

The saturation function allows you to restrict a set of values without limits, so that they do not exceed certain levels, in order not to surpass the maximum and minimum allowed values of a lever or motor, or to obtain a limited motion range. (For example, a human head cannot rotate indefinitely).

In order to do this, the saturation function is defined as follows:

$$y = Sat(x) = \begin{cases} M \text{ if } x \geq M \\ x \text{ if } x < M \text{ and } x > m \\ m \text{ if } x \leq m \end{cases}$$

where Y is the output value, X is the input value, M is the maximum value, and m is the minimum value. See Figure 4-3.

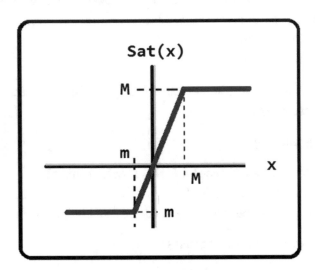

Figure 4-3. *Saturation function*

Although Figure 4-3 was made for illustrative purposes, note that the limits for M and m can be both positive and negative as preferred (see Listing 4-9). The saturation function is a logical function, so it can have other names, definitions, and similar functions. Among others see the following functions: signum function, heavyside function, step function, arctan function, on-off type activation function, binary step function, hyperbolic tangent function, and sigmoid function.

Listing 4-9. The Saturation function Seen as a Code

```
float sat (float val, float maxi, float mini)
{
    if(val>=maxi) val=maxi;
    else val=val;
    if(val<=min) val=min;
```

```
    else val=val;
    return val;
}
```

For example, suppose you have an orientation sensor that can measure values from -180 to 180 degrees, but to avoid damaging the equipment or to avoid reaching singular values, you want to limit the values to those between -45 and 45 degrees.

Listing 4-10. Saturating Values to Lesser Degrees

```
// it is assumed that the roll variable exists and
// that it can take values between -pi and pi radians
// see the upcoming section about the use of the inertial sensor

rolldeg=mapeo(-3.14,3.14,-180,180,roll);
rolls=sat(rolldeg,45,-45);
```

Implementation tips to remember are

- In the case of Listing 4-10, it is convenient to obtain maximum, minimum, and intermediate values if necessary. For this purpose, visualize each signal to be used with the serial monitor.

- The use of a LIPO battery adapter is recommended so that the radio stays on for longer. Some radios already come with this connector.

- In general, the binding process is necessary before using the transmitter and the receiver. This is to verify that they are compatible and use the same communication channel. For this purpose, each radio model has its own binding method.

Auxiliary Channels and Introduction to State Machines

As a standard, it is assumed that a radio is equipped with at least four channels: one for elevation or height (called throttle) and three others for guidance control. One is for turning on its own axis (yaw or rudder) and the rest are for moving indirectly within the XY plane by varying the angle of inclination of the vehicle (pitch and roll).

However, suppose you want to teleoperate other tasks. For example, you want to indicate the exact moment of takeoff, landing, ignition of some sprayer, etc.

For these situations, it is desirable that the remote control has auxiliary controls, which can be levers of two or three positions, buttons, or continuous rotation knobs.

If more auxiliary channels are available in the remote control, it is logical to say that more tasks can be assigned. However, if the remote control has more channels, it will also be more expensive. So it is useful to talk about state machines in order to increase the tasks to be performed with less communication channels.

Suppose that you have a six-channel radio. As mentioned, at least four of them should be used for vehicle movement, so there are two auxiliary channels. At first sight, you may assume that you only have capacity for two additional tasks. However, if these channels are ON/OFF lever types, you actually have a combination of four states for executing four different tasks:

```
Aux1 ON/Aux2 ON
Aux1 ON/Aux2 OFF
Aux1 OFF/Aux2 ON
Aux1 OFF/Aux2 OFF
```

You could also have an auxiliary channel of the ON/OFF lever type and another with three positions. This way, you have six possible combinations assignable to six tasks:

```
Aux1Pos1/Aux2  ON
Aux1Pos1/Aux2  OFF
Aux1Pos2/Aux2  ON
Aux1Pos2/Aux2  OFF
Aux1Pos3/Aux2  ON
Aux1Pos3/Aux2  OFF
```

The immediate action after making these deductions is to establish a sequence of operations and changes between tasks according to the positional logic of levers. This is called a state machine.

As an example, consider a drone window-cleaning sequence using two auxiliary channels and four tasks. You have a remote control that has two auxiliary channels with two-state type levers (ON/OFF). The four tasks are: (A) takeoff; (B) clean window; (C) regular landing (descend the vehicle once tasks are finished without any problem); (D) emergency stop (land immediately if there is any problem, interrupting any another task in turn).

The first step is to assign a combination of levers to each task. In order to make no intermediate combinations, it is convenient to assign a sequence where the change is made progressively and by activating one lever at a time. See Table 4-1.

Table 4-1. *Example of a State Machine*

State	Task	Combination AUX1, AUX2
(A)	Takeoff	0 , 1
(B)	Clean window	1 , 1
(C)	Regular landing	1 , 0
(D)	Emergency stop	0 , 0

The next step is to define the transition between states and discard unwanted transitions. For example, it is desirable to go from cleaning (B) to regular landing (C), but not from emergency stop (D) to takeoff (A), or from emergency stop (D) to cleaning (B). In those cases, the desirable action is simply to stay in that state.

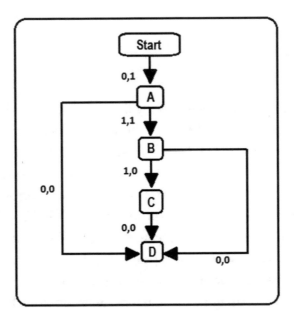

Figure 4-4. *The state machine of this example*

The diagram in Figure 4-4 is interpreted as follows:

- When the vehicle is stopped, the only way to take off is by using the combination of levers (0,1). All other combinations keep it stopped.

- When the vehicle is taking off (A), the only way to clean windows is through the combination (1,1). If the (0,0) combination is activated, then it proceeds to the emergency stop. If any other combination is activated, the vehicle stays in takeoff mode.

- When the vehicle is in cleaning mode (B), the only way to land in a regular way is through the combination (1,0). If the combination (0,0) is activated, the emergency stop is carried out. If any other combination is activated, the vehicle remains in the cleaning mode.

- When the vehicle is in regular landing mode (C), the aircraft will land smoothly unless the combination of emergency stop (0,0) is activated. Activating any other combination means the vehicle stays in the regular mode.

- Finally, when the vehicle is in emergency stop (D), any combination of levers will have no effect unless the battery is disconnected and reconnected.

The reader should notice that the logic of a state machine depends on the end user. Possibly, while being in state (D), it could be feasible for some readers to switch to takeoff (A) if the (0,1) combination is activated, or as seen in the previous example, taking off could not be feasible again until a battery reset.

This way, you have defined your operation sequence using combinatorial logic with two auxiliary levers. Notice that the commands necessary for each task are not yet defined. However, the steps to be followed once you detect the auxiliary channels are already defined. The code can be programmed with simple conditional commands like IF, WHILE, SWITCH, etc.

In the following chapters, you will return to what you have seen in this section, but it will be applied to the general example of a quadcopter flight, in order to design the controller for change between hover mode and follow-trajectory mode.

Implementation Tip   Sometimes programmers omit the realization of a state machine, following their own logic or simply thinking that this step could be omitted. Nevertheless, it is important to know how to design a state machine, or at least have notions of it, in order to make an operation diagram or flow chart. This makes it easier for other programmers to understand your code.

Position and Orientation Internal Sensors Reading

- **Devices**: Magnetometer, barometer, accelerometer, internal gyroscope

- **Components**: Only the Pixhawk, powered by a USB cable or LIPO battery

- **Description**: The Pixhawk has internal devices to measure position, altitude, orientation, linear acceleration, and angular speed. As will be noted in the code, obtaining this data requires the fusion of these sensors, except for the GPS, which allows an independent measurement based on satellite triangulation. This is necessary if you want to obtain a measurement in the X and Y planar positions.

Regarding altitude, which is an essential parameter to keep an unmanned aerial vehicle flying, Table 4-2 explains the ways to measure it.

Table 4-2. *Ways to Measure a Vehicle's Altitude*

Type of altitude measurement	Characteristics
GPS	For use in open areas, not in built or wooded areas Not suitable for landing or takeoff due to the centimetric resolution, in most cases Useful in large extensions, high altitudes, and open areas
Barometer	For use in laboratory or at intermediate heights (up to. 5 meters approx.) Not recommended for takeoff or landing due to its high noise level and drift error (cumulative error)
Analog	Examples are ultrasonic or LIDAR sensors Recommended for takeoff and landing (measurement resolution between 20 cm and 2 meters)
Serial	An example is a camera plus a Raspberry type development card. Serves for any case as long as the camera and the artificial vision algorithm are robust enough Allows serial data wireless communication

IMPLEMENTATION TIP

- If it is necessary to connect both the LIPO battery and the USB power, make sure to connect the LIPO first.

- Electrical noise is an inevitable phenomenon. It is generated by motor vibrations in a very similar way to how a blender or drill affects most TV screens. However, to attenuate it in some projects, it is convenient to add dissipating pads between the drone's frame and the autopilot.

- Drift is another inevitable phenomenon in certain sensors, such as the barometer (a device that measures height as a function of pressure). In this case, it is convenient to have different sensors to measure different altitude modalities. For example, use an analog-type sonar or laser to measure height during landing and takeoff, or other delicate proximity tasks during flight; and use the barometer in combination with the GPS and the inertial control unit to measure altitude in really high or clear flight ranges.

- Up to now, GPS still presents an unreliable resolution with respect to other sensors (in centimetric order). Therefore, it must be used in open field scenarios (it is not very operative in closed environments). Also, it must be used in situations where the resolution is not so important. For example, in wide-ranging movements (such as following road routes or exploring crops).

- Avoid flying near high voltage lines and transformers, because the IMU has a terrestrial field magnetometer whose measurements can be altered under the effects of electromagnetic induction.

- In order to regulate orientations, you need to consider situations called "singularities," especially in continuous movements such as the yaw angle. In situations with restricted movements such as roll and pitch in a standard multicopter, there is no need to worry about them. These situations are positions where the sensor, by its nature, has abrupt changes, such as the ones described in Figure 4-5. Notice that the illustration is presented in degrees to facilitate understanding, but the sensor commonly measures in radians. However, this does not change the nature of the problem, only the units used.

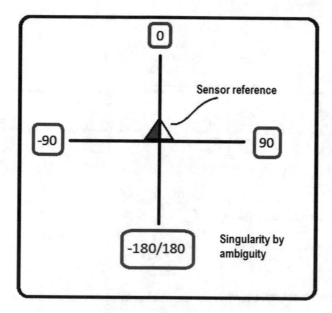

Figure 4-5. *A kind of angular singularity*

In this case, it is convenient to use a normalization method, which implies adjusting the values so that they have a continuous operating range. For these tests, you will use the angular normalization algorithm with left and right symmetry with respect to the measured value. It is performed as follows:

1. Calculate the angular error.

2. Apply the following membership rule. It indicates whether the angular movement is normalized to the left or right with respect to the measurement angle. See Figure 4-6.

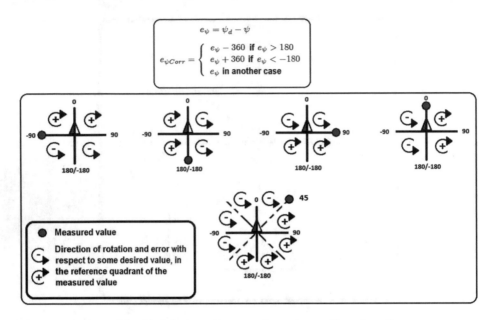

Figure 4-6. *A kind of dynamic angular normalization for avoiding singularities*

Notice that an inverse rotation algorithm, a transfer algorithm (-180°, 180°) to (0°, 360°), an algorithm that considers turns account, or an absolute reference algorithm may also exist. In this case, a relative reference algorithm was described with respect to the measured value. Also notice that the presented algorithm allows you to reduce the effect of the singularity with respect to these measured positions. For this purpose, we encourage you to test the given algorithm in a spreadsheet and corroborate the turning direction and the magnitude of error. The presented algorithm has the intention of minimizing the energy consumption of the drone, as well as rotation time, establishing rotation symmetry with respect to the measurement axis, which is dynamically updated and can be applied to any other type of vehicles. See Listings 4-11 and 4-12.

Listing 4-11 provides an example of angular reading. Note the following:

- The syntax are:

```
ahrs.roll;
ahrs.pitch;
ahrs.yaw;
for angles
const Vector3f  &get_gyro(void)
for angular velocities
```

You can find more information at: https://github.com/ArduPilot/ardupilot/blob/master/libraries/AP_AHRS/AP_AHRS.h

https://github.com/ArduPilot/ardupilot/blob/master/libraries/AP_AHRS/examples/AHRS_Test/AHRS_Test.cpp

https://github.com/ArduPilot/ardupilot/blob/master/libraries/AP_InertialSensor/AP_InertialSensor.h

https://github.com/ArduPilot/ardupilot/blob/master/libraries/AP_InertialSensor/examples/INS_generic/INS_generic.cpp

Listing 4-11. Orientation and Angular Velocity Readings

```
///////////////////////// DECLARATION /////////////////////////
//                  Put the header here
//                  see the appendix

//        verify or add these lines
static AP_GPS  gps;
static AP_Baro barometer;
static AP_InertialSensor ins;
static AP_SerialManager serial_manager;
static Compass compass;
#if CONFIG_SONAR == ENABLED
static RangeFinder sonar;
```

121

```
static bool sonar_enabled = true;
#endif

//////////////////// the code goes here ////////////////////

//         verify or add these lines

float roll, pitch, yaw;
float gyrox, gyroy, gyroz;
Vector3f gyro;

//////////////////////// INITIALIZATION ////////////////////////

void setup(){
//          verify or add these lines
    compass.init();
    compass.read();
    ahrs.set_compass(&compass);
}
//////////////////////// EXECUTION ////////////////////////

void loop(){
// angular reading
    ahrs.update();
    roll  = ahrs.roll;
    pitch = ahrs.pitch;
    yaw   = ahrs.yaw;

// angular velocities reading
    gyro  = ins.get_gyro();
    gyrox = gyro.x;
    gyroy = gyro.y;
    gyroz = gyro.z;

}

AP_HAL_MAIN(); // Ardupilot function call
```

Listing 4-12 provides an example of barometer reading. Note the following:

- The syntax are:

float barometer.get_altitude( );

and .get_climb_rate for vertical velocity

You can find more information at: https://github.com/ArduPilot/ardupilot/blob/master/libraries/AP_Baro/AP_Baro.h

Listing 4-12. Altitude and Vertical Velocity Readings with a Barometer

```
///////////////////////// DECLARATION /////////////////////////////
//                  Put the header here
//                      see the appendix

//////////////////////// the code goes here ////////////////////////

//       verify or add these lines

static AP_Baro barometer;
float baro_alt=0;

////////////////////////// INITIALIZATION //////////////////////////

void setup(){
//          verify or add these lines
    barometer.init();
    barometer.calibrate();
}
```

```
//////////////////////// EXECUTION ////////////////////////

void loop(){
    barometer.update();
    baro_alt = barometer.get_altitude();
}

AP_HAL_MAIN();// Ardupilot function call
```

External Position Sensors Reading (GPS)

- **Components**: GPS and Pixhawk

- **Description**: So far with Listing 4-11 and Listing 4-12, you have orientation and altitude measurements. However, in order to measure planar positions (X,Y) you can follow three paths:

    1. Use integrators or mathematical observers applied on accelerations and velocities to estimate them. In this case, acceleration measures are obtained by the ins command through its accel property: ins.get_accel ().

       However, this entails cumulative performance errors. These errors are caused by filtering delays and increased noise (an estimate based on a noisy signal will achieve only another noisy signal). The simplest algorithm (called dirty integration or rectangular approximation) is shown in Figure 4-7.

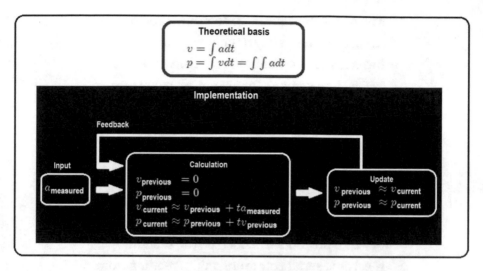

Figure 4-7. *An elementary dirty integrator algorithm to get positions and velocities from acceleration*

Without going into extensive details, it is based on a continually updatable sum, because the approximation of an integral is a succession of added rectangular areas. However, it has some important details:

a. Being a sum, it can overflow.

b. The approximation is usually deficient if the integration interval is very large.

c. If the movement profile is not smooth or is very noisy, the integral will also try to add up noise and abrupt changes, causing more error propagation.

The use of this option is recommended only in case of emergency or failure in the rest of the sensors. It is better to use a direct sensor (a GPS or a camera, for example). If you are interested in further details, there are innovative algorithms based on modifications of the dirty integral. One of them can be found at `http://x-io.co.uk/gait-tracking-with-x-imu/`.

2. Get the measurement from specialized sensors such as cameras with artificial vision or analog or serial position sensors (see the sections regarding serial communication, reading from analog sensors, and serial communication with development cards).

    The use of this option is recommended in interior spaces where the GPS signal does not arrive, or for more precise tasks such as takeoff, landing, or automatic contact with the environment (windows, walls, other nearby drones, etc.).

3. Use GPS. This option is highly recommended in outdoor spaces and especially in open areas (GPS does not work in enclosed spaces or among trees, buildings, walls, etc.).

    The use of this option is recommended for long distance flights in which accuracy is not a significant factor (standard GPS goes from metric errors to centimetric ones). Although there are GPSs with millimeter range, their cost rises considerably. See Listing 4-13.

Listing 4-13 provides an example of GPS reading. Note the following:

- The syntax are:

```
const Location &location( )
virtual void set_home(const Location &loc)
void set_initial_location(int32_t latitude, int32_t
longitude)
virtual const Vector3f&    get_position( )
virtual const Vector3f&    get_velocity( )
```

You can find more information at: https://github.com/ArduPilot/ardupilot/blob/master/libraries/AP_GPS/AP_GPS.h

https://github.com/ArduPilot/ardupilot/blob/master/libraries/AP_GPS/examples/GPS_AUTO_test/GPS_AUTO_test.cpp

https://github.com/ArduPilot/ardupilot/blob/master/libraries/AP_AHRS/AP_AHRS.h

https://github.com/ArduPilot/ardupilot/blob/master/libraries/AP_Compass/AP_Compass.h

https://github.com/ArduPilot/ardupilot/blob/master/libraries/AP_InertialNav/AP_InertialNav.h

Listing 4-13. To Read Planar Positions and Velocities by Using GPS (Also Altitude)

```
//////////////////////// DECLARATION ////////////////////////
//              Here goes the header
//                 See apendix

// verify or add this line
static AP_InertialNav_NavEKF inertial_nav(ahrs);
```

```
//////////////////////// your code is here ////////////////////////

//          verify or add these lines

static Vector3f pos_gps;
static Vector3f vel_gps;
static Vector3f pos;
static Vector3f vel;
static AP_GPS  gps;
static Compass compass;

/////////////////////// INITIALIZATION /////////////////////////////

void setup(){

//           verify or add these lines
    gps.init(NULL,serial_manager);
    ahrs.set_compass(&compass);
}
///////////////////////// EXECUTION /////////////////////////////////

//              Main loop
void loop(){
    update_GPS();
}

//           GPS auxiliary function

static void update_GPS(void){
      static uint32_t last_msg_ms;
      gps.update();
       if (last_msg_ms != gps.last_message_time_ms())
       {
           last_msg_ms = gps.last_message_time_ms();
           const Location &loc =gps.location();
```

```
        flag = gps.status();
     }

    uint32_t currtime = hal.scheduler->millis();
    dt = (float)(currtime - last_update) / 1000.0f;
    last_update = currtime;
// a delta t is required to internally calculate velocities
   inertial_nav.update(dt);

// this part verifies that there are at least 3 satellites to
// operate and turn on the led if this is affirmative,
// also changes a variable called flag2 to update speeds

    flag= gps.num_sats();

    if(pos.x!=0 && flag >=3 && flag2==1){
        const Location &loc = gps.location();
        ahrs.set_home(loc);
        compass.set_initial_location(loc.lat, loc.lng);
        toshiba_led.set_rgb(0,LED_DIM,0);   // green LED
        flag2 = 2;
     }

   pos_gps  = inertial_nav.get_position();
   vel_gps = inertial_nav.get_velocity();
// a gps of centimetric resolution is assumed
// and then it is transformed to meters

   pos.x=((pos_gps.x)/100);
   pos.y=((pos_gps.y)/100);
   pos.z=((pos_gps.z)/100);
   if(flag2==2){
       vel.x=((vel_gps.x)/100);
       vel.y=((vel_gps.y)/100);
   }
```

```
    vel.z=((vel_gps.z)/100);
    flag2==1;
```

```
// utility to display the GPS data, comment if it is not needed
//hal.console->printf("%f\t %f\t %f\t %f\t
//%d\n",pos_gps.x,pos_gps.y,vel_gps.x,vel_gps.y,gps.num_sats());
```

```
}
```

```
AP_HAL_MAIN(); // Ardupilot function call
```

Implementation Tip   Operate as long as there are at least six or more satellites available. The more satellites, the better the resolution and operation.

After a certain time, if the error between the current position and the previous position remains low (noise-free, almost constant, and seems not to change, tending to a value close to zero), or there is not an adequate number of satellites, you can use sensorial fusion; that is, to activate operation cycles where the position signal is updated either by a mathematical method or by another sensor on board (cameras, radars, lasers, etc.).

Reading Analog Sensors

- **Components**: Different analog sensors and Pixhawk

- **Description**: The Pixhawk allows the connection of various analog sensors, such as ultrasonic meters of distance, color, contact force, etc.

- **Connection**: Analog sensors in general have three pins: power, ground, and signal. However, not all analog sensors have the connection port of the Pixhawk. You may need to weld or adapt the sensor to this port.

Implementation Tip   To obtain the required operating ranges it is necessary to use mapping functions. This happens because sensors can have an arbitrary range of values. Linear mappings generally work, but it is advisable to review the manufacturer's technical sheets because certain sensors have highly non-linear behaviors (which do not behave as a straight line). In these cases, it is the readers' responsibility to establish their own correspondence rules.

In some cases, it is useful to establish saturation functions, in order to avoid the sensor reaching risk points. It could also be useful to simply establish a limited work area.

Do not forget to check the sensor's maximum and minimum electrical values and adapt them to those of the autopilot. If the sensor delivers a lot of current or voltage, the autopilot could literally be fried.

The Pixhawk has three analog inputs, one of 6.6V and two shared 3.3 V ports. For correct declaration, check port directions at http://ardupilot.org/copter/docs/common-pixhawk-overview.html.

For the example in Listing 4-14, use a sensor connected to pin 15.

Listing 4-14 provides an example of analog reading. Note the following:

- The syntax are:

```
ch=hal.analogin->channel(chan);
ch->set_pin(chan number);
ch->voltage_average( );
```

You can find more information at: https://github.com/ArduPilot/ardupilot/blob/master/libraries/AP_HAL/AnalogIn.h

https://github.com/ArduPilot/ardupilot/blob/master/libraries/AP_HAL/examples/AnalogIn/AnalogIn.cpp

Listing 4-14. Reading Analog Ports

```
/////////////////////////// DECLARATION ///////////////////////////
//                     Put the header code here
//                          see apendix

// verify this line or add it
AP_HAL::AnalogSource* ch;

/////////////////////////// INITIALIZATION ///////////////////////////

//           setup cycle
void setup(){

// verify these lines or add them

    ch = hal.analogin->channel(0);
    ch->set_pin(15);

}
/////////////////////////// EXECUTION ///////////////////////////

// Main loop and ADC function call
```

```
void loop(){
    adc();
}

//          ADC function definition

static void adc(){
    float v = ch->voltage_average();
    hal.console->printf("voltaje:%f \n",v);
}

AP_HAL_MAIN(); // Ardupilo function call
```

Signals Filtering

- **Components**: Any sensor

- **Description**: Many vehicles, especially those subject to vibrations, such as aerial or ground vehicles with irregular terrain, transfer their mechanical noise to electrical noise, particularly because they have motors. As a result, measurements made by their sensors are affected. To reduce the effects of the inevitable noise by mechanical vibrations or other sources of disturbances, the best known active method is signal filtering.

Although there are many analog and digital electronic filters, in this section we will describe computational filters incorporated into ArduPilot libraries, such as the low-pass filter. Without going into further details, we can say that they take a signal of interest and soften it.

The biggest problem with the use of filters is that they produce a delay on the filtered signal; see Figure 4-8. This means that the filtered signal will arrive later than the original signal, which may affect the vehicle's performance. This is why it is convenient to have a moderate filter or a specialized processor. The Pixhawk has both.

133

It is also convenient to design a filter that delays the output signal for the least amount of time possible with respect to the one introduced. In this case, ArduPilot libraries have a range of filters. Therefore, you can choose the one most appropriate for your application.

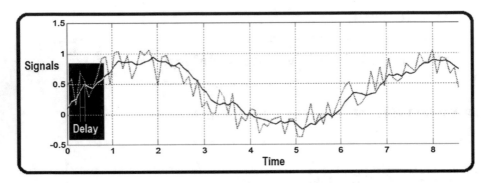

Figure 4-8. *A noisy signal and its filtered signal*

In Figure 4-8, you can see how the soft (filtered) signal looks more delayed than the noisy one (original). This means that the original signal occurred first and the filtered one occurred after processing (if the operation of the system is critical, a delay between both signals can be problematic). This way, filter design turns into a game between noise elimination and the delay of the filtered signal. See Listing 4-15.

Listing 4-15 provides an example of signal filtering. Note the following:

- The syntax are:

```
static LowPassFilter2pFloat NAME(SamplingFrequency,
CutFrequency);
filteredSignal = NAME.apply( originalSignal );
```

You can find more information at: https://github.com/ArduPilot/
ardupilot/tree/master/libraries/Filter/examples

https://github.com/ArduPilot/ardupilot/blob/master/
libraries/Filter/examples/LowPassFilter2p/LowPassFilter2p.cpp

Listing 4-15. Signal Filtering

```
///////////////////////// DECLARATION ///////////////////////////
//                      Place here the header
//                              see appendix

///////////////////////// place your code here ///////////////////////

// verify t.hat the following lines exist or add them
// this code uses part of the code related to the barometer

static AP_Baro barometer;

// in the following line the characteristics and name
// of the filer to be use are defined
static LowPassFilter2pfloat fil_posz(10,0.8);
float baro_alt=0, alt_fil:

///////////////////////// INITIALIZATION ///////////////////////////

void setup(){
//          verify or add the following lines
    barometer.init();
    barometer.calibrate();
}
///////////////////////// EXECUTION ///////////////////////////

void loop(){
    barometer.update();
    baro_alt = barometer.get_altitude();
```

```
// on the next line, the previously defined filter is applied
// to a signal of interest, in this case the one received by
// the barometer

    alt_fil=fil_posz.apply(baro_alt);

}

AP_HAL_MAIN(); // Ardupilot function call
```

Digital Reading and Writing

- **Components**: JTAG CABLES and two-state digital components (LEDs, push buttons, etc.)

- **Description**: Digital ports allow binary components (ON/ OFF type), such as LEDs, push buttons, pulse encoder readers or buzzers, to be used as indicators, sound or visual alerts, security or start buttons, or as task sequencers if several autopilots are connected among them (that is, depending on the binary signal read, an autopilot may or may not perform a given function). This type of port is known as GPIO (global purpose input and output).

- **Connection**: It is only necessary to use the ground pin and the signal pin. In these cases, it is convenient to leave the Pixhawk power port disconnected. See Listing 4-16.

Implementation Tip   According to the ArduPilot libraries webpage, digital ports have associated numbers. Go to `http://ardupilot. org/copter/docs/common-pixhawk-overview.html`.

As with any other port, it is convenient to review the electrical specifications of both the autopilot and the devices to be connected.

Listing 4-16 provides an example of digital input and output. Note the following:

- The syntax are:

```
pinMode(uint8_t pin, uint8_t output)
write(uint8_t pin, uint8_t value)
read(uint8_t pin)
```

You can find more information at: https://github.com/ArduPilot/ardupilot/blob/master/libraries/AP_HAL/GPIO.h

Listing 4-16. Reading and Writing Digital GPIO

```
//////////////////////// DECLARATION //////////////////////////
//                      Here paste the header code
//                              See appendix

//    If needed add this library: GPIO.h


/////////////////// example code is placed here ////////////////

//////////////////////// INITIALIZATION ////////////////////////

void setup(){

// add the following lines, for pin numbers consult
// http://ardupilot.org/copter/docs/common-pixhawk-overview.html
// in this part pins 54 and 55 are started as output and input
// respectively

      hal.gpio->pinMode(54, HAL_GPIO_OUTPUT);
      hal.gpio->pinMode(55, HAL_GPIO_INPUT);
      hal.gpio->write(54, 0);

}
```

```
/////////////////////////// EXECUTION ///////////////////////////

// this program sends a logical 1 or 0 to port 54
// physically connected to the 55
// reading the pin 55 and writing a message
// if 1 or 0 was received

void loop(){

    hal.scheduler->delay(7000);
    hal.gpio->write(54, 1);

    if (hal.gpio->read(55))
        {hal.console->printf("A\t\n");}
    else
        {hal.console->printf("B\t\n");}

    hal.scheduler->delay(1000);
    hal.gpio->write(54, 0);

    if (hal.gpio->read(55))
        {hal.console->printf("A\t\n");}
    else
        {hal.console->printf("B\t\n");}

}

AP_HAL_MAIN(); // Ardupilot function call
```

Battery Reading

- **Components**: Battery, battery monitor

- **Description**: This command allows the user to read the average current and voltage from the LIPO battery in order to later use these readings to activate an alarm in case of low battery or to design battery-dependent controllers. See Listing 4-17.

Listing 4-17 provides an example of battery reading. Note the following:

- The syntax is:

```
void read( );
```

You can find more information at: https://github.com/ArduPilot/ardupilot/blob/master/libraries/AP_BattMonitor/AP_BattMonitor.h

Listing 4-17. Reading the Battery State

```
//////////////////////// DECLARATION ////////////////////////
//                      Paste the header here
//                          See appendix

//////////////////// place your code here ////////////////////
// verify those lines or add them
static AP_BattMonitor battery;
float volt, corriente_tot;

//////////////////////// INITIALIZATION ////////////////////////
void setup(){
// verify those lines or add them

battery.set_monitoring(0,AP_BattMonitor::BattMonitor_TYPE_
ANALOG_VOLTAGE_AND_CURRENT);
    battery.init();
}
//////////////////////// EXECUTION ////////////////////////
void loop(){
    Read_battery();
}
```

```
// auxiliar function definition
static void Read_battery(){

    battery.read();
    volt=battery.voltage();
    corriente_tot=battery.current_total_mah();
}

AP_HAL_MAIN(); // Ardupilot function call
```

Implementation Tip   When the battery level is reduced, you should increase controller gains so that the system continues to operate as expected. This is, of course, until the point when the vehicle must stop due to safety considerations.

Never use LIPO batteries under the average voltage level (generally a LIPO with max voltage charge at 4.2V must not be used under 3.7V, but this can vary among battery models, so check this value on datasheets). This could damage them or imply an explosion risk. In order to monitor these values without using a Pixhawk, use an external monitor.

The Pixhawk uses batteries with at least three cells (so around 11.4V). The current will depend on the motors used and the limit load of the vehicle. In general, if the battery gives more current, the motor will only take the necessary amount and it will last longer. On the other hand, the system will be heavier.

In order to operate a charger, remember that they are usually sold as two different components: a power supply and the charger by itself.

Using Visual Alerts Through the Main LED

- **Components**: Pixhawk main LED

- **Description**: The Pixhawk has a RGB-type LED on
  board. It allows us to use a visual alert system (for
  starting a mission, for indicating low battery, for
  indicating which drone is a leader within a group of
  drones, etc.). The implementation is relatively simple;
  see Listing 4-18.

Listing 4-18 provides an example of the on-board LED. Note the following:

- The syntax is:

```
toshiba_led.set_rgb(red, green, blue);
```

You can find more information at: https://github.com/ArduPilot/
ardupilot/blob/master/libraries/AP_Notify/examples/ToshibaLED_
test/ToshibaLED_test.cpp

Listing 4-18. Main LED

```
//////////////////////// DECLARATION /////////////////////////
//                 Paste here the header
//                     see appendix

//////////////////////// here is your code ////////////////////

// add those lines or verify them
#define LED_DIM 0x11
static ToshibaLED_PX4 toshiba_led;

//////////////////////// INITIALIZATION ///////////////////////

void setup(){
// verify or add this line
```

```
    toshiba_led.init();
}
/////////////////////////// EXECUTION ///////////////////////////
void loop(){
    toshiba_led.set_rgb(0,LED_DIM,0);
}

AP_HAL_MAIN(); // Ardupilot function call
```

Chapter Summary

In this chapter you learned some of the most important and basic input and output operations:

- How to read and write from and to a serial terminal

- How to read the radio control

- How to read from analog ports

- How to use digital GPIO ports

- How to read the battery

- How to use the onboard main LED

- How to read position and orientation signals in order to later control a vehicle

- How to filter those signals, which usually are pretty noisy

In the next chapter, you will learn advanced commands by using ArduPilot libraries. Specifically, you'll learn how to use serial wired and wireless communications, and how to store flight data, as well as generalities on time management and how to use different kinds of motors.

CHAPTER 5

Advanced Operations

In this chapter, you will explore some advanced ArduPilot topics. In fact, this is one of the most valuable parts of the book because we break down the more complicated commands. We'll also cover wired and wireless UART serial communications, flight data storage, foundations of time management, and how to use several types of motors.

Wired and Wireless Serial Communication

- **Components**: Telemetry transmitter
- **Description**: This device allows wired or wireless intercommunication via serial type UART devices.

  - Wirelessly, this task demands power from the autopilot. In this way, in order to work correctly, you must use a LIPO battery supply or another adequate supply that is better than just your computer USB port.

  - It is advisable to use telemetry transmitters with this kind of wireless communication. However, the transmission speed is reduced to 57600 bps.

  - On the other hand, when a wired form is used, speed is limited only by the system's performance.

© Julio Alberto Mendoza-Mendoza, Victor Gonzalez-Villela 2020
J. A. Mendoza-Mendoza et al., *Advanced Robotic Vehicles Programming*,
https://doi.org/10.1007/978-1-4842-5531-5_5

- **Connection**: Wireless. The user must connect the
  transmitters to the corresponding port. However, they
  must share the same channel. For this, it is necessary to
  perform the following procedure:

  1. Connect the radio to the computer, using the
     miniUSB port. It should install automatically.
     Pay attention to which COM port is assigned
     during this step.

  2. If you do not obtain this information, you must
     look for it in the Windows device manager, in
     the COM ports section. It should be indicated
     as "USB serial port" or something similar. In
     Figure 5-1, it is assigned to COM6.

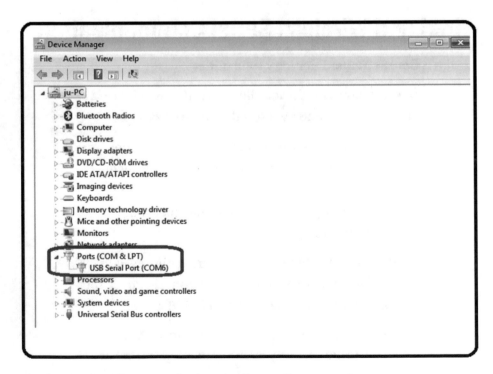

Figure 5-1. *Telemetry device configuration, step 2*

3. Indicate the assigned port number (in this example COM6) in Mission Planner, without clicking the Connect button. Then set the speed to 57600 (which is standard for wireless serial transmission). See Figure 5-2.

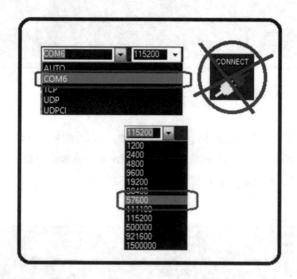

Figure 5-2. *Telemetry device configuration, step 3*

4. Go to the initial setup tab and select Optional Hardware. See Figure 5-3.

Figure 5-3. *Telemetry device configuration, step 4*

5. Press SiK Radio (or 3DRadio, in older versions). SiK is the generic name of the wireless serial telemetry protocol. See Figure 5-4.

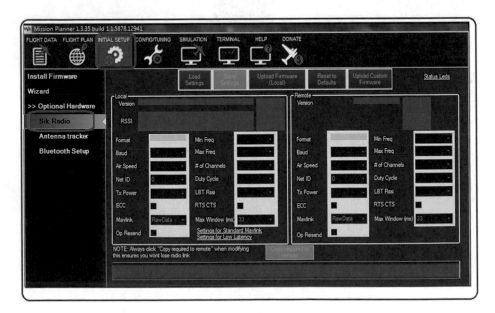

Figure 5-4. *Telemetry device configuration, step 5*

6.   Select Load Settings. The preloaded features
     of the connected telemetry radio should be
     loaded. If you plan to make the channels
     compatible with other equipment, print
     the screen and save it as an image for later
     comparisons and adjustments. See Figure 5-5.

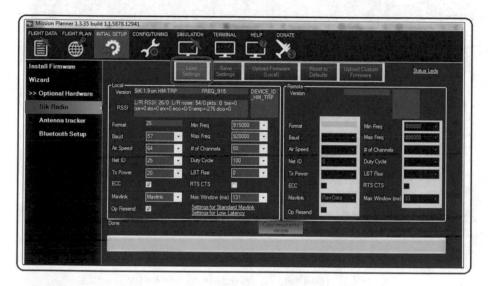

Figure 5-5.   *Telemetry device configuration, step 6*

7.   Repeat the process for the other radios
     (in the other example, COM7 was assigned).
     See Figure 5-6.

Figure 5-6. *Telemetry device configuration, step 7*

8. If it is necessary to change other parameters, such as net ID (so that, for example, three or five radios share a specific channel of operation), modify the corresponding box and save by pressing the Save Settings button. See Figure 5-7.

Figure 5-7. *Telemetry device configuration, step 8*

It is advisable only to change the net ID; to modify other parameters, see http://ardupilot.org/copter/docs/common-configuring-a-telemetry-radio-using-mission-planner.html.

The netID is assigned to 25 by default, but assuming that many users have the same number, perhaps you want a private channel, so you must modify that 25 to another number. This tool is also useful if you have a previously used telemetry radio and several of its parameters were altered with the intention of resetting them or updating certain transmission parameters that are not legal in some places.

As a physical connection, you must share ground between the devices (not necessarily power, unless the transmitter and the receiver share the same battery), and the TX and RX pins (transmit and receive) must be connected by a cross-wire.

Remember, if it is a wireless transmission, the UARTC port must be used, but if it's wired, the UARTD port must be used.

Communication Procedure

The serial communication standard requires transmission and reception of 8-bit data packages. For this, it is necessary to send data that does not exceed the number 255 or that contains negative or decimal numbers. This can be done by using the scaling with displacement method, and module and residue components. This is explained in the next sections.

Procedures for Sending Data

If the data you're sending contains a range of negative and positive values:

1. Apply scaling with casting (type conversion) to eliminate decimals. Since serial communication only admits integer numbers, scaling will influence precision. For example, the number 3.1416 scaled 10 times is 31.416 and once you've applied the casting, it is only 31. The same number, 3.1416, scaled 100 times is 314.16 and after casting, it is the integer 314.

2. Apply displacement. To do this, it is necessary to establish maximum and minimum limits to define an operation range (see the saturation function). For example, if the minimum value is -10.12 and the maximum value is 10.78, once they're scaled 100 times and the integer range of [-1012, 1078] is established, the absolute value of the minimum value (which is 1012) must be added to each limit. This way the new range is [0, 2090].

3. Obtain the module and residue (upper and lower parts). Remember that UART serial communication only supports groups of 8 bits, which is a maximum value of 256 elements (from 0 to 255). So if your range exceeds this, it is necessary to separate it into a module and a residue. In order to do this, you use the following operation:

   a) Module: It is the integer result of the next division (VALUE/256).

   b) Residual: It is the residual part of the next division (VALUE/256).

The module is known as the high part and the residual as the low part. For example, if the value is 2090,

- Module (2090/256) = 8. See Figure 5-8.

- Residual (2090/256) = 42. See Figure 5-9.

This way, the number sent corresponds to the following reconstruction:

```
VALUE = MODULE * (256) + RESIDUE
2090 = (8 * 256) + 42
```

Since groups of bits operate in binary values, the binary equivalent of these module and residue operations are shift operations (>> in C++) and AND masking (& in C ++).

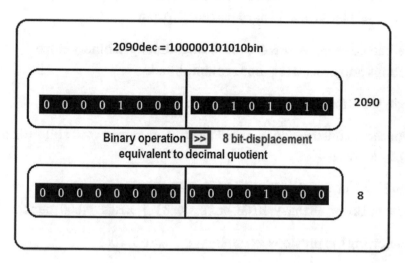

Figure 5-8. *Number fragmentation for sending data, module*

The value of 8 is chosen for the shift because 2 raised to the eighth power equals to 256.

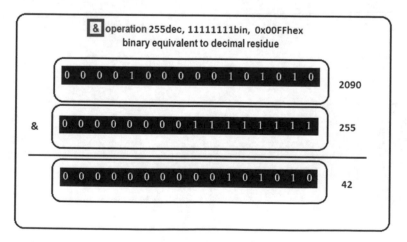

Figure 5-9. *Number fragmentation for sending data, residue*

The value of 255 is chosen because it is the largest number that can be formed with 8 bits. Thus,

```
HIGH part = MODULE = binary value >> 8
LOW part = RESIDUE = binary value & 0x00FF
```

As can be seen, we prefer proceeding directly in binary since operations and processing time are simplified.

```
4 High and low part reconstruction
```

For the reconstruction, you will use the operators << 8 and | (OR in C ++), as follows:

```
Decimal value = MODULE * (256) + RESIDUE
Binary value = (Binary HIGH part << 8) | Binary LOW part
```

Following the previous example, see Figure 5-10.

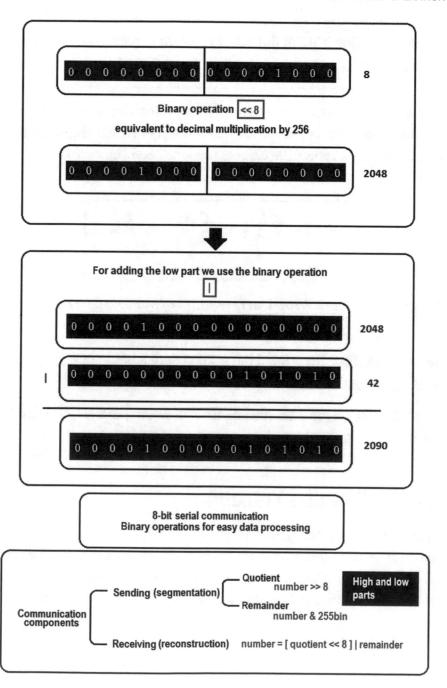

Figure 5-10. *Data reception process and recap*

Implementation Tip   If the data to be sent is only located in a range of positive values, execute only steps 1 and 3. Omit step 2.

The concepts of module and residue are better understood with a circumference. An angle of 810 degrees is simply two 360-degree turns (module) and a surplus of 90 degrees (residue). See Figure 5-11.

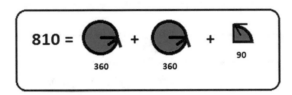

Figure 5-11. *Geometrical interpretation of module and residue*

Implementation Tip   Read the section dedicated to special types of data again to remember why uint_8 variable types are used.

Always clean values after reading from or writing to the UART. This avoids sending or reading junk or accumulated values.

Data Verification Procedure

Reading or sending data is not enough. You should also try to verify this data. In order to do this, we will teach you two very basic but useful methods called checksum and XOR checksum. Be careful, and remember that they are not corrective methods; they simply avoid receiving incorrect data.

Description of a Basic Checksum Method

1. **Sending**: Since data are collections of 8-bit integers sent sequentially, when sending them, it is convenient to send at least one additional byte (an 8-bit collection) that contains the sum of the data of interest.

   ```
   Data1 = 100
   Data2 = 15
   CheckSend = 115
   ```

2. **Reception**: In this case, you must add the received data by generating a checksum of reception, which must match with the checksum that was sent.

   ```
   Received1 = 100
   Received2 = 15
   Received3 = 115
   CheckReceived = Received1 + Received2 = 115
   Since Received3 = CheckReceived, sent data are
   accepted.
   ```

However, imagine that Data1 is corrupted in the sending process, getting the following:

```
Received1 = 90
Received2 = 15
Received3 = 115
CheckReceived = Received1 + Received2 = 105
```

In this case, since Received3 is different from CheckReceived, the transmission data are rejected or requested again.

This method has a problem. It can overflow and require sending two parts (high and low) or it can send more than a single checksum. Remember that the checksum can only reach a maximum value of 255.

```
Data1 = 200
Data2 = 300
CheckSend = 500
```

This way, the checksum cannot be sent directly and must be segmented.

Description of the XOR Checksum Method

The XOR type checksum is an improvement method that instead of using a standard sum uses a "logical binary sum." Its problem is that it can present ambiguities.

For this, you use the truth table of the XOR function.

```
Inputs      Output
X   Y       X (xor) Y
0   0          0
0   1          1
1   0          1
1   1          0
```

For example, you want to transmit the value 10011. You get the parity

```
1 (xor) 0 (xor) 0 (xor) 1 (xor) 1 = 1
```

You include the parity in the sending:

```
100111
```

In the receiver, you perform

```
1 (xor) 0 (xor) 0 (xor) 1 (xor) 1 = 1
```

You compare it with the last element received (in this case, the sixth to be read). Since they coincide, the reception was successful.

Now imagine that information was corrupted and you get

```
110111
1 (xor) 1 (xor) 0 (xor) 1 (xor) 1 = 0
```

Since this value is different from checksum, which is equal to 1, the received element is discarded or requested again.

This method presents two problems. First, the data may seem to be correct even if it is not. For example, if you get

```
010111
0 (xor) 1 (xor) 0 (xor) 1 (xor) 1 = 1
```

It is evidently wrong, but since it produced the same checksum, it is considered valid data. The second problem is, the same checksum can arrive incorrectly, avoiding the reception of a correct message. So instead of receiving 100111, you get 100110. Although the message arrived correctly, the checksum by itself discards the sent data.[1]

In summary, if the checksum on the receiver side matches the checksum on the transmitter side, you can say that they are "valid" data or, at least, usable. Although there are more sophisticated methods for performing this verification, we have presented two of the simplest. For our purposes, it is considered that a successful checksum recovers at least 50% of the sent data.

---

[1]For more information, you can consult https://en.wikipedia.org/wiki/Parity_bit

Polling

Up to now, you know how to read and write serial data, as well as how to verify sending integrity (at least in a very basic way). However, it is also convenient to know when you need to read and when you need to write (in the same way that you know when to talk and when to listen in a conversation). Note that this method is only valid when all the devices are able to send and receive data (as with most wireless Pixhawk radios).

For this, you will use a simple polling method, in which the members of a communication system emit turn signals to indicate when they should be emitters and when they should be receivers. The method follows this process (notice that this algorithm can vary among different communication topologies, and it is only illustrated for being easy to understand and apply):

1. All the devices write and read simultaneously looking for a special value (a letter or a number). This special value will dictate who starts the turn (for example, a group of three transmitters and receivers, each one sending the numbers 1, 2, and 3).

2. When that sequence initializer is detected (number 1, for example), only the corresponding device can write, while the rest is dedicated to reading. Once this device has written, the sequencer will change to number 2.

3. While the corresponding devices read and the sequencer has been changed to 2, now only device 2 can send data and the others must read. Once device 2 has written, the sequencer must change to number 3.

4. Now only device 3 can write data and the others must read. Once the writing is complete, the sequencer will be sent to number 1 and the cycle will be repeated.

TRANSMISSION AND RECEPTION CODE WITHOUT CHECKSUM OR POLLING

Listing 5-1 provides an example of wired or wireless UART serial communication. Note the following:

- The syntax are:

```
uartC->available( )
uint8_t  uartC->read( )
uartD->available( )
uint8_t  uartD->read( )
```

You can find more information at: http://ardupilot.org/dev/docs/
learning-ardupilot-uarts-and-the-console.html
https://github.com/ArduPilot/ardupilot/blob/master/
libraries/AP_HAL/examples/UART_test/UART_test.cpp

Listing 5-1. UART Communication, Wireless and Wired Receiver

```
//////////////////////////// DECLARATION ////////////////////////////////
//                    Paste the header here
//                        see appendix

//////////////////////// place your code here ////////////////////////

// verify or add this line
uint8_t _bufferrx[4]; // 4 values are readed
```

```
//////////////////////// INITIALIZATION ///////////////////////
void setup(){
        hal.uartC->begin(57600); // verify or add this line
                                 // remember,  C = Telem 1
                                 // or wireless
                                 // also 57600 is maximum
                                 // wireless speed

}
/////////////////////////// EXECUTION ///////////////////////////

void loop(){

    uint8_t i=0;
    // read if the port is available
    if(hal.uartC->available()){
        while(hal.uartC->available() &&  i<4)
            {
                _bufferrx[i]=hal.uartC->read();
                i=i+1;
            }
    }
    // data elements 1 and 2 are high and low parts of a bigger value
    // the operator + and |  are interchangeable in this case
    int constru=(_bufferrx[1]<<8) + (_bufferrx[2]);
    hal.console->printf("%d \n",constru);

// after each reading, the value of the buffers must be reset
// or keep the previous one according to the user
    _bufferrx[0]=0;
    _bufferrx[1]=0;
    _bufferrx[2]=0;
    _bufferrx[3]=0;
}

AP_HAL_MAIN(); // Ardupilot function call
```

Listing 5-2. Serial UART Communication, Wireless and Wired
Transmitter

```
///////////////////////// DECLARATION /////////////////////////
//            Paste the header here
//                    See appendix

/////////////////////// place your code here /////////////////////

// verify or add this line
uint8_t _buffertx[4]; // 4 values are sent

///////////////////////// INITIALIZATION /////////////////////////

void setup(){
       hal.uartC->begin(57600); // verify this line or add it
                                 // remember,  C = Telem 1
                                 // or wireless
                                 // 57600 is the full Wireless
                                 // speed
}
///////////////////////// EXECUTION /////////////////////////

void loop(){

    int envi1=2099; // value to be sent, it must be partitioned
    _buffertx[0]=5;
    _buffertx[1]=envi1>>8;        //high part to send
    _buffertx[2]=envi1 & 0x00FF; // low part to send
    _buffertx[3]=2;

    hal.uartC->write(_buffertx,4);  // send all data
// after each writing, the value of the buffers must be reset

    _buffertx[0]=0;
    _buffertx[1]=0;
    _buffertx[2]=0;
```

```
   _buffertx[3]=0;
}

AP_HAL_MAIN(); // Ardupilot function call
```

Listings 5-1 and 5-2 send and receive data without any order and can store erroneous data in the process. Improvement with a basic XOR type checksum is shown in Listings 5-3 and 5-4.

TRANSMISSION AND RECEPTION CODE WITH XOR CHECKSUM AND WITHOUT POLLING

Listing 5-3. Serial UART Communication, Wireless and Wired Transmitter

```
//////////////////////// DECLARATION ////////////////////////
//              Paste the header here
//                      See appendix

//////////////////// place your code here ////////////////////

// verify or add this line

uint8_t _buffertx[4];

//////////////////////// INITIALIZATION ////////////////////////

void setup(){
       hal.uartC->begin(57600); // verify this line or add it
                                // remember,  C = Telem 1
                                // or wireless
                                // 57600 is the full Wireless
                                // speed
}
```

```
//////////////////////// EXECUTION /////////////////////////////

void loop(){

    int envi1=2099;
    _buffertx[0]=5;
    _buffertx[1]=envi1>>8;         //high part to send
    _buffertx[2]=envi1 & 0x00FF; // low part to send

// note that the cheksum is only generated with the bits of
// interest they can be all except the same cheksum, or
// selective as in this case the bits 1 and 2 because they
// represent the high and low part of a more relevant data
    _buffertx[3]= _buffertx[1]^_buffertx[2];

    hal.uartC->write(_buffertx,4);

// after each writing, the value of the buffers must be reset
    _buffertx[0]=0;
    _buffertx[1]=0;
    _buffertx[2]=0;
    _buffertx[3]=0;
}

AP_HAL_MAIN();// Ardupilot function call
```

Listing 5-4. Serial UART Communication, Wireless and Wired Receiver

```
/////////////////////////// DECLARATION /////////////////////////////
//                  Paste the header here
//                         See appendix

//////////////////// place your code here ////////////////////

// verify or add this line

uint8_t _bufferrx[4];
```

```
/////////////////////// INITIALIZATION ///////////////////////

void setup(){
      hal.uartC->begin(57600); // verify this line or add it
                               // remember,  C = Telem 1
                               // or wireless
                               // 57600 is the full Wireless
                               // speed
}
/////////////////////// EXECUTION ///////////////////////

void loop(){
    int constru=0;
    uint8_t i=0;
    unsigned char checks = 0;
// char is equivalent to uint_8 this variable will contain the
// read checksum

    if(hal.uartC->available()){
        while(hal.uartC->available() &&  i<4)
           {
               _bufferrx[i]=hal.uartC->read();
               i=i+1;
           }
    }

// the checksum is generated with the data read by the receiver
    checks=_bufferrx[1]^_bufferrx[2];

// now is compared with the one coming from the transmitter and
// only in case they match the data is accepted

    if(checks==_bufferrx[3])
    {

    // data reconsruction
    // the operator + and | they are interchangeable in this case
```

```
        constru=(_bufferrx[1]<<8) + (_bufferrx[2]);
    }
```

```
// if they are not the same, we proceed to anything except
// receiving it, in this case for simplicity, we just assign zero
```

```
    else
    {
        constru=0;
    }
    hal.console->printf("%d \n",constru);
```

```
// after each reading, the value of the buffers must be reset
// or keep the previous one according to the user
    _bufferrx[0]=0;
    _bufferrx[1]=0;
    _bufferrx[2]=0;
    _bufferrx[3]=0;
}
```

```
AP_HAL_MAIN(); // Ardupilot function call
```

Now we will present the polling method that is based on permissions to determine when to read and when to write since the previous mode only writes or reads indistinctly as long as there is availability to do so. In this example, notice that that both devices can be transmitter and receiver alternately but not simultaneously. An extension to more than two devices can made by following the logic described in the previous paragraphs. See Listings 5-5 and 5-6.

FOR DEVICE1

Listing 5-5. Serial UART Communication, Wireless and Wired

```
///////////////////////// DECLARATION /////////////////////////
//                  Paste the header here
//                       See appendix

//////////////////////// place your code here //////////////////

// verify or add those lines

uint8_t _buffertx[4];
uint8_t _bufferrx[4];
int permit=1; // one of the devices starts as a writer

///////////////////////// INITIALIZATION ////////////////////////

void setup(){
        hal.uartC->begin(57600);
}
///////////////////////// EXECUTION //////////////////////////////

void loop(){

  if(permit==1)
  {
    writeSerial();
    permit=2;  // once device1 has written, it begins to read
  }

  else
  {
    readSerial();
  }

}
```

```
//              auxiliar functions
static void writeSerial(){

    int envi1=2099;
    _buffertx[0]=2; // sending its turn to device 2
    _buffertx[1]=envi1>>8;
    _buffertx[2]=envi1 & 0x00FF;
    _buffertx[3]= _buffertx[1]^_buffertx[2];
    hal.uartC->write(_buffertx,4);

    _buffertx[0]=0;
    _buffertx[1]=0;
    _buffertx[2]=0;
    _buffertx[3]=0;
}

static void readSerial(){
    int constru=0;
    uint8_t i=0;
    unsigned char checks = 0;

    if(hal.uartC->available()){
        while(hal.uartC->available() &&  i<4)
            {
                _bufferrx[i]=hal.uartC->read();
                i=i+1;
            }
    }

    checks=_bufferrx[1]^_bufferrx[2];
    if(checks==_bufferrx[3])
    {
        constru=(_bufferrx[1]<<8) + (_bufferrx[2]);
    }
```

```
    else
    {
        constru=0;
    }
    hal.console->printf("%d \n",constru);
    permit=_bufferrx[0]; // in this line the permission to write
                         // is retaken
    _bufferrx[0]=0;
    _bufferrx[1]=0;
    _bufferrx[2]=0;
    _bufferrx[3]=0;

}

AP_HAL_MAIN(); // Ardupiot function call
```

FOR DEVICE2

Listing 5-6. Serial UART Communication, Wireless and Wired

```
///////////////////////// DECLARATION /////////////////////////
//              Paste the header here
//                    See appendix

/////////////////// place your code here ///////////////////

// verify or add those lines

uint8_t _buffertx[4];
uint8_t _bufferrx[4];
int permit=0; // the other device starts as a reader

///////////////////// INITIALIZATION /////////////////////

void setup(){
      hal.uartC->begin(57600);
}
```

////////////////////////// EXECUTION //////////////////////////////

```
void loop(){

  if(permit==2)
  {
    writeSerial();
    permit=1; // once device2 has written, it begins to read
  }

  else
  {
    readSerial();
  }

}

//          auxiliar functions

static void writeSerial(){

    int envi1=1099;
    _buffertx[0]=1; // sending its turn to device 2
    _buffertx[1]=envi1>>8;
    _buffertx[2]=envi1 & 0x00FF;
    _buffertx[3]= _buffertx[1]^_buffertx[2];
    hal.uartC->write(_buffertx,4);

    _buffertx[0]=0;
    _buffertx[1]=0;
    _buffertx[2]=0;
    _buffertx[3]=0;
}

static void leeSerial(){
    int constru=0;
    uint8_t i=0;
    unsigned char checks = 0;
```

```
    if(hal.uartC->available()){
        while(hal.uartC->available() &&  i<4)
            {
                _bufferrx[i]=hal.uartC->read();
                i=i+1;
            }
    }

    checks=_bufferrx[1]^_bufferrx[2];
    if(checks==_bufferrx[3])
    {
        constru=(_bufferrx[1]<<8) + (_bufferrx[2]);
    }

    else
    {
        constru=0;
    }
    hal.console->printf("%d \n",constru);
    permit=_bufferrx[0];   // in this line the permission to
                           // write is retaken

    _bufferrx[0]=0;
    _bufferrx[1]=0;
    _bufferrx[2]=0;
    _bufferrx[3]=0;

}

AP_HAL_MAIN(); // Ardupilot function call
```

Notice that additional data are sent and the receiver must verify their validity
to decide whether to continue reading or to change roles. This technique is
particularly useful for communication among multiple vehicles. Its purpose is to
determine which one emits, and which ones receive, with a certain order (in the

same way that each member of a group of people should talk and listen). Note that the biggest disadvantage with this procedure is that if the transmission is lost or altered with respect to the turn data, a problem may occur. To reduce this possibility, it is convenient to include polling data into the checksum algorithm.

Implementation Tip   This procedure can be performed with as many wireless devices as needed. The theoretical limit is infinite devices and the virtual 128. However, at least a dozen will work without any problem. Furthermore, never use wireless transmitters without a LIPO battery or an external power source. Remember that wireless transmission demands electrical power, which if not satisfied will be translated into bad reception and sending.

Reading from External Devices Through Serial Communication and Development Boards

This section explains how to use external sensors that are not compatible with the Pixhawk autopilot but are compatible with other development boards or just to free up the Pixhawk processor from unnecessary load and allow another device to take care of it. For example, suppose a Raspberry Pi takes care of the object location process through artificial vision and then sends the position of that object exclusively to the Pixhawk. A second example is to transmit the vehicle's location to the Pixhawk through an external object monitoring module, via WiFi or Bluetooth.

In order to do this, the Pixhawk code could be the one of wired or wireless serial reading, whereas in the secondary card or equipment to be used you must program serial writing code. For example, if you use an Arduino, data can be sent using the `Serial.write()` command. Please remember that each development board or programmable device has

171

its own commands. For the examples in Listings 5-7 and 5-8, we used an Arduino, but you may choose any other device that you want to employ.

Listing 5-7. Pixhawk's Receptor Code

```
//////////////////////// DECLARATION //////////////////////////
//                      Paste header code here
//                             See apendix

//////////////////// place your code here ///////////////////////

// verify or add this line
uint8_t _bufferrx[4];

//////////////////////// INITIALIZATION /////////////////////////

void setup(){
      hal.uartC->begin(57600);
}

///////////////////////// EXECUTION //////////////////////////

void loop(){

    uint8_t i=0;
    if(hal.uartC->available()){
        while(hal.uartC->available() &&  i<4)
          {
              _bufferrx[i]=hal.uartC->read();
              i=i+1;
          }
    }
    int constru=(_bufferrx[1]<<8) + (_bufferrx[2]);
    hal.console->printf("%d \n",constru);

    _bufferrx[0]=0;
    _bufferrx[1]=0;
```

```
    _bufferrx[2]=0;
    _bufferrx[3]=0;
}

AP_HAL_MAIN(); // Ardupilot function call
```

Listing 5-8. Arduino's Transmitter Code

```
byte datos[4];
unsigned int envi1;

void setup() {
  Serial.begin(57600);
}

void loop() {
  datos[0]='R';
  envi1=2099;
  datos[1]=envi1>>8;
  datos[2]=envi1 & 0xFF;
  datos[3]=datos[1]^datos[2]^datos[3]^datos[4];

  if (Serial.available())
  {
      Serial.write(datos,4);
      datos[0]=0;
      datos[1]=0;
      datos[2]=0;
      datos[3]=0;

  }

}
```

To simplify, we omitted the polling and checksum processes. You should be able to add them using the previously mentioned code.

Now, look at the connection diagram in Figure 5-12. Notice that RX and TX pins are crossed. Also, notice that the auxiliary device is assumed to have its own power source. However, it is VERY important to share the ground pins.

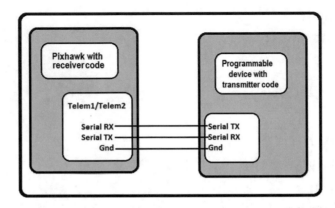

Figure 5-12. *Interfacing with development boards*

Info on the corresponding pins is located at http://ardupilot.org/copter/docs/common-pixhawk-overview.html.

Writing to Brushless Motors (BLDC Motors)

Knowing how to use motors does not guarantee in any way that you are able to use your vehicles. For this purpose, it is necessary to complete the following steps:

1. **Use of motors**: This subject is explained in the present section.

2. **Control tuning**: Although upcoming chapters of this book teach the basis of this subject, appropriate tuning will depend on your project.

3. **Definition of the allocation matrix**: As directly communicated in steps 1 and 2 (and other sections of this book teach its basis), the appropriate selection will depend on your project.

Components: Brushless DC motors, ESCs, power distributors, batteries or power supplies, propellers, battery monitors, bullet type connectors, silicon cable, connectors for batteries, battery chargers, BEC

Description: This command allows you to write values to motors in order to establish their speed, and indirectly, their thrust and torque.

Brushless motors test without using the Pixhawk: To make sure that your motors operate correctly, in addition to the proper welding of their pins (as indicated in the implementation tips of this same section), you must verify their correct mobility and overheating. For this purpose, we suggest the following procedure.

Equipment:

- Arduino (any model capable of generating a PWM output)

- Brushless motor properly welded with its corresponding ESC

- Jumpers to connect the Arduino to the ESC

- An adequate LIPO battery or a direct current power source that supports ESC's demand

Process:

1. Connect as indicated. Make sure that the grounds are properly connected. See Figure 5-13.

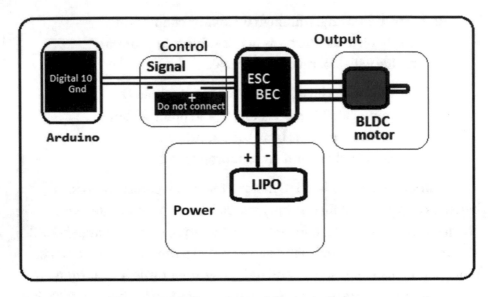

Figure 5-13. *Testing BLDC motors with an Arduino*

2. Compile and load the code in Listing 5-9 into the Arduino.

Listing 5-9. Writing to BLDC or Servos from an Arduino

```
///////

// by transductor in www.robologs.net

#include<Servo.h>  // library for RC type PWM

Servo ESC; //Servo object invocation

int vel = 1000; //initial pulse leng      th

void setup()
{
  //to assign a pin to the ESC object
  ESC.attach(10);
```

```
//To write the initial value at zero
ESC.writeMicroseconds(1000);
delay(5000);

//begin   serial port console
Serial.begin(9600);
Serial.setTimeout(10);

}

void loop()
{
  if(Serial.available() >= 1)
  {
    vel = Serial.parseInt(); //to read an integer, be sure that
                             //it has 1000-2000 values
    if(vel != 0)
    {
      ESC.writeMicroseconds(vel); //write previous data to ESC
                                  //and BLDC

      //delay(2);
    }
  }
}
```

3. Energize the system. Hold the brushless or fix it in a position that does not harm the motor or yourself. Never use propellers in this test.

4. It is not enough to look at the motor turning. Check that the motor is not overheated after testing at high speeds. If so, the motor will end up burning due to bad welding. Repeat the welding and try again.

5. With the motor fixed to a structure, perform the
    test with propellers. ATTENTION: This is your
    responsibility. Always verify that the system starts at
    zero PWM value to avoid injuries.

Once this quick test is finished, continue with the libraries. Notice that
the operation looks very similar. See Listing 5-10.

Listing 5-10 provides an example of BLDC writing. Note the following:

- The syntax is:

```
write(uint8_t channel, uint16_t microseconds period)
```

You can find more information at: https://github.com/ArduPilot/
ardupilot/blob/master/libraries/AP_HAL/RCOutput.h

Listing 5-10. Writing to BLDC Motors

```
//////////////////////////// DECLARATION ////////////////////////////
//                      Paste the header here
//                           See appendix

/////////////////////// place your code here ///////////////////////

///////////////////////// INITIALIZATION /////////////////////////

void setup(){

// add the following lines to the setup, they register the
// channels to be controlled this line sets the BLDC frequency
// of the first 4 channels
    hal.rcout->set_freq( 15, 490); //0xFF  0x0F->b'00001111'
// the following lines enable each of the first 4 channels
    hal.rcout->enable_ch(0);
    hal.rcout->enable_ch(1);
    hal.rcout->enable_ch(2);
    hal.rcout->enable_ch(3);
```

```
// since we will only use the first channel for this example,
// we write a ZERO on it (this value may vary for other engines,
// see datasheets)
    hal.rcout->write(0,900);
}
/////////////////////////// EXECUTION ///////////////////////////

void loop(){
// now just write and update, note that if a pause is not added
// your motor could be not // work or in extreme case it will
// burn HERE is written a sequence to engine 1 (numbered 0
// by convention)
    hal.rcout->write(0,900);
    hal.scheduler->delay(500);
    hal.rcout->write(0,1500);
    hal.scheduler->delay(100);
    hal.rcout->write(0,1700);
    hal.scheduler->delay(500);
}

AP_HAL_MAIN(); // Ardupilot function call
```

IMPLEMENTATION TIPS

- Remember that brushless motors are a three-phase type of motor. So, in order to connect them with the Pixhawk (whose control outputs are single-phase), it is necessary to use a converter called ESC, which receives a control input and sends its three-phase equivalent in return.

- There are two types of ESCs: optocoupled and standard. When using optocoupled ESCs, it is also convenient to use a BEC that allows energizing its control signals.

- To operate a multi-rotor, it is necessary to have a distributor, which allows connecting at least four motors to the main battery of the system.

- To invert the direction of spin rotation in a fixed way (which means that certain motors can only turn left and others only turn right), it is enough to cross the ESC's extreme cables. Also, there are ways to program an ESC such that it has a double direction of spin rotation (as long as the ESC has a bidirectional mode operation).

- The user must verify that the motors are clean. Debris can enter the motors and affect their performance. Be especially careful with areas with metal powder, because the motor has magnets and it is highly probable that the mechanical performance and the electrical integrity could be affected. In these cases, try to clean the work area.

- Welding connectors: Sometimes the ESCs come without connectors. In addition, batteries have connectors that are different from the ones compatible with the power module of the Pixhawk. In this case, follow an online resource. There are a lot of YouTube tutorials. Search "how to solder bullet connectors" or "how to solder XT60 connectors," etc.

- DANGER: Do not try to use any other type of cable. Those designed for batteries, motors, and ESCs resist high current levels. They are based on AWG standards and have special coatings. Using any other type of cable can produce an electrical risk to the equipment and the user.

- DANGER: Do not use propellers until you have properly tested the motors. Otherwise, you risk flesh cuts, mutilation, or serious injuries to living beings and structures. However, it is advisable not to test motors for long time periods without load. This is solved by placing paper sheets instead of propellers. It also helps to identify each engine's direction of rotation, and locate considerable vibrations or heating.

- Propellers can have more than two blades. This implies a thrust improvement but a consequent reduction of flight time and motor durability.

- Although there are highly resistant propellers, impacts are transferred to the motors. Therefore, know which is more important for your application: motors or propellers.

- Given the short duration of code execution, it is convenient to place a short delay to give time to the motors to react and prevent them from overheating due to abrupt changes in their electrical operation. This will not be necessary for real-time mode (it will be implicit).

- Always tighten propellers properly, because the force of thrust and torsion of the motor, which is proportional to its speed, can cause them to come out.

- When possible, always use a battery monitor.

- Remember that BLDC motors generally do not change the spin rotation's direction. To operate a drone, we use a combination of motors with the predefined direction of rotation. Some ESCs are connected in line, while others must be crossed. This way, those that are connected in line will rotate in one direction and the crossed ones in the opposite direction.

- When a drone is flying, the speed of each motor is never directly controlled, but the drone's pose (its position and its orientation) will be indirectly regulated by each motor's speed.

- Opt for non-optocoupled ESCs; otherwise use a BEC to operate correctly.

- If you want to change the direction of brushless motors (for example, a cart that has forward and backward operation), use reversible ESCs.

A reversible ESC can be calibrated so that its operating range (usually from 1000 to 2000) has a neutral point. This way the maximum left speed is achieved at 1000, the neutral point or motionless at 1500, and the maximum right speed at 2000. Note that the maximum achievable speed has been divided but now you have a motor with variable direction of rotation.

Radio control motor calibration: Its purpose is to make radio controls compatible with the motor that is being used. With the code in Listing 5-11, you can also understand the difference between RC input and RC output.

Listing 5-11. Writing to BLDC Motors from Radio Input

```
//////////////////////// DECLARATION ////////////////////////
//                      Paste the header here
//                         See appendix

/////////////////// place your code here ///////////////////

// verify or add those lines
int radio_roll, radio_pitch, radio_yaw, radio_throttle, aux_1,
aux_2;
uint16_t radio[6]; // the radio in this example has 6 channels
uint32_t time, timemod;
```

////////////////////// INITIALIZATION //////////////////////

```
void setup(){

// add the following lines to the setup, they register the
// channels to be controlled this line sets the BLDC frequency
// of the first 4 channels

    hal.rcout->set_freq( 15, 490); //0xFF  0x0F->b'00001111'

// the following lines enable each of the first 4 channels
    hal.rcout->enable_ch(0);
    hal.rcout->enable_ch(1);
    hal.rcout->enable_ch(2);
    hal.rcout->enable_ch(3);

// since we will only use the first channel for this example,
// we write a ZERO on it (this value may vary for other engines,
// see datasheets)
    hal.rcout->write(0,900);
}
```

/////////////////////// EXECUTION //////////////////////////

```
void loop(){

    time=hal.scheduler->micros();

// modulation to write every 3.5 milliseconds if you have
// servomotors, for BLDC motors this operation can be omitted
// and simply send directly the radio input to the motor

    timemod=time%3500;

// read radio channels
    for (uint8_t i = 0; i <6; i++)
    {radio[i] = hal.rcin->read(i);}
```

```
// using throttle channel to test an engine
    radio_throttle = radio[2];
```

```
// write the radio signal to the chosen motor according to the
// selected time base
    if(timemod==0)
    {
    hal.rcout->write(0,radio_throttle);
```

```
// it is possible that in some pixhawk models the value to be
// written to the motor must be converted in this way
// hal.rcout-> write (0, uint16_t (radio_throttle));
    }
}
```

```
AP_HAL_MAIN(); // Ardupilot function call
```

Keyboard motor calibration: Listing 5-12 is very useful because it is designed to manually find the minimum starting value of a brushless motor. This is carried out by using three increment keys and three decrement keys, in which speed increases and decreases are sent in the range of hundreds, tens, and units. This way, the user can find the starting value of a motor, which is useful in the design of the controller, as you will see later.

Listing 5-12. To Calibrate BLDC Motors by Using the Keyboard

```
//////////////////////////// DECLARATION ////////////////////////////
//                    Paste the header here
//                       See appendix
```

```
///////////////////// place your code here /////////////////////
```

```
// add these lines
```

```
char readk;
```

```
// value to increase or decrease, and to be sent to the
// selected motors
int incr=0;

/////////////////////////// INITIALIZATION ///////////////////////////

void setup(){

    hal.rcout->set_freq( 15, 490); //0xFF  0x0F->b'00001111'

    hal.rcout->enable_ch(0);
    hal.rcout->enable_ch(1);
    hal.rcout->enable_ch(2);
    hal.rcout->enable_ch(3);

    hal.rcout->write(0,900);
}

////////////////////////// EXECUTION //////////////////////////////

void loop(){
    readboard();
}

//              auxiliar functions

static void readboard(){
    readk= hal.console->read();

// q increases from 100 in 100 w of 10 in 10 and e of 1 in 1
// a reduces from 100 in 100 s to 10 in 10 and d to 1 in 1
// it is possible that in some pixhawk models the value to be
// written to the motor must be converted in this way
// hal.rcout-> write (0, uint16_t (incr));
```

```cpp
if (readk=='q')
 {
     incr=incr+100;
     hal.rcout->write(0,incr);
     hal.scheduler->delay(200);
 }

if (readk=='w')
 {
     incr=incr+10;
     hal.rcout->write(0,incr);
     hal.scheduler->delay(200);
 }

if (readk=='e')
 {
     incr=incr+1;
     hal.rcout->write(0,incr);
     hal.scheduler->delay(200);
 }

if (readk=='a')
 {
     incr=incr-100;
     hal.rcout->write(0,incr);
     hal.scheduler->delay(200);
 }

if (readk=='s')
 {
     incr=incr-10;
     hal.rcout->write(0,incr);
     hal.scheduler->delay(200);
 }
```

```
if (readk=='d')
{
    incr=incr-1;
    hal.rcout->write(0,incr);
    hal.scheduler->delay(200);
}

}

AP_HAL_MAIN(); // Ardupilot function call
```

Code Optimization

Although this section could have been placed in previous chapters, we decided to incorporate it here for practicality and to link it to the last section, since it helps to improve your code for writing to motors.

Simplified Function for Writing to Motors

As you may have noticed, writing to motors is a tedious procedure when repeated (nevertheless, in this book, for didactic purposes, we will maintain this modality). For that reason, an abbreviated way of writing to motors is the following one.

Note that this first optimization simply improves the code by removing the writing-to-motors commands from the if comparators, leaving just one writing-to-motors command at the end of all comparators. This optimization is not as relevant as the following, but it is illustrative. See Listing 5-13.

Listing 5-13. To Calibrate BLDC Motors by Using the Keyboard, First Optimization

```
/////////////////////////// DECLARATION ///////////////////////////
//                   Paste the header here
//                        See appendix

//////////////////////// place your code here ////////////////////////

// add these lines

char readk;
// value to increase or decrease, and to be sent to the
// selected motors
int incr=0;

/////////////////////////// INITIALIZATION ///////////////////////////

void setup(){

    hal.rcout->set_freq( 15, 490); //0xFF  0x0F->b'00001111'

    hal.rcout->enable_ch(0);
    hal.rcout->enable_ch(1);
    hal.rcout->enable_ch(2);
    hal.rcout->enable_ch(3);

    hal.rcout->write(0,900);
}

/////////////////////////// EXECUTION ///////////////////////////

void loop(){
    readboard();
}
```

```
//            auxiliar functions
static void readboard(){
    readk= hal.console->read();

// q increases from 100 in 100 w of 10 in 10 and e of 1 in 1
// a reduces from 100 in 100 s to 10 in 10 and d to 1 in 1
// it is possible that in some pixhawk models the value to be
// written to the motor must be converted in this way
// hal.rcout-> write (0, uint16_t (incr));

    if (readk=='q')
     {
         incr=incr+100;
     }

    if (readk=='w')
     {
         incr=incr+10;
     }

    if (readk=='e')
     {
         incr=incr+1;
     }

    if (readk=='a')
     {
         incr=incr-100;
     }

    if (readk=='s')
     {
         incr=incr-10;
     }
```

```
if (readk=='d')
{
    incr=incr-1;
}

hal.rcout->write(0,incr);
hal.scheduler->delay(200);

}

AP_HAL_MAIN(); // Ardupilot function call
```

Now let's code a second optimization that improves the writing process. Imagine you have two motors. The code must be updated as follows:

```
hal.rcout->write(0,incr);
hal.rcout->write(1,incr);
hal.scheduler->delay(200);
```

What would happen if you had ten motors and you had to update their writing in different processes as well?

Note that you need a function that facilitates motor writing. This function could be one shown in Listing 5-14.

Listing 5-14. To Calibrate BLDC Motors by Using the keyboard, Second Optimization

```
//////////////////////// DECLARATION //////////////////////////
//                 Paste the header here
//                      See appendix

//////////////////// place your code here ///////////////////

// add these lines
```

```
char readk;
// value to increase or decrease, and to be sent to the
// selected motors
int incr=0;
// motor label
int mot1,mot2,mo3,mot4;

//////////////////////// INITIALIZATION ///////////////////////

void setup(){

    hal.rcout->set_freq( 15, 490); //0xFF   0x0F->b'00001111'

    hal.rcout->enable_ch(0);
    hal.rcout->enable_ch(1);
    hal.rcout->enable_ch(2);
    hal.rcout->enable_ch(3);

    hal.rcout->write(0,900);
}

//////////////////////// EXECUTION ///////////////////////

void loop(){
    readboard();
}

//              auxiliar functions

static void r.eadboard(){
    readk= hal.console->read();

// q increases from 100 in 100 w of 10 in 10 and e of 1 in 1
// a reduces from 100 in 100 s to 10 in 10 and d to 1 in 1
// it is possible that in some pixhawk models the value to be
// written to the motor must be converted in this way
// hal.rcout-> write (0, uint16_t (incr));
```

```
if (readk=='q')
 {
     incr=incr+100;
 }

 if (readk=='w')
 {
     incr=incr+10;
 }

 if (readk=='e')
 {
     incr=incr+1;
 }

 if (readk=='a')
 {
     incr=incr-100;
 }

 if (readk=='s')
 {
     incr=incr-10;
 }

 if (readk=='d')
 {
     incr=incr-1;
 }
 mot1=incr;
 mot2=incr;
 mot3=incr;
 mot4=incr;
```

```
    tomotors (mot1,mot2,mot3,mot4);

}

static void tomotors(int m1, int m2, int m3 int m4){

    hal.rcout->write(0,m1);
    hal.rcout->write(1,m2);
    hal.rcout->write(2,m3);
    hal.rcout->write(3,m4);

    hal.scheduler->delay(200);

}

AP_HAL_MAIN(); // Ardupilot function call
```

Writing to Standard DC Motors (Brushed)

Knowing how to use motors does not guarantee in any way that you are able to use your vehicles. For this purpose, it is necessary to complete the following steps:

1. **Use of motors**: This subject is explained in the present section.

2. **Control tuning**: Although upcoming chapters of this book teach the basics of this subject, appropriate tuning will depend on your project.

3. **Definition of the allocation matrix**: As directly communicated in steps 1 and 2 (and other sections of this book teach its basics), the appropriate selection will depend on your project.

As mentioned, although the Pixhawk does not generate a PWM signal compatible with that required by a standard DC brushed motor, it is important to indicate how this connection is made when using different types of robots than aircraft. There are three ways. See Figure 5-14.

1. Directly use ESCs for brushed DC motors called brushed ESCs.

2. Use an intermediate transformation circuit between PWM servo and PWM-duty cycle. Although it can be any microcontroller, microprocessor, FPGA, or any other programmable device, here we use an Arduino with its `pulseInt()` function. It is necessary to clarify that in this case, the command's resolution operates at a minimum of 10 microseconds. Therefore, the 1000-2000 scale, instead of advancing 1 unit at a time, it will advance 10 units at a time. Another option is the `attachInterrupt()` function if you want to use more than one DC motor (for example, a cart driven by two or four motors on its wheels).

3. Use an embedded circuit. Search the Web for "servo to PWM converter," "Pixhawk brushed motors," or "DC motor RC input." For example, see `https://core-electronics.com.au/pololu-trex-jr-dual-motor-controller-dmc02.html`.

Meanwhile, DC motors also require a signal to determine the direction of rotation. In this case, in addition to the servo-type PWM signal from the Pixhawk, a logic signal from the GPIO rails of the same autopilot can be used. Also, if you prefer to use only the PWM outputs, a mapping could be helpful. Note that when using a brushed ESC, there are also motors with reversible direction from the ESC.

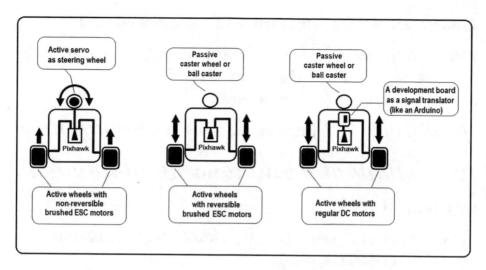

Figure 5-14. *Kinds of brushed motors and Pixhawk autopilot connection*

The following code consists of two files: the main, which drives the motors and is uploaded into the Pixhawk, and the other that simply uses an Arduino as an interpreter to write the RC-type PWM signal (1000-2000) of the Pixhawk to a PWM duty-cycle type of DC motors (0-255). Although we use an Arduino, any other programmable device capable of detecting pulse changes or interruptions can be used. It must be understood that the Arduino, or any other device used, only serves as an interpreter between the two PWM types. In order to be able to use standard DC motors, all vehicle control is carried out directly on the Pixhawk, including reading sensors, GPS, data storage, etc. See Listings 5-15 and 5-16.

If you prefer the Arduino option, the `pulseInt` command is the simplest way to achieve this task, but there are more efficient ways to do so. See `www.benripley.com/diy/arduino/three-ways-to-read-a-pwm-signal-with-arduino/`.

Listing 5-15. Writing to Brushed DC Motors, Pixhawk Code

```
/////////////////////// DECLARATION /////////////////////////
//                  Paste the header here
//                        See appendix

////////////////////// put your code here //////////////////////


/////////////////////// INITIALIZATION //////////////////////////

void setup(){

    hal.rcout->set_freq( 15, 50); //0xFF  0x0F->b'00001111'
    hal.rcout->enable_ch(0);
    hal.rcout->enable_ch(1);
    hal.rcout->enable_ch(2);
    hal.rcout->enable_ch(3);

}
/////////////////////////// EXECUTION //////////////////////////

// HERE a sequence is written to each motor from 1 to 4
// (numbered 0 to 3 by programming convention) NOTE that this
// code abuses of the delay command, the correct action is to
// use the timer based on milliseconds or microseconds lapses or
// the real time, see the use of time section or the real time
// section to know how to to do it ALSO NOTE that a brushed
// motor does not operate at such high frequencies with
// respect to a BLDC, for this reason it is convenient to
// update the signal every 50 hz modifying the setup
// set_freq, in order to write to the motors every 20
```

```
// milliseconds, the delay given in this example is 500
// milliseconds so there is no problem in the execution and
// the DC motor should operate correctly

void loop(){

    hal.rcout->write(0,1000);
    hal.rcout->write(1,1000);
    hal.rcout->write(2,1000);
    hal.rcout->write(3,1000);

    hal.scheduler->delay(500);

    hal.rcout->write(0,1200);
    hal.rcout->write(1,1200);
    hal.rcout->write(2,1200);
    hal.rcout->write(3,1200);

    hal.scheduler->delay(500);

    hal.rcout->write(0,1500);
    hal.rcout->write(1,1700);
    hal.rcout->write(2,1300);
    hal.rcout->write(3,1100);

    hal.scheduler->delay(500);

    hal.rcout->write(0,1900);
    hal.rcout->write(1,1860);
    hal.rcout->write(2,1390);
    hal.rcout->write(3,1300);

    hal.scheduler->delay(500);

    hal.rcout->write(0,2000);
    hal.rcout->write(1,2000);
```

```
    hal.rcout->write(2,1000);
    hal.rcout->write(3,1000);

    hal.scheduler->delay(500);

}

AP_HAL_MAIN(); // Ardupilot function call
```

Listing 5-16. Writing to Brushed DC Motors, Arduino Code

```
double chan[4];

void setup() {
  pinMode(2,INPUT);
  pinMode(3,INPUT);
  pinMode(4,INPUT);
  pinMode(5,INPUT);
  Serial.begin(9600);

}

void loop() {

// the RC PWM  from the pixhawk motor ports is read
// command arduino pulseInt

  chan[0]=pulseIn(2,HIGH);
  chan[1]=pulseIn(3,HIGH);
  chan[2]=pulseIn(4,HIGH);
  chan[3]=pulseIn(5,HIGH);

    // once read, then is printed, but it can be scaled with a
    // mapping function so that the range 1000-2000 can be
    // translateby the arduino as -255 to 255
    // once done this, data can be sent to the required DC
    // brushed motors by connecting to the arduino a direction
```

```
// pin (-1 or 1) and an speed pin (0 to 255), observe that
// this establish a zero reference at 1500 RC from pixhawk
// and 0 at arduino
Serial.print(chan[0]);
Serial.print(",");
Serial.print(chan[1]);
Serial.print(",");
Serial.print(chan[2]);
Serial.print(",");
Serial.println(chan[3]);
}
```

Using the Arduino's serial plotter you can see the signals sent by the Pixhawk in Figure 5-15. If you prefer to send these signals directly to the motors, make sure you have the corresponding mapping as well as the required power stage.

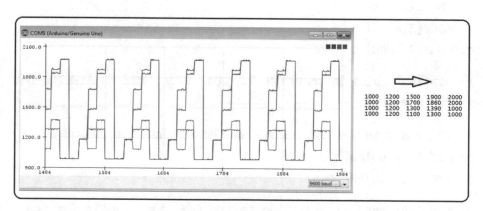

Figure 5-15. *RC output signals sent by a Pixhawk autopilot and read by an Arduino*

The following code is complementary. Its purpose is to send two Pixhawk PWM signals to two DC motors connected to the Arduino. In this example, we used the Arduino-one and the L298 driver, so each motor required one digital input for reading RC PWM from the Pixhawk, one digital output for PWM duty-cycle speed signal, and two digital output pins for sending the direction signals. Since the Arduino-one has only 14 digital pins and we need four digital pins for each motor, we can only use this code for applications with up to three DC brushed motors. See Listing 5-17.

Listing 5-17. Writing to DC Brushed Motors, Arduino code

```
// 2 channel for reading PWM RC 1000-2000 from the pixhawk
   double cha[2];
// 2 outputs for DC brushed motors PWM duty cycle 0-255
   double mo[2];
// 2 ouputs for motor sign or spin direction
   double simo[2];

void setup() {

// pins to receive the signals generated in the RC output from
// the pixhawk
pinMode(2,INPUT);
pinMode(4,INPUT);

// available pins to generate PWM type duty cycle in Arduino-uno
// 3 5 6 9 10 11

// in this case for two motors we choose the pins 10 and 11
pinMode(10, OUTPUT);
pinMode(11, OUTPUT);

// the L298 needs in addition to the PWM, two signals for the
// direction of rotation of each motor

pinMode(5, OUTPUT);
pinMode(6, OUTPUT);
```

```
pinMode(7, OUTPUT);
pinMode(8, OUTPUT);

Serial.begin(9600);
}

void loop() {

// spin sense by default
simo[0]=0;
simo[1]=0;

// reading of the pixhawk connected to digital pins 2 and 4
cha[0]=pulseIn(2,HIGH);
cha[1]=pulseIn(4,HIGH);

// mapping of the pixhawk RC PWM 1000-2000 to the arduino dutyc
// cycle PWM -255 to 255 (the sign is separated later)
mo[0] = map(cha[0],1000, 2000, -255, 255);
mo[1] = map(cha[1],1000, 2000, -255, 255);

// here the sign is separated, if the value is positive it is
// sent 1, if it is negative stays at zero

if (mo[0]>=0)
{
   simo[0]=1;
}

if (mo[1]>=0)
{
   simo[1]=1;
}
```

```
// the absolute value is written to each motor
analogWrite(10, abs(mo[0]));
analogWrite(11, abs(mo[1]));

// the corresponding sign is written to each motor
// remember that the L298 requires two values, the original and
// the denied

digitalWrite(5,simo[0]);
digitalWrite(6,!simo[0]);

digitalWrite(7,simo[1]);
digitalWrite(8,!simo[1]);

}
```

The connection is illustrated in Figure 5-16.

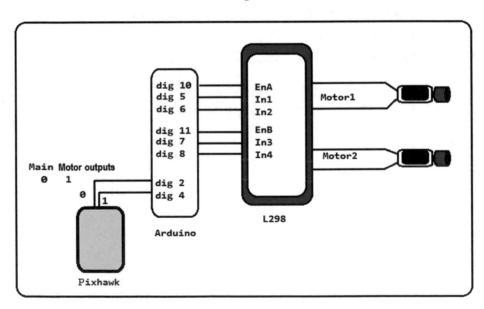

Figure 5-16. *An Arduino employed as an interpreter for commanding standard DC motors from the Pixhawk autopilot*

This code can be improved at both the hardware and software levels in the following ways:

- By reducing the number of pins used, so that for each motor there is only one pin for magnitude or PWM duty-cycle and one pin for motor's direction of rotation

- By using the Arduino's registers or interrupt functions

- By using a miniature Arduino for each motor as a "brushed ESC"

- By using a microcontroller instead of the Arduino to improve the translation from RC to duty-cycle

- By taking advantage of a PPM modulator to reduce the effort of reading interruptions in the Arduino

For more, see

- www.youtube.com/watch?v=63JmO4Mc8NM

- https://github.com/xkam1x/Arduino-PWM-Reader

- http://blog.solutions-cubed.com/using-radio-control-transmitters-for-motor-control/

- www.instructables.com/id/Rc-Controller-for-Better-Control-Over-Arduino-Proj/

A useful text in Spanish: Esteban Joel Rabuffetti. "Diseño y construcción de un ROV para aplicaciones de sensorización medioambiental." www.hooked-on-rc-airplanes.com/brushed-vs-brushless-esc.html. 2016.

Using Stepper Motors

Knowing how to use motors does not guarantee in any way that you are able to use your vehicles. For this purpose, it is necessary to complete the following steps:

1. **Use of motors**: This subject is explained in the present section.

2. **Control tuning**: Although upcoming chapters of this book teach the basics of this subject, appropriate tuning will depend on your project.

3. **Definition of the allocation matrix**: As directly communicated in steps 1 and 2 (and other sections of this book teach its basics), the appropriate selection will depend on your project.

When using stepper motors with the Pixhawk and ArduPilot libraries, the logic is similar to that found in the previous section. In addition to commanding the direction of rotation, you need two parameters: the number of steps to be taken, and the speed of rotation. They are both given as a function of the RC PWM signal. This way, it is convenient to use an Arduino or any other device that interprets these requirements.

There are two ways to use a stepper motor with the Pixhawk:

1. Maintaining constant speed and varying the number of steps given as a function of the PWM-RC signal. In this case, the stepper motor will behave like a servo because its position will be controlled.

2. Maintaining a constant number of steps (for example, a whole revolution) and varying the execution speed as a function of the PWM-RC signal. In this case, the stepper motor will behave like a BLDC motor because its speed will be regulated.

As you may have already noticed, this requires two code files: the Pixhawk standard code for writing to BLDCs, and the code from the development board connected to the Pixhawk which serves as a translator.

For programming the development board (Arduino, microcontroller, etc) we recommend the following project: `http://chipkit.net/wiki/index.php?title=Driving_Steppers_from_RC_Reciever`.

A project that is no longer supported and that carried out the required implementation with an Arduino: `www.cunningturtle.com/wiki/index.php?title=Radio_Controlled_Stepper`.

Another project that is somewhat complex to understand but useful: `http://chromatex.me/arduino-stepper-motor-wiring-diagram.html/easy-driver-hook-up-guide-learn-sparkfun-com-stunning-arduino-stepper-motor-wiring-diagram/`.

That said, if you do not want to deal with algorithms and code, you can buy electronic modules that directly transform the RC signal and send it to a stepper motor. In this case, coding the ArduPilot BLDC writing programs and connecting the corresponding outputs from the Pixhawk to the electronic module is enough. Here is an example: `www.pololu.com/product/3131`.

To learn more about this subject, search the Web for "rc to stepper," "servo signal to stepper," and "rc to stepper Arduino." Change the word Arduino to any other term of interest such as "microcontroller," "raspberry pi," etc.

Using Servomotors for Auxiliary Tasks

Knowing how to use motors does not guarantee in any way that you are able to use your vehicles. For this purpose, it is necessary to complete the following steps:

1. **Use of motors**: This subject is explained in the present section.

2. **Control tuning**: Although upcoming chapters of this book teach the basics of this subject, appropriate tuning will depend on your project.

3. **Definition of the allocation matrix**: As directly communicated steps 1 and 2 (and other sections of this book teach its basics), the appropriate selection will depend on your project.

- **Components**: Pixhawk, battery, BEC, servomotors

- **Description**: This command is identical to the one in the "Writing to BLDC" section, with the difference that the writing frequency must be performed at 50 Hz, while it is performed at 490 Hz with BLDC motors. Its usefulness lies in the use of vectorizers (see the appendix on vectorization) for redirecting the thrust of each motor, wings, stabilizers for cameras, the use of robotic tweezers for the collection of objects, etc.

Although servomotors control positions and BLDC control speeds, they both admit the same RC-type PWM signal of approximately 1000-2000 range values. This may vary slightly among different commercial models.

The Pixhawk has six additional outputs that can be used interchangeably but not at the same time as auxiliaries for servomotors or GPIO ports. If used to control servomotors, they are invoked with different numbers than their corresponding GPIO pins (from 8 to 13). See Listing 5-18.

Implementation Tip   Given that the execution of a large block of code only takes a few milliseconds in the system, sending information to servomotors can lead to burning them. Therefore, it is advisable to perform this in safe time intervals. The simplest way to test them is by using delays, but this entails jeopardizing the execution of functions and the drone's integrity. See the time management section further in this book.

A servomotor demands more power than that given by the Pixhawk's auxiliary outputs. For this reason, you can use a BEC after verifying the consumption of both the servomotor and the autopilot port. If you do not consider this, two scenarios are feasible: the first where the servomotor simply won't move and the second where the autopilot port will burn.

To avoid problems when BLDC motors are used simultaneously with some type of BEC in their ESCs and servos that demand more voltage, current, or both than BLDC motors, you should use only the signal output and the Pixhawk's ground by plugging the Pixhawk to the servomotor without using the BEC.

Listing 5-18. Writing to Servomotors

```
///////////////////////// DECLARATION /////////////////////////
//                    Paste the header here
//                        See appendix

/////////////////// place ypur code here ///////////////////

/////////////////////// INITIALIZATION ///////////////////////

//
void setup(){

// add the following lines to the setup, they register the
// channels to be controlled remember that the main lines are
// numbered from 0 to 7
    hal.rcout->enable_ch(0);
    hal.rcout->enable_ch(1);

// the next line only sets the frequency of the main outputs
// the auxiliaries are not affected since they only support
// 50hz operation
// the 3 in binary is 0000 0011 that is to say the motors 1 and
// 2 numbered as 0 and 1 the servos can also be used in the
// main outputs by modifying the corresponding channels to 50,
// for example if we want to place a servo on the 3rd main
// channel seen as 0000 0100 we should place a second command
// set_freq with first argument equal to 4 and second equal to 50

    hal.rcout->set_freq( 3, 490);

// this line enables auxiliary output number 2
// the numbering of auxiliaries is from 8 to 13, ie aux1 to aux6
// remember that the auxiliary outputs do not require the set_
// freq, as in generala servomotor operates at 50hz
```

```
    hal.rcout->enable_ch(9);

// starting the two respective BLDCs and the servo
    hal.rcout->write(0,900);
    hal.rcout->write(1,900);
    hal.rcout->write(9,900);

    hal.scheduler->delay(1000);

}

/////////////////////////// EXECUTION ////////////////////////////

// HERE is written a sequence to each motor from 1 to 2
// (numbered 0 to 1 by programming convention) and to a servo
// motor connected to the auxiliary channel 2 numbered 9
// NOTE that this code abuses of the delay command, the correct
// action will be to use the timer based on millis or micros
// or the realtime scheduler, see the section about use of
// times or real time to know how to do it
// ALSO NOTE that a servomotor does not operate at such high
// frequencies with respect to a BLDC, for which it is
// convenient to update the signal every 50 hz modifying the
// setup in order to write to the motors every 20 milliseconds
// the delay given in this example is 1000 milliseconds so
// there is noproblem in the execution and the servo motor
// should not be damaged

void loop(){
    hal.rcout->write(0,1000);
    hal.rcout->write(1,1000);
    hal.rcout->write(9,2000);

    hal.scheduler->delay(1000);
```

```
    hal.rcout->write(0,1200);
    hal.rcout->write(1,1200);
    hal.rcout->write(9,1500);

    hal.scheduler->delay(1000);

    hal.rcout->write(0,1500);
    hal.rcout->write(1,1700);
    hal.rcout->write(9,1000);

    hal.scheduler->delay(1000);

    hal.rcout->write(0,1900);
    hal.rcout->write(1,1860);
    hal.rcout->write(9,1200);

    hal.scheduler->delay(1000);

    hal.rcout->write(0,2000);
    hal.rcout->write(1,2000);
    hal.rcout->write(9,1000);

    hal.scheduler->delay(1000);
}

AP_HAL_MAIN(); // Ardupilot function call
```

The monitored signal by using the Arduino's serial monitor is graphed in Figure 5-17. Compare it to the previous code.

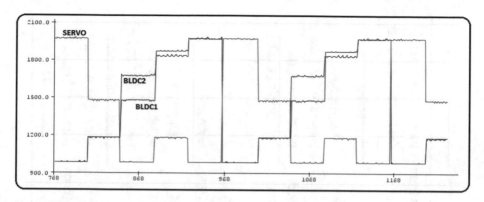

Figure 5-17. *An Arduino displaying Pixhawk autopilot simultaneous BLDC and servo outputs (main and auxiliar)*

Summary of ArduPilot Compatible Motors

In the following table there is a brief summary on the use of different types of motors.

Table 5-1. Summary of ArduPilot-Compatible Motors

Motor type	Required signals	Required code	Output signals from the Pixhawk	Output signals from the translator device
BLDC	RC-type PWM	The Pixhawk's	RC-type PWM	Not needed
BDC or "standard"	-Generally duty-cycle type PWM, sometimes RC-type PWM -Direction of rotation signal	-The Pixhawk's -The one for conversion of RC-type PWM to duty-cycle type PWM through an interpreter device (Arduino, Raspberry Pi, microcontroller, etc.)	-Mapping mode RC-type PWM -No mapping mode RC-type PWM and GPIO signal for direction of rotation	-Mapping mode duty-cycle PWM and direction of rotation -No mapping mode duty-cycle PWM
Servomotor	50 Hz RC-type PWM	The Pixhawk's	50 Hz RC-type PWM	Not needed
Stepper motor	-Number of pulses (with constant speed) or speed (with constant number of pulses) -Direction of rotation	-The Pixhawk's -The one for conversion of RC-type PWM to number of pulses or speed of rotation through an interpreter device (Arduino, Raspberry Pi, microcontroller, etc.)	-Mapping mode RC-type PWM -No mapping mode PWM RC and GPIO signal for direction of rotation	-Mapping mode Number of fixed or variable pulses and Direction of rotation -No mapping mode Number of fixed or variable pulses

Data Use and Storage

Components: microSD memory, memory card adapter, Mission Planner

Description: The commands we will present allow writing data into the autopilot's SD memory. Look at the following storage sequence:

- Package data type declaration

- Header declaration (how data will be saved in the SD memory)

- Initialization

- Saving sequence

In the declaration procedures and in the saving sequence, you must be careful with the names you use. The names must not be the same, but they must be related (by varying a letter or using a combination of capital letters and lowercases, as you will see in the example code).

Be especially careful with the header declaration because it does not use standard C or C ++ code. Consequently, an error would be undetectable by the compiler.

Although this code can go in the main program (for example `MainSD.pde`), given its complexity, it is easier to handle it in an auxiliary file inside the same folder (for example `Data.pde`). See Listings 5-19 and 5-20.

Implementation Tips   Data are stored in a maximum of 13 packages, with the objective of not saturating or slowing down the main task (in the Pixhawk and ArduPilot versions used with this book, this number of data packages worked well). Therefore, it is advisable to send a separator. Among others, data packages can be sensor reading packages, control packages, radio reading packages, error packages, additional data packages, etc.

The Pixhawk is not usable if you have not placed your SD card properly. Once data are extracted to the computer, make sure to place it correctly into the autopilot.

Always verify data and data types sent into the memory. If something fails, the compiler will not emit a warning. You will only know if there is an error at the moment of flight. This happens because correct data writing is the user's responsibility. Anything can be stored, but that does not mean that it is stored correctly.

Listing 5-19 provides an example of data storage. Note the following:

- The syntax is:

```
void WriteBlock(const void *pBuffer, uint16_t size);
```

You can find more information at: https://github.com/ArduPilot/ardupilot/blob/master/libraries/DataFlash/DataFlash.h

Listing 5-19. Saving Data in SD, MainSD.pde

```
//////////////////////////// DECLARATION ////////////////////////////
//                    Paste the header here
//                        See appendix
///////////////////////// place your code here /////////////////////////

//////////////////////////// INITIALIZATION ////////////////////////////

void setup(){
    init_flash();  // invocation of the initialization function
                   // defined in Data.pde
}
```

```
/////////////////////////// EXECUTION ///////////////////////////

void loop(){
    Save_data();// auxiliary function defined furher in this
                // program to store data
}

//              Auxiliar function

static void Save_data(){
    Log_Write_Pose(); // function to save pose data defined in
                      // Data.pde
    Log_Write_Control(); // function to save control data
                         // defined in Data.pde
    Log_Write_Errors(); // function to save error data defined
                        // in Data.pde
}
AP_HAL_MAIN(); // Ardupilot function call
```

Listing 5-20. Saving Data in SD, Auxiliary Code Data.pde

```
// register definition, see arducopter.pde code
#define LOG_POSE_MSG 0x01
#define LOG_ERR_MSG 0x0C
#define LOG_CONTROL_MSG 0x05

// DATA PACKAGE DECLARATION
// Number of packages 3, Pose, Control and Error

static uint16_t log_num;    //Dataflash

struct PACKED log_Pose{
    LOG_PACKET_HEADER;
    float    alt_barof;
    float    Roll;
    float    Pitch;
```

```
    float      Yaw;
    float      z_pos;
    float      vel_x;
    float      vel_y;
    float      vel_z;
    float      x_pos;
    float      y_pos;
    float      giroz;
    float      girox;
    float      giroy;
};

struct PACKED log_Control {
    LOG_PACKET_HEADER;
    float   time_ms;
    float   u_z;
    float   tau_theta;
    float   tau_phi;
    float   tau_psi;
    float   comodin_1;
    float   comodin_2;
    float   comodin_3; // data wildcards useful for whatever
    float   comodin_4; // you want to add
};

struct PACKED log_Errors {
    LOG_PACKET_HEADER;
    uint32_t    time_ms;
    float      error_x;
    float      error_y;
    float      error_z;
    float      voltaje;
```

```
    float    corriente;
    float    comodin_5;
    float    comodin_6;
    int    comodin_7;
    float    alt_des;
    float    x_des;
    float    y_des;
};

//          HEADER DECLARATION

static const struct LogStructure log_structure[] PROGMEM = {
        LOG_COMMON_STRUCTURES,
      {LOG_POSE_MSG, sizeof(log_Pose),
       "1", "ffffffffffffff", "a_bar,ROLL,PITCH,YAW,
       Z_POS,V_X,V_Y,V_Z,X_POS,Y_POS,G_Z,G_X,G_Y"},
       { LOG_CONTROL_MSG, sizeof(log_Control),
        "2", "fffffffff", "T_MS,UZ,T_TH,T_PHI,T_PSI,TAUX,TAUY,
        S_PHI,S_PSI"},
        { LOG_ERR_MSG, sizeof(log_Errors),
        "3", "IffffffIfff", "T_MS,E_X,E_Y,E_Z,VOLT,AMP,nav_z,
        nav_zp,con_alt,ZDES,XDES,YDES"},
};

//          INITIALIZATION

static void init_flash() {
    DataFlash.Init(log_structure,sizeof(log_structure)/
    sizeof(log_structure[0]));
    if (DataFlash.NeedErase()) {
        DataFlash.EraseAll();
    }
    log_num=DataFlash.StartNewLog();
}
```

```
//    SAVING SEQUENCE DATA, BY PACKAGE, Pose, Control, Errors
// DATA TO THE RIGHT is assumed previously defined in the main
// cycle or auxiliary functions

static void Log_Write_Pose()
{
    struct log_Pose pkt = {
        LOG_PACKET_HEADER_INIT(LOG_POSE_MSG),
        alt_barof    : baro_alt,
        Roll         : ahrs.roll,
        Pitch        : ahrs.pitch,
        Yaw          : ahrs.yaw,
        z_pos        : pos.z,
        vel_x        : vel.x,
        vel_y        : vel.y,
        vel_z        : vel.z,
        x_pos        : pos.x,
        y_pos        : pos.y,
        giroz        : gyro.z,
        girox        : gyro.x,
        giroy        : gyro.y,
    };
    DataFlash.WriteBlock(&pkt, sizeof(pkt));
}

static void Log_Write_Control(){
    struct log_Control pkt = {
        LOG_PACKET_HEADER_INIT(LOG_CONTROL_MSG),
        time_ms      : (float)(hal.scheduler->millis()/1000),
        u_z          : ctrl.z,
        tau_theta    : (ctrl.x+c_pitch),
        tau_phi      : (ctrl.y+c_roll),
```

```
        tau_psi     : c_yaw,
        comodin_1      : 0,
        comodin_2      : 0,
        comodin_3    : 0,
        comodin_4    : 0,
    };
    DataFlash.WriteBlock(&pkt, sizeof(pkt));
}
static void Log_Write_Errors(){
    struct log_Errors pkt = {
        LOG_PACKET_HEADER_INIT(LOG_ERR_MSG),
        time_ms         : (hal.scheduler->millis()/100),
        error_x         : error.x,
        error_y         : error.y,
        error_z         : error.z,
        voltaje         : volt,
        corriente       : corriente_tot,
        comodin_5        : 0,
        comodin_6       : 0,
        comodin_7        : radio_throttle,
        alt_des       : ref.z,
        x_des         : ref.x,
        y_des         : ref.y,
    };
    DataFlash.WriteBlock(&pkt, sizeof(pkt));
}
```

Next we describe how to use Mission Planner to save the data into your computer or to view them directly at the same interface.

Caution   In both cases, you need to remove the SD card from the autopilot and read it through a memory adapter.

Using the Mission Planner GUI to Plot SD Data

Although the microSD card can be programmed to store navigation data while the vehicle is in operation (see the previous section), the question that arises is how to later use this data for either monitoring or reporting.

This is achieved through the Mission Planner interface. The steps to obtain the information are the following:

1. Carefully remove the microSD card from the Pixhawk. See Figure 5-18.

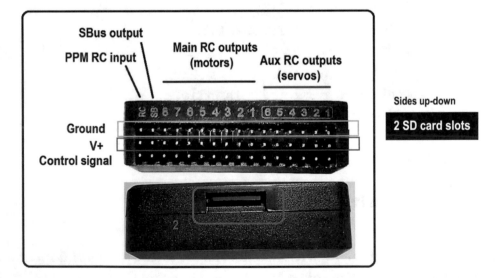

Figure 5-18. *Plotting flight data from SD, part 1*

2. Whether the computer which you plan to work the
    data has a microSD card port or an adapter for that
    purpose, connect said card as if it is USB memory.
    Notice the presence of the APM folder and the LOGS
    folder inside it. See Figure 5-19.

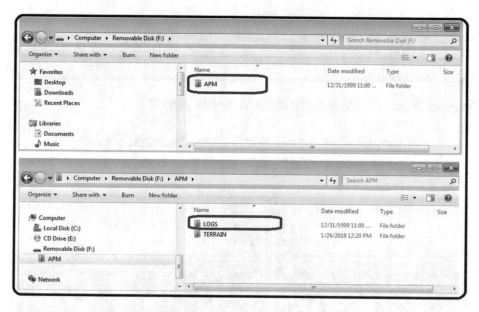

Figure 5-19. *Plotting flight data from SD, part 2*

3. All the updated navigation files that you have
    programmed for storage are in the LOGS folder. To
    find the most recent one, look for the file LASTLOG.
    TXT (in this example, lastlog tells us that it is the file
    called 77). See Figure 5-20.

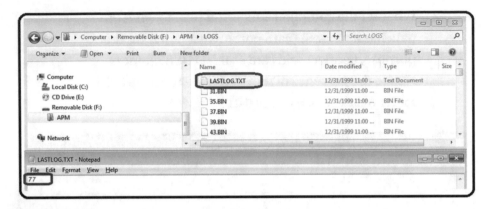

Figure 5-20. *Plotting flight data from SD, part 3*

4. Open Mission Planner and click the Terminal button (never press the Connect button). See Figure 5-21.

Figure 5-21. *Plotting flight data from SD, part 4*

5.   Click the Log Download button. See Figure 5-22.

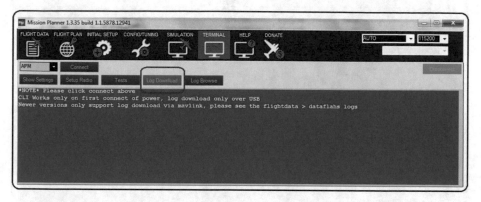

Figure 5-22. *Plotting flight data from SD, part 5*

6.   If the message in Figure 5-23 appears, just ignore it
      by clicking the OK button.

Figure 5-23. *Plotting flight data from SD, part 6*

7.   In the auxiliary window, look for and click the Bin to
      log button. (The bin format is exclusively designed
      to be small and to contain navigation information.
      However, it must be decoded to a log format in
      order for it to be used and its data extracted to a
      computer). See Figure 5-24.

Figure 5-24. *Plotting flight data from SD, part 7*

8. You will be asked for the location and name of the file
    to convert. In our example, it is the 77 file in the APM/
    LOGS folder. Select it and open it. See Figure 5-25.

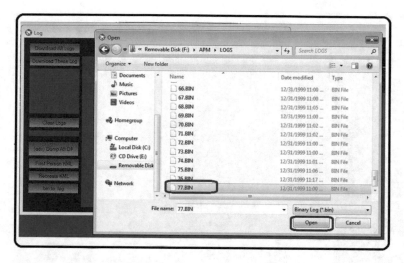

Figure 5-25. *Plotting flight data from SD, part 8*

9. In the following window, indicate the name and a
    folder where you want to save the file (remember
    that the output .log file is already a text file that
    can be used with any editor such as notepads,
    spreadsheets, equation editors, plotting programs,
    etc.). See Figure 5-26.

Figure 5-26. *Plotting flight data from SD, part 9*

10. Finally, close all tabs and, if necessary, Mission
    Planner. Look for your .log file and verify its
    contents. In this example, it is saved as compu77.
    log on the Desktop (since it is a text file, it can also
    be saved or renamed with extensions .txt or .dat if
    the program you use requires it). See Figure 5-27.

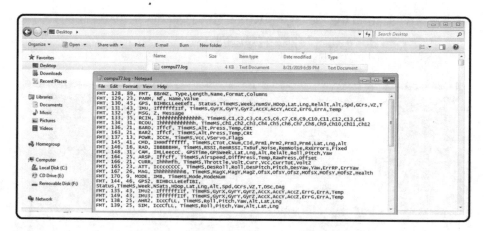

Figure 5-27. *Plotting flight data from SD, part 10*

11. If you do not have a spreadsheet or an equation
     editor, or you want just a quick interpretation of the
     data stored in the `.log` file, you can do the following:

     a) Open Mission Planner. Go to the Terminal tab and click the
         Log Browse button. See Figure 5-28.

Figure 5-28. *Plotting flight data from SD, alternative procedure
part A*

b) Search for, select, and open the .log file (called compu77.log in this example). See Figure 5-29.

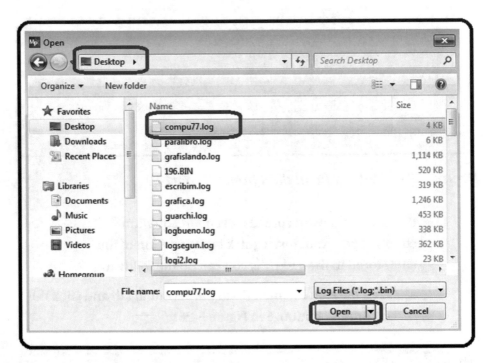

Figure 5-29. *Plotting flight data from SD, alternative procedure part B*

c) A window like the one shown in Figure 5-30 will appear. The data of interest will appear in the form of packages numbered from 1 to n (remember that it works well up to 13 packages).

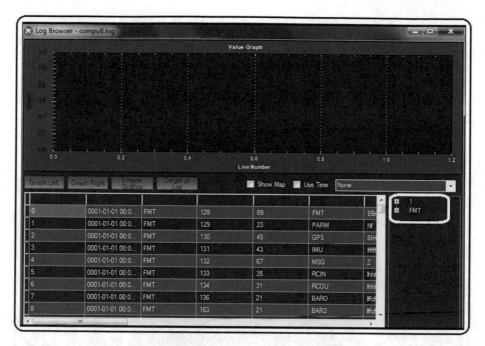

Figure 5-30. *Plotting flight data from SD, alternative procedure part C*

d) The data available will appear by clicking the package number. See Figure 5-31.

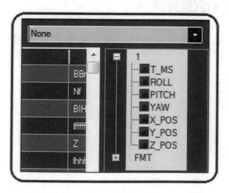

Figure 5-31. *Plotting flight data from SD, alternative procedure part D*

e) Select the data of interest and plot it. It can be stored as some common type of image by right-clicking the graph. See Figure 5-32.

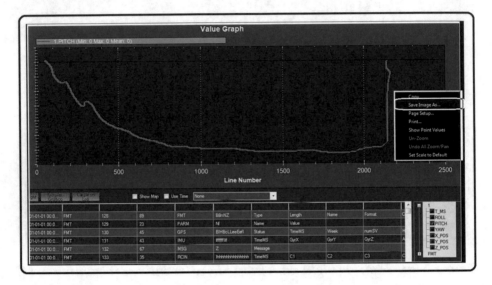

Figure 5-32. *Plotting flight data from SD, alternative procedure part E*

Time Management

There are five ways to use time in the ArduPilot libraries. See Table 5-2.

Table 5-2. *ArduPilot Libraries Time Management*

Type	Usual ArduPilot commands	Characteristics
Delay	`hal.scheduler->delay(time)`	It pauses the system completely.
System's clock	`hal.scheduler->millis()` `hal.scheduler->micros()`	It uses the system's clock since it is activated without pausing any activity. It is a basis for real time.
Inactive cycles	`for, while, do while, if`	It is the basis for delay and implies the same disadvantages.
Accumulator	`var=var+1`	It does not stop any process, but if one is blocked, so is the accumulator. It's another basis for real time.
Real time	Scheduler sequence	It allows the parallelization of tasks, it is the most powerful way of time management

1. **By invoking delays (the analog form of using an alarm):** In this case, the delay function allows you to enter empty time until the delay ends. It is the least recommended because the system remains totally inactive for as long as you decide. Once the delay is finished, the system returns to the normal execution of its tasks. Generally, delays are used to give some time for a physical task to be executed (for example, if commands are continuously sent to a motor, it can burn up; the delay gives time for the motor to react smoothly). See Listing 5-21.

Listing 5-21 provides an example of time management by using delays. Note the following:

- The syntax is:

```
void delay(uint16_t miliseconds);
void delay_microseconds(uint16_t microseconds)
```

You can find more information at: https://github.com/ArduPilot/ardupilot/blob/master/libraries/AP_HAL/Scheduler.h

Listing 5-21. Time Management by Using Delays in Milliseconds and Microseconds

```
//////////////////////// DECLARATION ////////////////////////
//                  Paste the header here
//                      See appendix

//////////////////// place your code here ////////////////////


///////////////////////// INITIALIZATION /////////////////////


void setup(){
    // copy the basic setup see appendix
}
//////////////////////////// EXECUTION ///////////////////////

// HERE the previous functions for reading orientations are used
// and each reading is separated in a period of 3000
// milliseconds or 3s note that the system does not do
// anything during that time only the data displaying

void loop(){
```

```
    ahrs.update();
    roll  = ahrs.roll;
    pitch = ahrs.pitch;
    yaw   = ahrs.yaw;
    hal.console->printf("%f\t %f\t %f\t\n",roll,pitch,yaw);
    hal.scheduler->delay(3000);
}

AP_HAL_MAIN(); // Ardupilot function call
```

2. **By invoking global meters (the analog form of
   using a clock)**: In this case, you can know the
   "exact" elapsed time since the system was turned
   on until the invocation of the command. One of
   its main functions is the calculation of speed. This
   method, along with that of accumulators, is the
   basis of real time. See Listing 5-22.

Listing 5-22 provides an example of time management by using the
system clock. Note the following:

- The syntax are:

```
millis( );
micros( );
```

You can find more information at: http://ardupilot.org/dev/docs/
learning-ardupilot-the-example-sketches.html

Listing 5-22. Time Management by Using the System Clock

```
/////////////////////////// DECLARATION ///////////////////////////
//                      Paste the header here
//                         See appendix

////////////////////// place your code here //////////////////////

// integers that contain time, their variable types are without
// sign because time is always positive and also of value 32
// which can reach a maximum value of 4,294,967,296 milliseconds,
// a type 16 could be used but it would be useful just one
// minute or approximately 65536 milliseconds

uint32_t timec, timecmod;

/////////////////////////// INITIALIZATION ///////////////////////////

void setup(){
    // copy the basic setup see appendix

}

/////////////////////////// EXECUTION ///////////////////////////

// HERE the previous functions for reading orientations are used
// and each reading is separated in a period of 3000
// milliseconds or 3s note that the system continues with
// its normal tasks and data display is done just when the
// global time module equals 3s

void loop(){

    timec=hal.scheduler->millis();
    timecmod=timec%3000;

    ahrs.update();
    roll  = ahrs.roll;
```

```
pitch = ahrs.pitch;
yaw   = ahrs.yaw;

if(timecmod==0)
{
    hal.console->printf("%f\t %f\t %f\t\n",roll,pitch,yaw);
}

}

AP_HAL_MAIN(); // Ardupilot function call
```

3. **By inactive cycles**: This method uses combinations of logical or sequential structures (for, if, while), for generating dead time. It is the basis of the delay, but it is not as useless because it is performed by an event count (number of times the program has passed through a line of code, for example).

4. **By accumulators (the analog form of a counter)**: An event count must be performed (number of times the program has passed through a line of code, for example) to increase variables called accumulators. Its disadvantage is that each increment is affected by the length of the program (the longer the code, the more time the accumulator's update takes). Thus if some task is blocked, so is the accumulator. This method, along with the global meter, is the basis of real time.

5. **By the real-time scheduler (the analog form of a chronometer)**: This is one of the most powerful methods of time management. It allows you to rank and prioritize tasks. Given its importance, it will be seen in the next section of this book.

Chapter Summary

In this chapter, you learned the following ArduPilot libraries advanced operations:

- Wired and wireless UART serial communication

- How to interface your Pixhawk autopilot with other development cards (such as an Arduino)

- How to optimize your code

- Different ways of time management

- How to save and use flight data

- How to use different types of motors with your autopilot

In the next chapter, you will learn how to control a vehicle, in this case a quadcopter. For this you will use the previously seen commands, and we teach you in a basic way to model and control this sort of vehicle so you can follow similar steps with another kind of robot.

CHAPTER 6

Quadcopter Control with Smooth Flight Mode

In this chapter, we will teach you how to program a vehicle with the previous knowledge acquired. This chapter will guide you through the basics of automatic control, modeling, and the tool known as an allocation matrix, which is very useful for linking theory with practice. All this will be shown with a specific use-case: the quadcopter. By the end of this chapter, you'll be able to use the skills learned with any other type of robotic vehicle.

Suggested requirements include first loading the code in Listing 6-1 to the Pixhawk. This code will send the signals of the remote control and distribute them in the drone's BLDC motors.

© Julio Alberto Mendoza-Mendoza, Victor Gonzalez-Villela 2020
J. A. Mendoza-Mendoza et al., *Advanced Robotic Vehicles Programming*,
https://doi.org/10.1007/978-1-4842-5531-5_6

Listing 6-1. Reading the Remote Control and Writing to Each Engine of the Vehicle as a Combination

```
///////////////////////// DECLARATION /////////////////////////
//                      Paste the header here
//                        See appendix

////////////////////////// place your code here ////////////////

// add or verify those lines

uint16_t radio[6];
float m1,m2,m3,m4;
int radio_roll, radio_pitch, radio_yaw, radio_throttle, aux_1,
aux_2;

/////////////////////////// INITIALIZATION /////////////////////

void setup(){
// verify or add those lines
    hal.rcout->enable_ch(0);
    hal.rcout->enable_ch(1);
    hal.rcout->enable_ch(2);
    hal.rcout->enable_ch(3);
    hal.rcout->set_freq( 15, 490);
}
/////////////////////////// EXECUTION ///////////////////////////

void loop(){

/////    starting BLDC in zero

    hal.rcout->write(0,0);
    hal.rcout->write(1,0);
    hal.rcout->write(2,0);
    hal.rcout->write(3,0);
```

///// reading all the radio channels, radio must be in mode 2
///// or helicopter mode

```
for (uint8_t i = 0; i < 6; i++)
    {radio[i] = hal.rcin->read(i);}
```

///// assignment of each channel

```
radio_roll  = (radio[0]-1500)/3;
radio_pitch = (radio[1]-1510)/3;
radio_throttle = radio[2];
radio_yaw = (radio[3]-1510)/2;
aux_1 = radio[4];
aux_2 = radio[5];
```

///// values to write from
///// remote control to each engine through its corresponding
///// allocation matrix type X (see further sections), notice
///// the saturation to the engines so that they do not exceed
///// the minimum and maximun security values

```
m1 = satu((radio_throttle-radio_roll+radio_pitch+
radio_yaw),1700,1100);
m2 = satu((radio_throttle+radio_roll-radio_pitch+
radio_yaw),1700,1100);
m3 = satu((radio_throttle+radio_roll+radio_pitch-
radio_yaw),1700,1100);
m4 = satu((radio_throttle-radio_roll-radio_pitch-
radio_yaw),1700,1100);
```

// emergency stop using a two-position auxiliary lever,
// when the lever is on, it is written to each motor
// otherwise, the motors are switched off

```
    if (aux_1<1500)
    {
        hal.rcout->write(0,uint16_t(m1));
        hal.rcout->write(1,uint16_t(m2));
        hal.rcout->write(2,uint16_t(m3));
        hal.rcout->write(3,uint16_t(m4));
    }

    else
    {
        hal.rcout->write(0,900);
        hal.rcout->write(1,900);
        hal.rcout->write(2,900);
        hal.rcout->write(3,900);
    }

    hal.scheduler->delay(50);

}

//        Auxiliar functions

AP_HAL_MAIN(); // Ardupilot function call

///    saturation function

static float satu(float nu, float maxi, float mini){
    if(nu>=maxi) nu=maxi;
    else nu=nu;
    if(nu <= mini) nu=mini;
    else nu=nu;
    return nu;
}
```

Note   The non-arbitrary way to send RC PWM signals to the motors uses something we'll cover later in this chapter called an allocation matrix.

The code shown in Listing 6-1 corresponds to a variation on the Pixhawk type X configuration. To use it, verify that the motors are properly connected to the autopilot as indicated in Figure 6-1. Verify the direction of rotation as well.

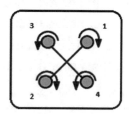

Figure 6-1. *Motor configuration for the Pixhawk type X variation*

Once you finish loading the code, check if the direction of the remote control levers is correct. For this purpose, assemble a quadcopter-type drone and *without the propellers* check the following by placing the vehicle in your hands (See allocation matrix section).

By exclusively moving the throttle, all motors should change their speed in a similar way with respect to each other (an almost identical speed must be observed in all motors). See Figure 6-2.

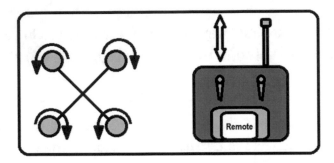

Figure 6-2. *Motor effect when moving throttle lever*

When moving the yaw lever in one direction, two motors should go faster than those rotating in the opposite direction (diagonal). When moving the yaw lever in the other direction, the motors with opposite direction of rotation should rotate faster than the first ones. See Figure 6-3.

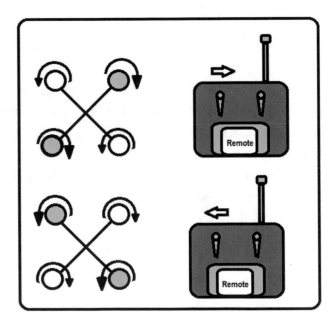

Figure 6-3. *Motor effect when moving yaw lever*

When moving the levers of advance in X and Y (roll and pitch), you should notice that two motors dominate their opposites (the rear ones vs. the frontal ones, the left ones vs. the right ones). The objective is that if you want to move to the right and you have an opposite behavior to that shown in the figure, then the command is inverted and you must change the signs of the associated channel. See Figure 6-4.

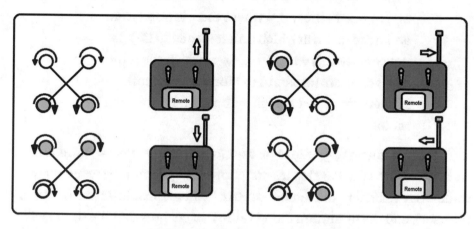

Figure 6-4. *Motor effect when moving roll and pitch levers*

The previous steps were used to calibrate the remote control. Now you need to find the starting value for each BLDC:

a.   Assemble an aeropendulum (a solid pendulum whose suspended mass is a BLDC motor). See http://aeropendulum.arizona.edu/ to guide your own design.

b.   The distance from the motor to the center of the pendulum should measure the same as the arm of the quadcopter.

c.   The added weight must be equal to one quarter part of the weight of the assembled drone (including the motors).

d. Load one of the code files for testing a motor by
    using a keyboard (the one with Arduino or the one
    with Pixhawk, previously described).

e. Write down the value reached when each motor
    starts to rotate and also the value needed to raise the
    pendulum (to be more specific, increase PWM units
    one by one in the range where there is no movement
    and write down at which unit it started to lift). Do
    not confuse this with the value at which the motor
    starts to rotate (around 1100 for most motors).
    However, it is best to register both values for each
    motor.

At this moment, the code to be sent to the motors has two groups of
values. You can later develop a semiautomatic operation by using these
values: one related to the remote control (with manual intervention from
the user), and the minimum lifting value that ensures that the drone will at
least manage to take off.

Next, you will design other important values: the attitude control,
the altitude one, and the planar position, which will provide automatic
operation.

Basic Modeling of a Multicopter

Although this section is simplified, if you do not have the appropriate
mathematical context, read the "Allocation Matrix" section since it plays an
essential role in programming the drone and any vehicle in general.

1. **Reference frames**: This first step involves
    identifying the three reference frames to perform
    the multicopter modeling: base, world, global, or
    inertial frame, depending on the consulted source.

It is the global reference that you impose for your drone's movement. It can be the center of a room, a given corner, a landing platform, etc.

Body, local, mobile, vehicle, or not-inertial frames depend on the consulted source. A local reference frame is generally placed on the approximate position of the vehicle's center of gravity. Some criteria to establish local frames are indicated in Table 6-1.

Table 6-1. *Criteria for Choosing Usual Body Frames*

Point to choose to locate the body frame	Criteria
Geometric center	Use it when the vehicle has high radial symmetry and the weight is more or less balanced to its radial center. Also, use it when making slow movements of negligible masses. This center is common to use with cart wheeled robots.
Center of masses	Use it when a vehicle's shape or inertia changes with moderate speed variations (a slow quadruped walking robot, for example).
Center of gravity	Use it when a vehicle's shape or inertia changes with abrupt speed variations (a rollercoaster car or an acrobatic quadcopter, for example).
Center of flotation	Use it for aquatic vehicles.
Center of pressure	Use it for vehicles or objects with high aerodynamic variation (projectiles or aircraft in turbulent conditions, for example).
Base point	Use it with anchored bodies, the base of a robotic arm fixed to the ground, or to a heavy load, for example.

245

Propulsion, propeller, motor, or engine frames are reference frames that describe thrust and torque of each propeller or motor. Note that every vehicle has a propulsion frame. In the case of wheeled robots, it is called a wheel frame.

All the frames are related in the following way; see Figure 6-5.

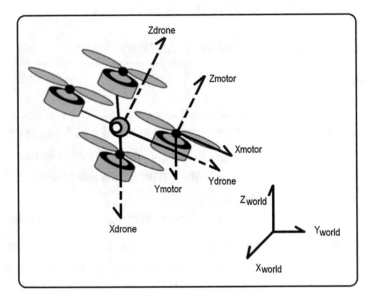

Figure 6-5. *Quadcopter coordinate frames*

The propulsion frame indicates how the thrust and torque of each propeller will affect the center of gravity, where their equivalent effects will be transferred.

Once it has transferred the equivalent dynamic effects of all motors, the body frame will be cinematically related to the base frame, through the entire movement of the vehicle.

2. **Propulsion matrix**: Also known as an allocation matrix, mixer, or matrix relation between speeds (the speeds of the actuators with respect to those of the analysis center of the vehicle). It establishes the dynamic connection between the center of gravity (or any other center, but this is most suitable for the design and control of an aircraft) and those effects originated by the propellers and motors (a tricopter, an octocopter, etc.). Its purpose is to establish a relationship between the designed forces and moments (remember that in a three-dimensional Cartesian space there are only three forces and three torques) and those that are sent to the motors individually. Therefore, the analysis is performed in the body frame.

To better understand the importance of the propulsion matrix, let's analyze the following figures. In Figure 6-6, note how each blade's thrust moves to the center of the propeller, resulting in a central thrust force plus a central torque dependent on the propeller's radius (notice that the horizontal forces are canceled, provided that the blades are well balanced).

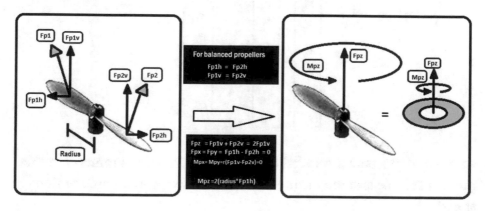

Figure 6-6. *Forces and moments in a propeller*

Let's repeat the process for each propeller towards the center of the drone. Notice that the thrust and torque of each propeller work as a thrust force and three torsional pairs in the center of the vehicle. Also notice that the forces in X and Y are equal to zero (similarly, the torques in those same axes, given that the propellers and the vehicle are supposed to be well balanced and these effects are mutually canceled). See Figure 6-7.

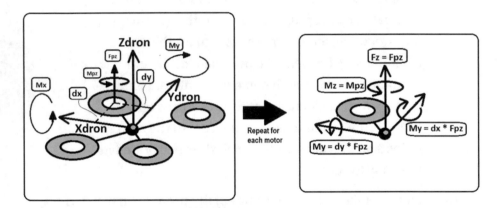

Figure 6-7. *Forces and moments in the body of a multicopter*

If you express this graphical deduction through a matrix, you have

$$
\begin{bmatrix} F_x \\ F_y \\ F_z \\ \tau_x \\ \tau_y \\ \tau_z \end{bmatrix} = \begin{bmatrix} F_x \\ F_y \\ F_z \\ \tau_\phi \\ \tau_\theta \\ \tau_\psi \end{bmatrix} = P_{6xn} \begin{bmatrix} m_1 \\ m_2 \\ m_3 \\ \vdots \\ m_n \end{bmatrix}_{nx1}
$$

where m represents the speed of each motor. You must remember that the thrust force and the torque of the motor are proportional to that speed.

The allocation matrix is the link between the theoretical design of the system controller and the practical execution of the task. Once the torques and forces have been translated to the center of interest of the drone or vehicle, it will be enough to perform the following operation to program each motor:

$$
\begin{bmatrix} m_1 \\ m_2 \\ m_3 \\ \vdots \\ m_n \end{bmatrix}_{n \times 1} = P^{-1} \begin{bmatrix} F_x \\ F_y \\ F_z \\ \tau_x \\ \tau_y \\ \tau_z \end{bmatrix}
$$

From here you can notice four problems:

A. The most important problem is that the interaction of the motors with the center of gravity is considered, but the interaction among the motors themselves is not (ground effects, vortex, suction, etc.). This is neglected or minimized by design in most cases. We will assume that in this book, but this problem should be considered and explored in specialized designs or in aggressive tasks or those performed near objects.

B. When there are more or fewer motors than Cartesian mobility degrees, computational optimization and pseudoinverse problems arise. In the case of a quadcopter, these problems are solved elegantly by making task dependences, in which the stabilization of roll and pitch angles becomes a dependency of the XY planar stabilization, as you will see later in the section of control design.

However, for hexacopters that have only four possible movements and six motors, this translates into computational problems.

C.   When there is a vectorization method such as those described in this chapter's corresponding appendix, the propulsion matrix has values that are not constant and, even more importantly, values dependent on the motors themselves. This demands that the allocation matrix recalculates permanently.

D.   Some vehicles' motors, especially those of aerial vehicles, only admit positive operation values, while the forces and the product with the same propulsion matrix are usually negative and positive, so you must work with a bias value, also known as a translation value.

According to point B and the interdependence of the XY planar tasks along with those of roll and pitch, the global propulsion equation of a quadcopter-type drone is (the particular versions will be defined in the following paragraphs)

$$
\begin{bmatrix} F_z \\ \tau_\phi \\ \tau_\theta \\ \tau_\psi \end{bmatrix} = P_{4x4} \begin{bmatrix} m_1 \\ m_2 \\ m_3 \\ m_4 \end{bmatrix}
$$

What is stated in the previous paragraph is also supported because you only have a thrust force and three torsional moments in the body frame. This way, the other two thrusts (in the XY plane) are dependent on roll, pitch, and yaw torques.

Note   All mobile robotic systems have a matrix of allocation, propulsion, or mixer. The type of impeller (propellers, wheels, legs, turbines, etc.) is the only factor that changes. However, this matrix always relates the impellers with some point of interest in the vehicle (center of masses, of gravity, of geometry, of flotation, etc.).

The allocation matrix calculation is affected by the following factors:

A.   Geometric shape configuration of the motors (that is, the way in which the motors are placed with respect to the coordinate frame located in the drone's reference center)

B.   The position of the coordinate frame in the drone's reference center. In this case, defining the name of each axis as well as its direction is highly important.

C.   The number assignation of the motors

D.   The direction of rotation of the motors

E.   The attitude angle's positive direction of rotation (which is assigned by following rules of right or left hand or simply assigning positive rotations in a clockwise or counterclockwise type rotations).

F.   The vehicle's symmetry

Now you will see a guided example of how to obtain a propulsion matrix in a simplified + type quadcopter. This example is simplified because most of the quadcopters are those of x type. We invite you to repeat this example with an x type drone or consult the Quan Quan book found in the references.

Step 1: Establish the symmetry of the vehicle. This influences how to place the body frame, as well as how the motors influence certain movements. This is performed based on the guide-mark of the autopilot, which indicates the zero reference in the yaw angle from your IMU sensor or the magnetic north of the compass in other models. See Figure 6-8.

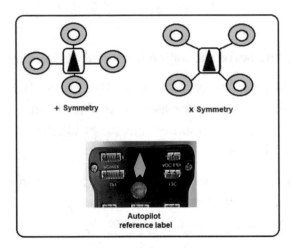

Figure 6-8. *Step 1 to obtain the propulsion or allocation matrrix*

Step 2: Assign a number to each motor. This affects even the way in which the motors will be connected to the autopilot. See Figure 6-9.

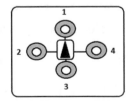

Figure 6-9. *Step 2 to obtain the propulsion or allocation matrrix*

Step 3: Choose the direction of rotation of the motors. Remember that in order to not produce a self-rotating effect, half of the drone's motors must turn in a clockwise direction and the other half in a counterclockwise direction. (When dealing with a vehicle with odd-numbered motors, one of them is used as a vectorizer. See the appendix on thrust vectoring). In general, there are several ways to achieve this, but the most usual is a diagonal sequence (see Figure 6-10). There are efficiency studies on which motors must have a certain direction of rotation. Moreover, you are free to experiment. However, in this example and for a certain degree of standardization we will choose the direction of rotation shown in Figure 6-10.

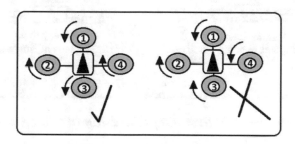

Figure 6-10. *Step 3 to obtain the propulsion or allocation matrix*

Step 4: Choose the geometric configuration. In this case, place the arms at the same distance to the center of the vehicle, with square angles (0 and 90 degrees) and at the same height with respect to the center of the vehicle. Very unequal distances, very different angles, or significantly different heights change the propulsion matrix considerably. Nevertheless, if the differences are moderate, this does not influence the operation of the vehicle. See Figure 6-11.

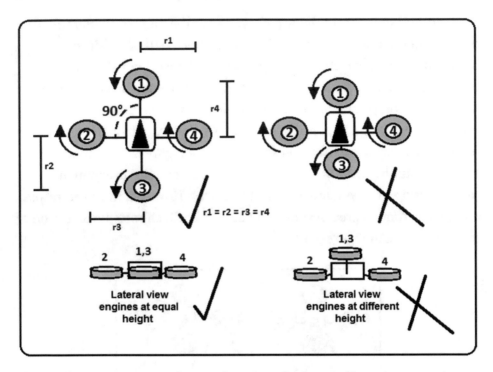

Figure 6-11. *Step 4 to obtain the propulsion or allocation matrix*

Step 5: Place the coordinate frame of the drone (that is the body frame) and label the axes. This influences the vehicle's movement and control design. The choice will depend on the test of the remote control levers. See Figure 6-12.

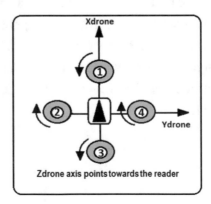

Figure 6-12. *Step 5 to obtain the propulsion or allocation matrix*

Step 6: Relate the rotational frames and their direction of rotation. In this example, you will associate the pitch with the X axis of the drone, the roll with the Y axis, and the yaw with Z. The positive direction of the rotation of the planar axes X and Y is the one in which it moves towards the positive zone of the axes when the vehicle is tilted. The direction of rotation of the Z axis is free, but the right hand rule is usually employed. (Point the right thumb in the same direction as the axis of interest points. The direction in which the rest of the fingers point in a closed fist is the positive direction of rotation). Just as the previous step influences vehicle's movement and control, this will also depend on the lever test of the remote control. Therefore, if the levers are inverted with respect to a desired movement, the proposed direction of rotation must be modified. Notice that the proposed situation changes for the design of omnidirectional vehicles, and it is convenient that all the rotating axes are selected according to the rule of the right hand. See Figure 6-13.

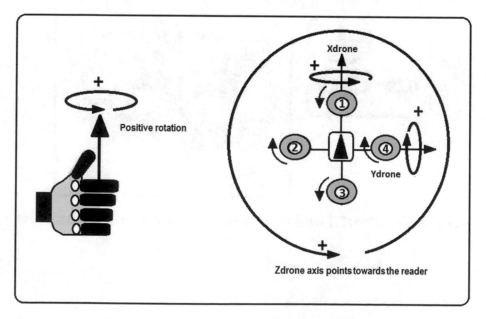

Figure 6-13. *Step 6 to obtain the propulsion or allocation matrix*

Step 7: Answer the following questions.

1. Which motors provide direct displacement on the X axis of the drone?

    In this case, none, $F_x = 0$, because by being well balanced, each propeller only transmits a vertical force and a torsional moment. You can also assume that the vehicle is well balanced, which means that the whole mass of the vehicle is concentrated at its geometric center where the autopilot reference mark is placed and its arms have the same length. See Figure 6-14.

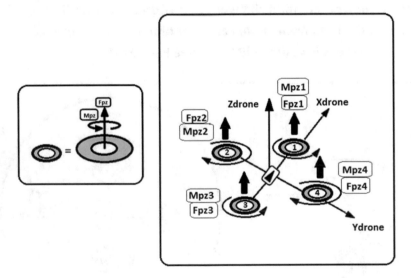

Figure 6-14. *Steps 7.1 and 7.2 to obtain the propulsion or allocation matrix*

2. Which motors provide direct displacement on the
    Y axis of the drone?

    None, $F_y = 0$, because by being well balanced,
    each propeller only transmits a vertical force and
    a torsional moment. You can also assume that the
    vehicle is well balanced, which means that the
    whole mass is concentrated at the center of the
    aircraft and the reference mark of the autopilot, and
    its arms have the same length. See Figure 6-14.

3. Which motors provide direct displacement on the
    Z axis of the drone?

    In this case, all of them, that is $F_z = \omega_1 + \omega_2 + \omega_3 + \omega_4$.
    See Figure 6-15.

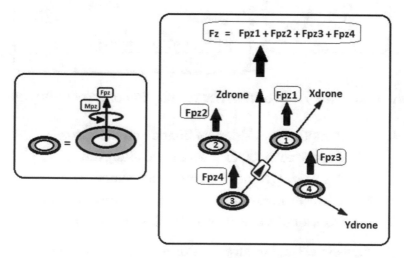

Figure 6-15. *Step 7.3 to obtain the propulsion or allocation matrix*

4. Which motors provide an inclination in the X axis
    of the drone so that it displaces tilted along the
    positive Y axis? (Notice that the displacement in
    Y is indirectly made by an inclination of the drone
    on the X axis for this type of vehicle).

    Increase w2 and reduce w4; this means $\tau_x = \omega_2 - \omega_4$.
    See Figure 6-16.

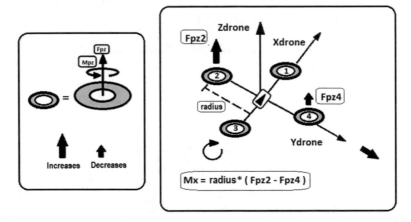

Figure 6-16. *Step 7.4 to obtain the propulsion or allocation matrix*

5. Which motors provide an inclination on the Y axis
    of the drone so that it displaces tilted along the
    positive X axis? (Notice that the displacement in
    X is indirectly made by an inclination of the drone on
    the Y axis for this type of vehicle). See Figure 6-17.

    Increase w3 and reduce w1; this means $\tau_y = \omega_3 - \omega_1$.

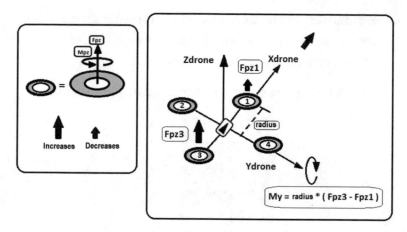

Figure 6-17. *Step 7.5 to obtain the propulsion or allocation matrix*

6. Which motors contribute on the Z axis of the drone so that it rotates in the positive direction of yaw?

Increase w1 and w3, and reduce w2 with w4, so $\tau_z = \omega_1 + \omega_3 - \omega_2 - \omega_4$. See Figure 6-18.

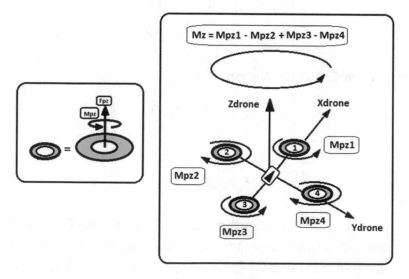

Figure 6-18. *Step 7.6 to obtain the propulsion or allocation matrix*

Remember that if this behavior is reversed with the levers, in the remote control tests, the signs of the altered axis must also be reversed.

Step 8: Group the equations obtained in a matrix form.

$$F_x = 0$$
$$F_y = 0$$
$$F_z = \omega_1 + \omega_2 + \omega_3 + \omega_4$$
$$\tau_x = \omega_2 - \omega_4$$
$$\tau_y = \omega_3 - \omega_1$$
$$\tau_z = \omega_1 + \omega_3 - \omega_2 - \omega_4$$

$$
\begin{bmatrix} F_x \\ F_y \\ F_z \\ \tau_x \\ \tau_y \\ \tau_z \end{bmatrix}
=
\begin{bmatrix}
0 & 0 & 0 & 0 \\
0 & 0 & 0 & 0 \\
1 & 1 & 1 & 1 \\
0 & 1 & 0 & -1 \\
-1 & 0 & 1 & 0 \\
1 & -1 & 1 & -1
\end{bmatrix}
\begin{bmatrix} \omega_1 \\ \omega_2 \\ \omega_3 \\ \omega_4 \end{bmatrix}
$$

Once simplified, this results in

$$
\begin{bmatrix} F_z \\ \tau_x \\ \tau_y \\ \tau_z \end{bmatrix}
= P_{4x4}
\begin{bmatrix} m_1 \\ m_2 \\ m_3 \\ m_4 \end{bmatrix}
=
\begin{bmatrix}
1 & 1 & 1 & 1 \\
0 & 1 & 0 & -1 \\
-1 & 0 & 1 & 0 \\
1 & -1 & 1 & -1
\end{bmatrix}
\begin{bmatrix} \omega_1 \\ \omega_2 \\ \omega_3 \\ \omega_4 \end{bmatrix}
$$

To remember the importance of the correct selection of the allocation matrix, note for the previous example that there are four possible ways to number the motors, two possible ways to select their direction of rotation, 24 ways to choose the positive XYZ axes, and at least six ways to choose the positive aircraft's axes rotations. This way, by combinatory theory, only for this type of drone there are several possibilities to choose the allocation matrix and only one is correct. If your choice is wrong, the vehicle will have incorrect or even catastrophic behavior.

Second Example: Bicopter (with Coaxial Motors Analysis)

The bicopter or PVTOL (planar vertical takeoff and landing) is a drone designed to move only along the vertical Z and horizontal Y axis. A real bicopter can move in all three dimensions but to prevent going forward and backward on the X axis, let's analyze the following example with coaxial motors, which are sold as coupled motors that share the same axis but rotate in opposite directions. See Figure 6-19.

$$\omega_2 = -\omega_3$$
$$\omega_1 = -\omega_4$$

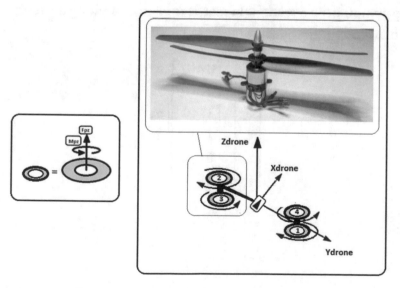

Figure 6-19. *References for obtaining the allocation matrix of a coaxial bicopter*

This this way, due to the opposite direction of rotation, the thrust forces are duplicated while the torques are canceled. If you apply these criteria and analyzing as if the vehicle has a single right motor and a single left motor, you get the following:

$$F_x = 0$$
$$F_y = 0$$
$$F_z = 2(\omega_2 + \omega_4)$$
$$\tau_x = 2(\omega_2 - \omega_4)$$
$$\tau_y = 0$$
$$\tau_z = 0$$

Remember that the torque in X is the necessary tilt on the X axis of the drone so that it advances on the positive Y axis of the drone. In this case, this is achieved by increasing the speed of motor 2 and reducing the speed of motor 4. There is no direct displacement on the Y axis of the drone and this is only achieved by tilting it on its X axis.

By grouping the equations in matrix form and omitting the multiplier 2, you obtain

$$\begin{bmatrix} F_x \\ F_y \\ F_z \\ \tau_x \\ \tau_y \\ \tau_z \end{bmatrix} = \begin{bmatrix} 0 & 0 \\ 0 & 0 \\ 1 & 1 \\ 1 & -1 \\ 0 & 0 \\ 0 & 0 \end{bmatrix} \begin{bmatrix} \omega_2 \\ \omega_4 \end{bmatrix}$$

Once simplified, this results in

$$\begin{bmatrix} F_z \\ \tau_x \end{bmatrix} = \begin{bmatrix} 1 & 1 \\ 1 & -1 \end{bmatrix} \begin{bmatrix} \omega_2 \\ \omega_4 \end{bmatrix}$$

Remember that

$$\begin{bmatrix} \omega_3 \\ \omega_1 \end{bmatrix} = \begin{bmatrix} -\omega_2 \\ -\omega_4 \end{bmatrix}$$

Therefore for coaxial vehicles you will have two allocation matrices: one of action, which correlates the effect of the motors with respect to the center of the vehicle, and one of opposition, which deals with the copy-motors, that is to say those used to compensate for unwanted self-rotation effects.

Although the forces and moments are duplicated in magnitude, this is omitted because it is a simple scaling factor that can be adjusted by the controller.

Notice that the control analysis of the center of the vehicle was only made with half of the motors. This is only possible while the copy-motors (in this case 1 and 3) are not placed far from the action-motors (in this case 2 and 4).

Notice that the action part of the propulsion or allocation matrix is similar to a differential wheeled robot.

Without the copy-motors of the coaxial system, if you increase the speed of motor 2 and reduce the speed of motor 4, in addition to torque on the X axis of the drone, you would also have torque on its Z axis. See Figure 6-20.

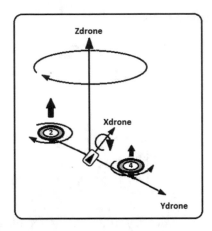

Figure 6-20. *References for obtaining the allocation matrix of a non-coaxial bicopter*

Therefore you would have a different system (remember the right-hand rotation criteria for the Z axis of the drone):

$$\begin{bmatrix} F_z \\ \tau_x \\ \tau_z \end{bmatrix} = \begin{bmatrix} 1 & 1 \\ 1 & -1 \\ -1 & 1 \end{bmatrix} \begin{bmatrix} \omega_2 \\ \omega_4 \end{bmatrix}$$

This implies a pseudoinverse problem and therefore a more complex computational optimization problem. Notice that, unlike a hexacopter which has more engines and only four possible independent movements, in this case you have fewer motors than feasible movements (only two of them to be used with three possible independent movements), falling into an underactuated robotics problem.

The propulsion matrix for the X-type multirotor recommended by the Pixhawk is shown in Figure 6-21. Pixhawk developers recommend the following quadcopter (notice the motor numbers and their directions of rotation, as well as the connection to the autopilot). Note that the X configuration is preferable because the action of the four motors is involved in all axes, and the power is distributed a bit more uniformly than the + configuration (look at this + configuration one more time to observe how only two motors are active in some movements).

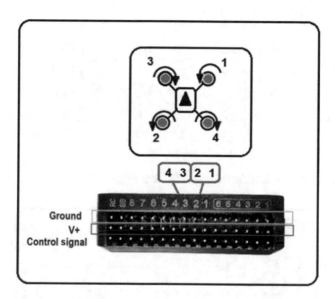

Figure 6-21. *References for obtaining the allocation matrix of a Pixhawk type X quadcopter*

You can deduce on your own the propulsion or allocation matrix associated with this drone, under the movement criterion shown (established by the compatibility with your remote control's levers, which is inverted for the displacements on X). See Figure 6-22.

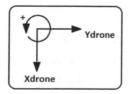

Figure 6-22. *References for the positive advance (this could be different for you)*

The aforementioned allocation matrix is the following (the square root terms of 2 over 2 are a consequence of an approximated 45-degree angle on each arm and its respective sine and cosine projections):

$$
\begin{bmatrix} F_z \\ \tau_x \\ \tau_y \\ \tau_z \end{bmatrix} = \begin{bmatrix} 1 & 1 & 1 & 1 \\ \dfrac{-\sqrt{2}}{2} & \dfrac{\sqrt{2}}{2} & \dfrac{\sqrt{2}}{2} & \dfrac{-\sqrt{2}}{2} \\ \dfrac{\sqrt{2}}{2} & \dfrac{-\sqrt{2}}{2} & \dfrac{\sqrt{2}}{2} & \dfrac{-\sqrt{2}}{2} \\ 1 & 1 & -1 & -1 \end{bmatrix} \begin{bmatrix} \omega_1 \\ \omega_2 \\ \omega_3 \\ \omega_4 \end{bmatrix}
$$

For example, for motor number 3, see Figure 6-23.

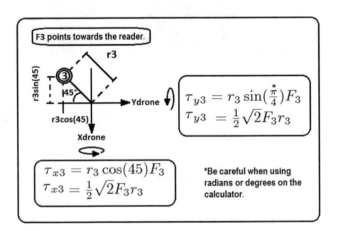

Figure 6-23. *A geometrical explanation for deducing the allocation matrix*

Remember that torques and thrust are a proportion of the speeds of the motors. Additionally, the radial term associated with the distance of the arm is also normalized (it is considered of value 1 by the symmetry of the other arms and because it is a value that can be directly overcome by the control, so it is not necessary to drag it during calculations). Also note that the constant of proportionality between the speeds of the motors and the thrust force of propellers is normalized. This happens because it is a constant in practically all the terms of the equation. However, you, as an interested reader, should perform a more formal way to calculate or estimate it:

$$F_3 \approx \kappa\omega_3 \quad \kappa \approx 1 \quad r_3 \approx 1$$

$$\tau_{x3} \approx \frac{\sqrt{2}}{2}\omega_3 \quad \tau_{y3} \approx \frac{\sqrt{2}}{2}\omega_3$$

Remember that this process has to be repeated for each motor and the result is practically the sum of the components of each motor.

Normalization is a very common process in programming and control. It consists on obtaining the sign of a given value, which is transformed into 1, -1, or 0, and only performed in conditions where said given value is constant, presents high symmetry, and/or where it is shared by many terms in a system of equations. This way you can assume that the control can absorb it without prior knowledge of its existence. The aim of normalization is to reduce the terms to be dragged during a succession of calculations in order to make them simpler.

You normalize the magnitudes (by obtaining their approximation to 1, which cannot always be done but it's done by symmetry in this example, since it appears in many terms of the equation, and because the root of 2 divided by 2 is approximately 0.707, which can be rounded to 1, and by the control's effect, which you will see later).

$$\begin{bmatrix} F_z \\ \tau_x \\ \tau_y \\ \tau_z \end{bmatrix} = \begin{bmatrix} 1 & 1 & 1 & 1 \\ -1 & 1 & 1 & -1 \\ 1 & -1 & 1 & -1 \\ 1 & 1 & -1 & -1 \end{bmatrix} \begin{bmatrix} \omega_1 \\ \omega_2 \\ \omega_3 \\ \omega_4 \end{bmatrix}$$

This way, the mixer that must be applied to each motor is the following. (Notice that magnitudes are also omitted. Mathematically, this is equivalent to applying the sign function.)

$$
\begin{bmatrix} \omega_1 \\ \omega_2 \\ \omega_3 \\ \omega_4 \end{bmatrix} = signum \left(\begin{bmatrix} 1 & 1 & 1 & 1 \\ -1 & 1 & 1 & -1 \\ 1 & -1 & 1 & -1 \\ 1 & 1 & -1 & -1 \end{bmatrix}^{-1} \begin{bmatrix} F_z \\ \tau_x \\ \tau_y \\ \tau_z \end{bmatrix} \right)
$$

When developed as matrix, it is

$$
\begin{bmatrix} \omega_1 \\ \omega_2 \\ \omega_3 \\ \omega_4 \end{bmatrix} = \begin{bmatrix} 1 & -1 & 1 & 1 \\ 1 & 1 & -1 & 1 \\ 1 & 1 & 1 & -1 \\ 1 & -1 & -1 & -1 \end{bmatrix} \begin{bmatrix} F_z \\ \tau_x \\ \tau_y \\ \tau_z \end{bmatrix}
$$

To reduce computational complexity, this is written to the motors in a developed way:

$$
\begin{bmatrix} \omega_1 \\ \omega_2 \\ \omega_3 \\ \omega_4 \end{bmatrix} = \begin{bmatrix} -\tau_x + \tau_y + \tau_z + F_z \\ \tau_x - \tau_y + \tau_z + F_z \\ \tau_x + \tau_y - \tau_z + F_z \\ -\tau_x - \tau_y - \tau_z + F_z \end{bmatrix}
$$

Propulsion matrix for the cases in which a non-zero yaw variation happens or is desired, and general case for a planar multicopter.

Now, suppose that you want a drone to follow a straight line but the wind tries to deflect it. See Figure 6-24.

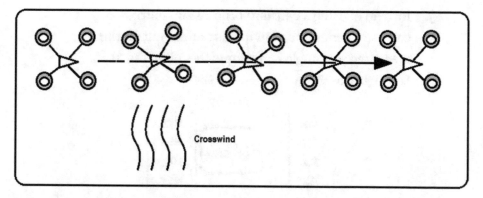

Figure 6-24. *A problem where yaw variable modifies either the allocation matrix or the control components*

You have two options:

A).   You can use a base allocation matrix like the ones already seen, but with projective terms introduced in the respective torques, which is useful for control demonstrations.

$$\begin{bmatrix} F_z \\ \tau_\phi \\ \tau_\theta \\ \tau_\psi \end{bmatrix} = P_{4x4} \begin{bmatrix} m_1 \\ m_2 \\ m_3 \\ m_4 \end{bmatrix}$$

$$\begin{bmatrix} F_z \\ \tau_\phi \sin\psi - \tau_\theta \cos\psi \\ \tau_\phi \cos\psi + \tau_\theta \sin\psi \\ \tau_\psi \end{bmatrix} = P_{4x4} \begin{bmatrix} m_1 \\ m_2 \\ m_3 \\ m_4 \end{bmatrix}$$

B). Instead of using a constant propulsion matrix, you can use a generic version that is dependent on the measured yaw angle and adopts the following form. See Figure 6-25.

$$
\begin{bmatrix} F_z \\ \tau_\phi \\ \tau_\theta \\ \tau_\psi \end{bmatrix} = \boxed{P(\psi)_{4x4}} \begin{bmatrix} m_1 \\ m_2 \\ m_3 \\ m_4 \end{bmatrix}
$$

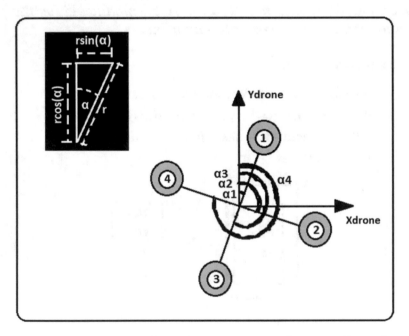

Figure 6-25. *How the angle with respect to each arm affects the allocation matrix components*

$$
\begin{bmatrix} F_z \\ \tau_x \\ \tau_y \\ \tau_z \end{bmatrix} = \begin{bmatrix} 1 & 1 & 1 & 1 \\ A_y r_1 \cos(\alpha_1) & A_y r_2 \cos(\alpha_2) & A_y r_3 \cos(\alpha_3) & A_y r_4 \cos(\alpha_4) \\ A_x r_1 \sin(\alpha_1) & A_x r_2 \sin(\alpha_2) & A_x r_3 \sin(\alpha_3) & A_x r_4 \sin(\alpha_4) \\ R_h & R_h & R_h & R_h \end{bmatrix} \begin{bmatrix} \omega_1 \\ \omega_2 \\ \omega_3 \\ \omega_4 \end{bmatrix}_*
$$

where, see Table 6-2.

Table 6-2. *Conditions and Possible Values to Assign in a*
Yaw-Dependant Allocation Matrix

Condition	Value
The motor rotates following the right-hand rule.	Rh = 1 (Rh means "Right hand")
The motor rotates opposite to the right-hand rule.	Rh = -1
The motor must increase its speed to advance on the positive Y axis.	Ay = 1 (Ay means "Along Y")
The motor must reduce its speed to advance on the positive Y axis.	Ay = -1
The motor must increase its speed to advance on the positive X axis.	Ax = 1 (Ax means "Along X")
The motor must reduce its speed to advance on the positive X axis.	Ax = -1

The correct use of indexes should correctly be Ay1, Ay2, up to Ayn. The same principle applies to Ax and Rh. Since the variables apply to every motor, if you use different indexes excessively, you lose readability. Also, note that the projections may vary depending on which axis has been called X and which axis is Y.

For this example, suppose that only motors 1 and 3 rotate following the right-hand rule. Normalize the radii to 1 for them to be symmetrical and use the following definition of symmetric quadcopter angles:

$$\alpha_1 = \psi$$
$$\alpha_2 = \psi + 90$$
$$\alpha_3 = \psi + 180$$
$$\alpha_4 = \psi + 270$$

This way, by replacing the indicated conditions and values, your "generic" equation becomes as follows (remember that the trigonometric terms will depend on how you define the drone's reference axes):

$$
\begin{bmatrix} F_z \\ \tau_x \\ \tau_y \\ \tau_z \end{bmatrix} = \begin{bmatrix} 1 & 1 & 1 & 1 \\ -\cos(\psi) & \cos(\psi+90) & \cos(\psi+180) & -\cos(\psi+270) \\ -\sin(\psi) & -\sin(\psi+90) & \sin(\psi+180) & \sin(\psi+270) \\ 1 & -1 & 1 & -1 \end{bmatrix} \begin{bmatrix} \omega_1 \\ \omega_2 \\ \omega_3 \\ \omega_4 \end{bmatrix}_{**}
$$

Notice that it is also necessary to establish a quadrant logic (maybe an arctan function) to define when a motor should increase its speed and when to decrease it; that is, to define each Ax and Ay as a function of the yaw angle and a base value of yaw. However, this was omitted here since the selection is valid for a movement over one quadrant of the plane (approximately 90 degrees), which is only useful if you do not want to go beyond this range of mobility.

Although mathematically equivalent, the first form, which is based on control's projection, is more efficient because the value of a vector is updated, while in the second form, the matrix must be updated continuously and perform demanding matrix operations such as inverses. This can also lead to obtaining singular matrices or indefinite values.

However, we show you this second alternative in this book because this is the generic way of calculating the terms of an allocation matrix for a multicopter (see the Quan Quan book in the references section).

Velocity Kinematic Relations

Here you impose the kinematic (movement) restrictions and directly interrelate the global and local frames. These equations are previous and necessary to find the dynamic equations.

The first thing to establish is a convention about which angles will be related to which planar axes. In this case, you will respect the convention from the propulsion matrix (this is the tetha angle or pitch with the Y axis; fi angle or roll with the X axis).

The second is to set a sequence for the Euler angles. In this case, let's use ZYX as a suggested sequence to have some degree of standardization. However, you are free to choose the one that suits you (without forgetting that this will affect your equations and that the results shown in this book should be modified to fit the model that you choose).

$$R = R_{z_\psi} R_{x_\phi} R_{y_\theta}$$

$$R = \begin{bmatrix} c\psi\, c\theta - s\phi s\psi\, s\theta & -c\phi s\psi & c\psi\, s\theta + s\phi s\psi\, c\theta \\ s\psi\, c\theta + s\phi c\psi\, s\theta & c\phi c\psi & s\psi\, s\theta - s\phi c\psi\, c\theta \\ -c\phi s\theta & s\phi & c\phi c\theta \end{bmatrix}$$

Remember to consult the subject regarding to rotation matrices and rotation sequences on any linear algebra book or related web page. Also, remember that the notations $c*$, $s*$, $t*$, and so on are abbreviations of cos $(*)$, sin $(*)$, and tan $(*)$, respectively, in the robotics field.

This way, the relation among translational velocities is simply

$$\begin{bmatrix} \dot{x} \\ \dot{y} \\ \dot{z} \end{bmatrix} = R \begin{bmatrix} \dot{x}_b \\ \dot{y}_b \\ \dot{z}_b \end{bmatrix}$$

Attention: The obtained R matrix will also be useful to later establish the relationship between the thrust force in the drone frame and in the global frame.

Once you establish the relation among frames and translational velocities, you must establish the relation among angular velocities. You do this by using the analysis of three-dimensional kinematics of the rigid body by means of Euler angles (see *Dynamics* by Beer and J in the bibliography section). This is also known as quasi-velocities relation and can be obtained geometrically, by vectorial succession, and by means rotation matrices properties. You can search the web for "Euler angles angular velocities."

You must be careful when using our convention or your own, because the order in which the Euler angles are established will define both kinematic relations. In fact, to find them without using geometry but analytical operations, the following equation is necessary (notice that it depends on the rotation matrix used for translational kinematic relations):

$$\dot{R} = \frac{dR}{dt} = \omega \times R = \hat{\omega} R = \begin{bmatrix} 0 & -\omega_{zB} & \omega_{yB} \\ \omega_{zB} & 0 & -\omega_{xB} \\ -\omega_{yB} & \omega_{xB} & \end{bmatrix} R$$

Therefore, the terms of p, q, and r can be found with the inverse of the rotation matrix and then by solving for the corresponding terms:

$$\begin{bmatrix} 0 & -\omega_{zB} & \omega_{yB} \\ \omega_{zB} & 0 & -\omega_{xB} \\ -\omega_{yB} & \omega_{xB} & \end{bmatrix} = \dot{R} R^T$$

Keywords: Vector angular velocity, cross product expressed as an antisymmetric matrix product (skew matrix), inverse of a rotation matrix

Notice that when the flight tends to be soft and therefore angular variations are small, the speed relationship of the local frame with respect to the global frame tends to be simple equivalences (approximation of small angles). This is why you must adequately revise this section if you are going to perform a flight mode with high angular variations (acrobatics).

$$\begin{bmatrix} p \\ q \\ r \end{bmatrix} = \begin{bmatrix} c\theta & 0 & -c\phi s\theta \\ 0 & 1 & s\phi \\ s\theta & 0 & c\phi c\theta \end{bmatrix} \begin{bmatrix} \dot{\phi} \\ \dot{\theta} \\ \dot{\psi} \end{bmatrix}$$

$$\begin{bmatrix} p \\ q \\ r \end{bmatrix} = \begin{bmatrix} 1 & 0 & 0 \\ 0 & 1 & 0 \\ 0 & 0 & 1 \end{bmatrix} \begin{bmatrix} \dot{\phi} \\ \dot{\theta} \\ \dot{\psi} \end{bmatrix}$$

Dynamic Translation Equations

This consists of adapting Newton's second law to a rotating frame (the aircraft thrusts vary their effect in proportion to the aircraft attitude). For the convenience of the reader and for achieving compatibility with the sensors, this is performed in the fixed frame (the translations of the drone are measured with respect to the world).

The base equation is the one that corresponds to Newton's second law:

$$F = ma$$

This equation is then expressed in terms of position, remembering that the acceleration is equal to the second derivative of the position. Notice the use of Newton's notation to rewrite the derivative. This is done for reasons of convenience and is often found in dynamic systems and control theory.

$$F = ma = m\frac{d^2\xi}{dt^2} = m\ddot{\xi}$$

If now you take into consideration a three-dimensional Cartesian spatial position, you can notice the use of a vector whose components are the X, Y, and Z axes. Note that this assumes the concept of point mass for the modeling of the quadcopter. This due to its high degree of symmetry.

$$
\begin{bmatrix} F_x \\ F_y \\ F_z \end{bmatrix} = F = m\ddot{\xi} = m \begin{bmatrix} \ddot{x} \\ \ddot{y} \\ \ddot{z} \end{bmatrix}
$$

When you add the concept of a body in free fall (that is, adding the gravitational component), note that this component only affects the Z axis of the fixed frame.

$$
F + \underline{mG} = m\ddot{\xi} \rightarrow \begin{bmatrix} F_x \\ F_y \\ F_z \end{bmatrix} + \begin{bmatrix} 0 \\ 0 \\ -mg \end{bmatrix} = m \begin{bmatrix} \ddot{x} \\ \ddot{y} \\ \ddot{z} \end{bmatrix}
$$

Remember that you are situated in the fixed frame. This way, you must find a relation between the forces of the drone or base frame and those of the fixed frame (the forces are generated by the drone or base frame, but the model is made with the fixed frame or world). See Figure 6-26.

$$
F = \underline{R}F_B
$$

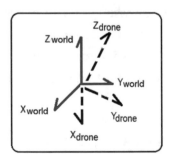

Figure 6-26. *The reason why a rotation matrix is needed to relate the world frame with the vehicle frame*

where

$$F_{xB} = 0$$
$$F_{yB} = 0$$
$$F_{zB} = u$$

This happens because the drone must tilt in order to move. You must apply a matrix that projects the unique thrust force of the drone (in its Z body axis) in each of the inertial axes or a fixed frame, through a rotation matrix based on Euler angles (roll, pitch, and yaw. See Bedford's dynamics).

$$F + mG = m\ddot{\xi} \rightarrow RF_B + mG = m\ddot{\xi} = R \begin{bmatrix} 0 \\ 0 \\ u \end{bmatrix} + \begin{bmatrix} 0 \\ 0 \\ -mg \end{bmatrix} = m \begin{bmatrix} \ddot{x} \\ \ddot{y} \\ \ddot{z} \end{bmatrix}$$

Dynamic Rotational Equations

This is the adaptation of Newton's second law to a rotating frame (Euler's second law of motion). For the convenience of the reader and for achieving compatibility with the sensors, this is performed in the body frame (the rotation measures taken by the sensors are made with respect to the body or drone frame).

Although there are at least three ways to find these equations, this book will use the one based on Euler angles. To study the other two methods (the one based on rotation matrices and the one based on quaternions), look for the Quan Quan book in the reference section.

When talking about the body frame, angular velocities are easier to obtain than the angles themselves, since they fulfill a so-called non-holonomic relation. They are, in fact, a direct function of the kinematic relation of angular velocities that link the angular velocities of the body with those of the fixed frame (the latter are expressed in Euler angles).

This way, the Euler motion equations defined in terms of the angular velocity of the body are (notice that the derivative of the angular velocity is the angular acceleration)

$$J\dot{\omega} + \underline{\omega \times (J\omega)} = J\alpha + \omega \times (J\omega) = \tau$$

where J is the inertial matrix of the drone (remember that inertia is the rotational equivalent of the mass). Note that this is the equivalent of Newton's second law in rotational motion.

The term $\omega \times (J\omega)$ is the vectorial representation of the centrifugal force, whose module or scalar representation is $J\omega^2$. Later you will see that it is usually discarded for your applications, but if you are looking for aggressive trajectories, it must be included in the design.

Also notice that

$$\tau = \begin{bmatrix} \tau_p \\ \tau_q \\ \tau_r \end{bmatrix} \quad \omega = \begin{bmatrix} \omega_{xB} \\ \omega_{yB} \\ \omega_{zB} \end{bmatrix} = \begin{bmatrix} p \\ q \\ r \end{bmatrix}$$

We use the pqr notation because it is very common in the aircraft field.

Notice that the equation is relatively simple and it does not require a transformation or rotation matrix in its torques because it is done directly at the body level. Also, it does not involve a gravitational term due to its symmetry (ideally it is done with respect to the center of a balanced and cross-shaped vehicle).

It is necessary to establish a relation between Euler angles (which correspond to the fixed frame; remember that the desired variables are designed with respect to this frame, although measurements takes place in the body frame), and the pqr variables (which corresponds to the body frame).

This is as follows (previously defined):

$$\begin{bmatrix} \dot{\phi} \\ \dot{\theta} \\ \dot{\psi} \end{bmatrix} = A\omega = A \begin{bmatrix} p \\ q \\ r \end{bmatrix}$$

Then, you state that the relation is non-holonomic because there is no way to find a direct relation in the desired variables but in their speeds.

When the angles are small and the movements are not acrobatic or aggressive (small speeds),

$$A = \begin{bmatrix} 1 & 0 & 0 \\ 0 & 1 & 0 \\ 0 & 0 & 1 \end{bmatrix}; \begin{bmatrix} \tau_p \\ \tau_q \\ \tau_r \end{bmatrix} \approx \begin{bmatrix} \tau_\phi \\ \tau_\theta \\ \tau_\psi \end{bmatrix}; \omega \times (J\omega) \approx 0$$

The first two relations are due to the trigonometric properties of the small angles. The last corresponds to the fact that while having small speeds, the square of a small value equals an even smaller value, therefore it's negligible.

Considering these approximations, the main rotational equation becomes quite simple and usual:

$$J\dot{\omega} + \omega \times (J\omega) = \tau \rightarrow J \begin{bmatrix} \ddot{\phi} \\ \ddot{\theta} \\ \ddot{\psi} \end{bmatrix} = \begin{bmatrix} \tau_\phi \\ \tau_\theta \\ \tau_\psi \end{bmatrix}$$

This is equivalent to performing the equations directly in terms of the fixed frame (remember that it is only valid for smooth flights; that is, at relatively low speeds and without reaching excessive inclinations, no greater than 45 degrees in roll and pitch, for example).

---

* See Jinhyun et al in the references section for extended versions in both coordinate frames and the reason why it is preferred to use the ones described.

In summary, you have a dynamic system of equations on which you design the control, a system of kinematic equations on which you restrict the trajectories to be followed, and a system of allocation equations of forces and torques on which you program the control to the motors. See Figure 6-27.

$$
\begin{bmatrix} F_z \\ \tau_\phi \\ \tau_\theta \\ \tau_\psi \end{bmatrix} = P_{4x4} \begin{bmatrix} m_1 \\ m_2 \\ m_3 \\ m_4 \end{bmatrix}
$$
Allocation equations
Theoretical-practical link

$$
R = \begin{bmatrix} c\psi c\theta - s\phi s\psi s\theta & -c\phi s\psi & c\psi s\theta + s\phi s\psi c\theta \\ s\psi c\theta + s\phi c\psi s\theta & c\phi c\psi & s\psi s\theta - s\phi c\psi c\theta \\ -c\phi s\theta & s\phi & c\phi c\theta \end{bmatrix}
$$
Euler matrix
Fixed and body frame relationship

$$
\begin{bmatrix} \dot{x} \\ \dot{y} \\ \dot{z} \end{bmatrix} = R \begin{bmatrix} \dot{x}_b \\ \dot{y}_b \\ \dot{z}_b \end{bmatrix}
$$
Translational kinematics

$$
\omega = \begin{bmatrix} \omega_{xB} \\ \omega_{yB} \\ \omega_{zB} \end{bmatrix} = \begin{bmatrix} p \\ q \\ r \end{bmatrix} = \begin{bmatrix} c\theta & 0 & -c\phi s\theta \\ 0 & 1 & s\phi \\ s\theta & 0 & c\phi c\theta \end{bmatrix} \begin{bmatrix} \dot{\phi} \\ \dot{\theta} \\ \dot{\psi} \end{bmatrix}
$$
Rotational kinematics

$$
R \begin{bmatrix} 0 \\ 0 \\ u \end{bmatrix} + \begin{bmatrix} 0 \\ 0 \\ -mg \end{bmatrix} = m \begin{bmatrix} \ddot{x} \\ \ddot{y} \\ \ddot{z} \end{bmatrix}
$$
Translational dynamics

$$
J\dot{\omega} + \omega \times (J\omega) = \tau
$$
Rotational dynamics

Figure 6-27. *The full set of a quadcopter non-linear equations*

If you desire to operate the system in a soft mode, that is, with small tilt angles and with non-aggressive or acrobatic maneuvers, as is the case of the examples in this book, the set of equations becomes as shown in Figure 6-28.

$$\begin{bmatrix} F_z \\ \tau_\phi \\ \tau_\theta \\ \tau_\psi \end{bmatrix} = P_{4x4} \begin{bmatrix} m_1 \\ m_2 \\ m_3 \\ m_4 \end{bmatrix}$$ **Allocation equations**
Theoretical-practical link

$$R = \begin{bmatrix} c\psi c\theta - s\phi s\psi s\theta & -c\phi s\psi & c\psi s\theta + s\phi s\psi c\theta \\ s\psi c\theta + s\phi c\psi s\theta & c\phi c\psi & s\psi s\theta - s\phi c\psi c\theta \\ -c\phi s\theta & s\phi & c\phi c\theta \end{bmatrix}$$ **Euler matrix**
Fixed and body frame
relationship

$$\begin{bmatrix} \dot{x} \\ \dot{y} \\ \dot{z} \end{bmatrix} = R \begin{bmatrix} \dot{x}_b \\ \dot{y}_b \\ \dot{z}_b \end{bmatrix}$$ **Translational**
kinematics

$$\begin{bmatrix} p \\ q \\ r \end{bmatrix} = \begin{bmatrix} 1 & 0 & 0 \\ 0 & 1 & 0 \\ 0 & 0 & 1 \end{bmatrix} \begin{bmatrix} \dot{\phi} \\ \dot{\theta} \\ \dot{\psi} \end{bmatrix}$$ **Rotational**
kinematics

$$R \begin{bmatrix} 0 \\ 0 \\ u \end{bmatrix} + \begin{bmatrix} 0 \\ 0 \\ -mg \end{bmatrix} = m \begin{bmatrix} \ddot{x} \\ \ddot{y} \\ \ddot{z} \end{bmatrix}$$ **Translational**
dynamics

$$J \begin{bmatrix} \ddot{\phi} \\ \ddot{\theta} \\ \ddot{\psi} \end{bmatrix} = \begin{bmatrix} \tau_\phi \\ \tau_\theta \\ \tau_\psi \end{bmatrix}$$ **Rotational**
dynamics

Figure 6-28. *Full set of a quadcopter linear-attitude equations*

To sum up, see Table 6-3.

Table 6-3. *Resume of Quadcopter, and In General Almost Any Other Vehicle, Equations*

Equations	Use
Propulsion, allocation, or mixer	A link between programming (practice) and control (theory). It communicates to the motor with the desired effect in the local frame of reference (center of gravity, for example).
Kinematics or of speeds and movement	A link between local and global movement variables. In multicopters of aggressive, acrobatic, or omnidirectional movements, it establishes the relations between the sensor's local measurements (body velocities) and the global ones (Euler angle velocities). Inside the controller, it allows the feedback desired or measured variables.
Dynamics or of forces	It allows establishing the framework of theoretical forces and torque design in the local frame of reference, being able to analyze the effects to overcome in order to achieve the correct operation of the vehicle. In some cases, such as wheeled robots, this design is often neglected, giving more importance to the kinematics. For robust controllers, this analysis is also usually negligible, since dynamic effects overcome with brute force, as long as the engines can deal with it. Also, they are high-importance equations to make simulations, since they are the mathematical representation of the behavior of an object or system.

Flight Modes

Do not confuse flight modes with control methods or with decoupled tasks. Flight modes supply the general objective. Decoupled tasks answer which particular objectives will be achieved. Control methods answer what tools will be used to achieve the objectives.

Figure 6-29 shows the relation among flight modes, control methods, and decoupled tasks, applied to an acrobatic flight mode with different control methods to achieve the required decoupled tasks (remember, there can be an enormous amount of methods for achieving each task).

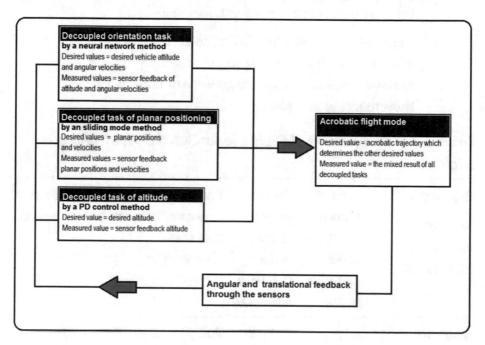

Figure 6-29. *An example of the relationship among control methods, task planning, and flight modes*

Currently, there are three large classifications of flight modes based levels of aggressiveness; see Table 6-4.

- **Soft**: The objective is for the drone to perform a smooth flight, like that of an airplane, without abrupt changes in its angular performance, but with "total" mobility in the XYZ space.

- **Kinodynamic**: The objective is for the drone to perform a flight with considerable but slow changes in its angular performance, maintaining "total" mobility in the XYZ space. The purpose of these slow but considerable changes is to achieve an interaction with the environment (move objects, for example).

- **Aggressive**: The objective is for the drone to perform a flight with full spatial and angular mobility, as well as fast execution, allowing aggressive or complicated movements to take place.

Table 6-4. *Classification of Flight Modes Based on Rudeness of the Flight*

Flight mode Featured author(s)/base control book	Desired value of positions in the Cartesian space	Desired value of velocities in the Cartesian XYZ space	Desired value of orientations, also called tilt angles or inclinations	Desired value of angular velocities
Common name of the variables	X, Y, Z	Vx, Vy, Vz	Roll, pitch, yaw	Wx, Wy, Wz
Soft **Rogelio Lozano/** **Khalil**	Any	Any (gradually)	0, except for yaw, which can take any value	0
Kinodynamic **Dongjun Lee/** **Kokotovic**	Any	Any	Any (in a range of security and mobility)	0 or low values (it is unable to follow continuous trajectories but it can do it point to point)
Aggressive **Taeyoung Lee,** **Pedro Castillo,** **Vijay Kumar/Bullo**	Any	Any	Any	Any (it can follow any trajectory, as long as the aircraft resists)

Note   that a flight mode is interrelated with planning the trajectory.

Now that you know the three great families of flight modes, we will introduce the main characteristics of some of their most-used subfamilies. Note that these subfamilies include the flight's degree of automation. (This is if you use the remote control, or an autonomous mode, or one semi-dependent of the sensors, etc. Also, if you use an automatic mode once a remote control lever has been pushed, if the control is GPS-dependent, etc.). Look at the following links for a complete description, and see Table 6-5:

http://ardupilot.org/copter/docs/flight-modes.html#full-list-of-flight-modes, http://ardupilot.org/plane/docs/flight-modes.html

Table 6-5. *Some Subfamilies of Flight Modes Based on the ArduPilot Libraries Webpage Classification*

Name	Hover control (altitude)	Attitude control (orientation)	Planar control (X,Y)
ACRO	Semiautomatic (with remote control)	Semiautomatic (with remote control)	None
LOITER	Automatic	Automatic	Automatic
AUTO (like loiter but made to follow trajectories)	Automatic	Automatic	Automatic
RTL (a way to return to the takeoff zone)	Automatic	Automatic	Automatic
ALT HOLD	Automatic	Semiautomatic (with remote control)	None
POS_HOLD	Automatic	Semiautomatic (with remote control)	Automatic (once the remote control is inactive)

Decoupled Tasks

There are four main tasks:

- **Orientation**: This is also known as angular or attitude control (do not confuse the word attitude with altitude). It consists of regulating the spatial orientation of the vehicle to achieve the desired orientation value.

- **Position**: This is also known as steering or planar control. It consists of commanding the position on the flight plane or with respect to the ground (usually the XY plane). In the particular case of a planar multicopter (in which the motors are aligned in the same plane, as in a standard quadcopter), the position task is dependent on the orientation. However, in linear operation or small angles flight, a decoupling of this dependence occurs (see the following sections in this chapter).

- **Altitude**: This is also known as floating control or hovering. It simply consists of controlling flight elevation.

- **Remote Control**: This consists of manually commanding the drone through a wireless or wired device.

There are also two dependent or optional tasks:

- **Trajectory**: This is the succession of positions, orientations, and altitudes.

- **Motor**: This is the direct control of each motor. This is assumed as a dependent task since it is modified as a function of altitude, position, and orientation through the propulsion matrix. There are currently attempts to make direct and independent motor controllers, but given the complexity, cost, weight, and volume to be incorporated, most commercial drones operate motors dependently.

Note that the combination of these decoupled tasks or particular objectives forms the basis of the flight mode; that is the general objective. In other words, the flight mode is a sequence of the decoupled tasks. (See Kumar's MOOCs about quadcopters in the reference section).

Table 6-6 displays the main characteristics of each task.

Table 6-6. *Usual Tasks of Flight Control*

Task	Rank	Synonyms	Manual or auto	Type of control loop
Remote control	1	Manual control It is divisible in the throttle related to altitude (also called gas), ruder related to yaw, remote roll, and remote pitch.	Manual and also optional, because the operation can be purely automatic	Closed by the user
Attitude	2	Orientation, angular	Automatic	Closed by the computer or autopilot
Altitude	3	Hovering, elevation, vertical, height	Automatic	Closed by the computer or autopilot

(*continued*)

Table 6-6. (*continued*)

Task	Rank	Synonyms	Manual or auto	Type of control loop
Planar	4	Horizontal, surface, steering	Automatic	Closed by the computer or autopilot
Trajectory	5	Path planning	Automatic or manual (by remote control)	Closed by the computer or autopilot (or by the user if it is through the remote control)
Motors	6 (because it is dependent on the others tasks)	Actuators, engine control	Automatic	Open

As you will see later in the controller implementation section, the total control is the sum of the decoupled tasks and it defines the flight mode. That is to say, see Figure 6-30.

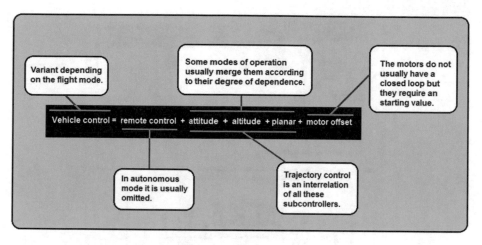

Figure 6-30. *Control components*

Figure 6-31 shows the desired automatic effect on the motors for the corresponding correcting behaviors in attitude, altitude, and planar movement for a quadcopter in the + configuration. Notice that these effects can be tested without propellers only by observing or feeling the effect of the motors when moving the vehicle away from the desired area. Remember, if the configuration changes, more or less motors are used, or the number sequence or direction of rotation of the motors is different, consider these changes to visualize the desired effect.

Also, notice that the direction of rotation of the roll and pitch effects do not necessarily have to coincide with those of the XY plane. This will depend on the used sensors as well as on the compatibility with the remote control levers operation. However, this is a practical way to determine if your designed automatic control at least behaves in the correct way. Moreover, notice that the remote effect can be opposite in roll, pitch, and yaw with respect to the automatic control. The calibration of the automatic tasks must be carried out separately from that of the manual ones.

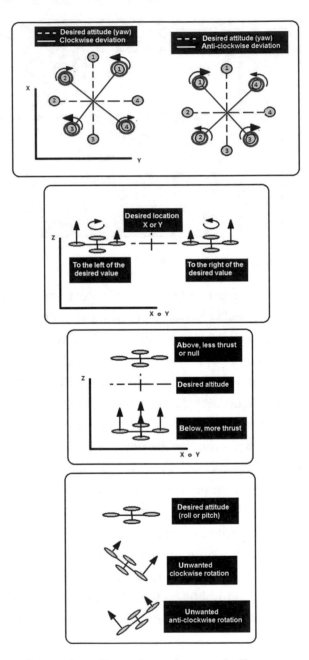

Figure 6-31. *Physical explanation of control effects*

Control Methods

The following are the ways in which you will achieve your tasks, among others: linear or non-linear, robust or adaptable, intelligent or classic, saturated or continuous, nested or sequential, etc.

Closed Loop vs. Open Loop

A closed loop is based on feedback, which means that a given system can be injected with a reference value and then supervise that the real value reaches its reference by using a third action that corrects the control in case of not reaching such reference. An open loop is based on proportionality, which is basically an empirical control. For example, by means of experiments and charts you can know that if you apply 1V to a certain motor along with its propeller, it may rise 1 meter; if you apply 3V, it will rise 3 meters; therefore, if you want it to reach 2 meters, it would be enough to apply 2V.

As you can notice, the problem with the open loop is that it does not adapt to changes such as a damaged motor or a damaged propeller, whether or not there is strong wind, whether the current on the battery is low or not, etc.

Currently most drones have both types of control loops. The closed loop is at the pose level (position plus orientation of the center of gravity or some other point of interest). However, the open loop is at the motor level (see Figure 6-32) since it is difficult to have the means that guarantee that the exact desired speed is sent to each motor (because placing a sensor on each motor is expensive and heavy). Nevertheless, you can measure its effects and correct them if the desired pose is achieved or not. There are currently some attempts of making both loops closed. (One of them is sensor-free. It is based on the fact that the brushless motor repeats a sequence of steps to rotate to a certain position, then they count the time of this sequence and determine motor measurements).

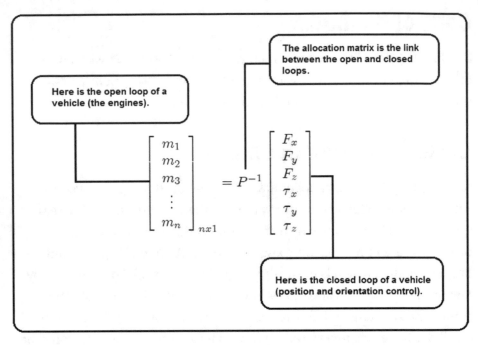

Figure 6-32. *Open and closed loops and their relationship with the allocation matrix*

Within the most commonly known closed loops of control is the PD, and this is just the one that we will use, because adding more terms such as an integral one implies improvements at the theory level, but implies more processing errors and considerations at the implementation level. Therefore, if we follow our simplifying philosophy, it is adequate and, above all, didactic. However, you can experiment on your own with other controllers.

It should be noted that in order to exemplify this work, the PD type control will be used in its saturated version (due to the limit values of the motors). Now let's proceed to the introductory explanation; note that we also choose this method since it is the most basic way of introducing control. For more specific references on other control methods with applications to aerial vehicles, see the reference section.

The control of a vehicle is performed only at one point of interest, in this case, at the center of gravity, assuming that the rest of the vehicle imitates the operation of this point of interest (rigid body assumption).

Saturated PD Control (Soft-Mode Basic Control of Flight)

Next, we will explain the design of control. Its correct tuning is your responsibility since it depends on the drone's mass, its shape (this influences its inertia), its irregularity or symmetry (also influences its inertia), the forces and torques that its motors can give, the amount of remaining battery, the type of propeller used, the conditions of the environment (wind conditions, for example), the quantity and quality of the engines used, the quantity and quality of the sensors used, the level of noise that the autopilot receives, etc.

In automatic control theory and practice, there are three systems (see Figure 6-33): a real one, which is the one you want to control; an injected one, which contains the desired behavior designed by the mathematical modeling of the real system; and a link system, which is where the injected system is induced to the real system through a transformation ratio (in this case, the propulsion or allocation matrix).

The PD is a spring-damper type system. Its objective is that the real system (the drone) behaves like the injected system (the spring-damper) as time goes by. The link system is usually underestimated but without it, physical implementation would not exist, only simulations. The link system is subject to computational resources optimization, so it is preferred in its most reduced expression. It is the relation between the equations that model a system with and its real actuators (in this case, the propulsion or allocation matrix).

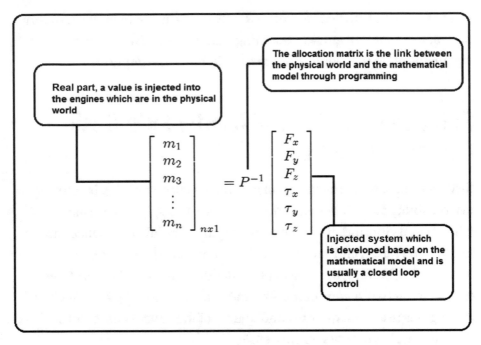

Figure 6-33. *Relationship between theory and practice trough allocation matrix*

The proportional part acts as a spring, forcing the system to move to a given point. However, as the injected system is virtual, it is also necessary to inject a dissipative component that allows the injected system to stop at this given point, and not just oscillate around that operation point. That dissipative component, associated with a damper, is the so-called differential part; see Figure 6-34. It is said that it is virtual because the user programs its effect through a code, which does not become real until the motors materialize said effect.

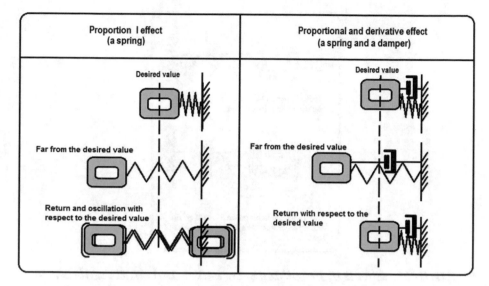

Figure 6-34. *P and PD controller analogies with spring and damper*

By switching the motors on and off (in the case of aerial vehicles, turbines, or motors with propellers), almost any behavior can be injected. In this case, you introduce a virtual spring-damper system, but you can also insert a constant value, or a sinusoidal behavior (in the case of injecting a purely proportional component, the system behaves like a sinusoidal signal), etc.; see Figure 6-35.

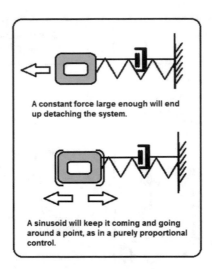

Figure 6-35. *Effects of introducing constant and sinusoidal forces*

In general, the injected system is designed to be stable, but the system to be controlled is usually not stable. In the case of drones, they are, in fact, highly unstable systems, so how do the real and virtual systems interact?

The answer is through mathematical stabilization methods, both linear and non-linear. Among the most commonly known are the root locus and Lyapunov methods. All the available methods are based on estimation or domination of disturbances and undesired phenomena (wind effect, vibrations, etc.). In the first case, they try to mathematically calculate the disturbances. In the second, only one controller that overcomes the undesirable phenomena is established (usually free of mathematical models and only dependent on the error). In the PD case, the controller used is of the dominant type (also known as robust). For this reason, many terms were previously omitted or normalized; they will not be directly compensated but will be overcome by the magnitude of the motors (some sort of brute force).

By imposing the previous condition, you can simply assume that the motors have enough thrust and torque to achieve the desired task. The tuning process can be performed in a heuristic way by respecting the fact that the P and D gains are greater than zero and some other considerations that you can find in a linear control book. It is also advisable to take into consideration the linearized model of the quadcopter in order to help with the gain-tuning process.

Consider the previously obtained dynamic translational and rotational models.

$$R \begin{bmatrix} 0 \\ 0 \\ u \end{bmatrix} + \begin{bmatrix} 0 \\ 0 \\ -mg \end{bmatrix} = m \begin{bmatrix} \ddot{x} \\ \ddot{y} \\ \ddot{z} \end{bmatrix}$$

$$J \begin{bmatrix} \ddot{\phi} \\ \ddot{\theta} \\ \ddot{\psi} \end{bmatrix} = \begin{bmatrix} \tau_\phi \\ \tau_\theta \\ \tau_\psi \end{bmatrix}$$

You expand according to the definition of R:

$$m \begin{bmatrix} \ddot{x} \\ \ddot{y} \\ \ddot{z} \end{bmatrix} = \begin{bmatrix} 0 \\ 0 \\ -mg \end{bmatrix} + \begin{bmatrix} c\psi s\theta + s\phi s\psi c\theta \\ s\psi s\theta - s\phi c\psi c\theta \\ c\phi c\theta \end{bmatrix} u$$

$$J \begin{bmatrix} \ddot{\phi} \\ \ddot{\theta} \\ \ddot{\psi} \end{bmatrix} = \begin{bmatrix} \tau_\phi \\ \tau_\theta \\ \tau_\psi \end{bmatrix}$$

Remember that due to drone symmetry,

$$J = \begin{bmatrix} J_{xx} & 0 & 0 \\ 0 & J_{yy} & 0 \\ 0 & 0 & J_{zz} \end{bmatrix}$$

And using the following small angle approximations (they are the base of the linear approximation, but remember to be careful, because sin approximations in some cases are 0 and in other cases are the angle),

$$
\begin{aligned}
s(*) &\approx 0 \approx * \\
c(*) &\approx 1
\end{aligned}
$$

Substituting these values, you obtain (notice that those small angle approximations are only made for roll and pitch, because they tend to zero, while the yaw angle has free mobility)

$$
m \begin{bmatrix} \ddot{x} \\ \ddot{y} \\ \ddot{z} \end{bmatrix} = \begin{bmatrix} 0 \\ 0 \\ -mg \end{bmatrix} + \begin{bmatrix} \theta c\psi + \phi s\psi \\ \theta s\psi - \phi c\psi \\ 1 \end{bmatrix} u
$$

$$
\begin{bmatrix} J_{xx}\ddot{\phi} \\ J_{yy}\ddot{\theta} \\ J_{zz}\ddot{\psi} \end{bmatrix} = \begin{bmatrix} \tau_\phi \\ \tau_\theta \\ \tau_\psi \end{bmatrix}
$$

This way you can design the most basic flight controller (a collection of PDs). We assume that you know how to tune a control, which is not included in the scope of this book. It can be performed using the geometric place of the polynomial roots, using state transition matrix properties, using the Lyapunov's linear method, etc. Consult the reference section or any other text or resource on linear systems control.

It is convenient to use the following notation:

$$PD_* = K_{P*}(*_d - *) + K_{D*}(\dot{*}_d - \dot{*})$$

For example

$$PD_X = K_{Px}(x_d - x) + K_{Dx}(\dot{x}_d - \dot{x})$$

$$PD_\psi = K_{P\psi}(\psi_d - \psi) + K_{D\psi}(\dot{\psi}_d - \dot{\psi})$$

To continue, make the following assumption:

$$\psi = \psi_d \approx 0$$

Also notice that the simpler dynamics are

$$\begin{bmatrix} m\ddot{z} \\ J_{zz}\ddot{\psi} \end{bmatrix} = \begin{bmatrix} -mg + u \\ \tau_\psi \end{bmatrix}$$

while the most complicated ones, by their chained dependencies are

$$\begin{bmatrix} m\ddot{x} \\ m\ddot{y} \\ J_{xx}\ddot{\phi} \\ J_{yy}\ddot{\theta} \end{bmatrix} = \begin{bmatrix} (\theta c\psi_d + \phi s\psi_d)u \\ (\theta s\psi_d - \phi c\psi_d)u \\ \tau_\phi \\ \tau_\theta \end{bmatrix} = \begin{bmatrix} \theta u \\ -\phi u \\ \tau_\phi \\ \tau_\theta \end{bmatrix}$$

This way, the first set of control equations to be imposed is that related to the independent dynamics, in this case altitude and yaw:

$$u = mg + PD_Z$$
$$\tau_\psi = J_{zz}(PD_\psi)$$

Substituting into these equations

$$\begin{bmatrix} m\ddot{z} \\ J_{zz}\ddot{\psi} \end{bmatrix} = \begin{bmatrix} -mg+u \\ \tau_\psi \end{bmatrix} = \begin{bmatrix} -mg+mg+PD_Z \\ J_{zz}(PD_\psi) \end{bmatrix}$$

Properly selecting the gains, and under certain considerations of movement (quasi-constant velocities and therefore accelerations tending to zero),

$$\begin{array}{ccc} e_z \rightarrow 0 = z_d - z & & z \rightarrow z_d \\ & \textbf{Therefore} & \\ e_\psi \rightarrow 0 = \psi_d - \psi & & \psi \rightarrow \psi_d \end{array}$$

The same thing happens with speed errors.

Substituting the value of u in the remaining four equations and considering that PDz tends to 0 as the desired value tends to the measured value,

$$\begin{bmatrix} m\ddot{x} \\ m\ddot{y} \\ J_{xx}\ddot{\phi} \\ J_{yy}\ddot{\theta} \end{bmatrix} = \begin{bmatrix} \theta u \\ -\phi u \\ \tau_\phi \\ \tau_\theta \end{bmatrix} = \begin{bmatrix} \theta mg \\ -\phi mg \\ \tau_\phi \\ \tau_\theta \end{bmatrix}$$

Simplifying

$$\begin{bmatrix} \ddot{x} \\ \ddot{y} \\ J_{xx}\ddot{\phi} \\ J_{yy}\ddot{\theta} \end{bmatrix} = \begin{bmatrix} g\theta \\ -g\phi \\ \tau_\phi \\ \tau_\theta \end{bmatrix}$$

Proposing the following PDs for roll and pitch:

$$
\begin{bmatrix} \ddot{x} \\ \ddot{y} \\ J_{xx}\ddot{\phi} \\ J_{yy}\ddot{\theta} \end{bmatrix} = \begin{bmatrix} g\theta \\ -g\phi \\ \tau_\phi \\ \tau_\theta \end{bmatrix} = \begin{bmatrix} g\theta \\ -g\phi \\ J_{xx}(PD_\phi) \\ J_{yy}(PD_\theta) \end{bmatrix}
$$

This way, under the correct tuning of gains and with angular speeds tending to zero (smooth flight),

$$
\begin{aligned} \theta &\to \theta_d \\ \phi &\to \phi_d \end{aligned}
$$

Substituting in the remaining dynamic equations,

$$
\begin{bmatrix} \ddot{x} \\ \ddot{y} \end{bmatrix} = \begin{bmatrix} g\theta \\ -g\phi \end{bmatrix} = \begin{bmatrix} g\theta_d \\ -g\phi_d \end{bmatrix}
$$

This way, you can notice that the X and Y controls can be performed through the desired values of roll and pitch angles (this is called nested control):

$$
\begin{aligned} \theta_d &= \frac{PD_X}{g} \\ \phi_d &= -\frac{PD_Y}{g} \end{aligned}
$$

Substituting and simplifying, you get

$$
\begin{bmatrix} \ddot{x} \\ \ddot{y} \end{bmatrix} = \begin{bmatrix} g\theta_d \\ -g\phi_d \end{bmatrix} = \begin{bmatrix} PD_X \\ PD_Y \end{bmatrix}
$$

So with the proper tuning of PD gains, you get

$$
\boxed{
\begin{aligned}
x &\rightarrow x_d \\
y &\rightarrow y_d
\end{aligned}
}
$$

Finally, the control that is injected into the pitch and roll, and thereby indirectly controls the X and Y positions, is

$$
\boxed{
\begin{aligned}
J_{yy}(PD_\theta) &= J_{yy}(K_{P\theta}(\theta_d - \theta) + K_{D\theta}(\dot{\theta}_d - \dot{\theta})) \\
J_{xx}(PD_\phi) &= J_{xx}(K_{P\phi}(\phi_d - \phi) + K_{D\theta}(\dot{\phi}_d - \dot{\phi}))
\end{aligned}
}
$$

Expanding:

$$
\boxed{
\begin{aligned}
J_{yy}(PD_\theta) &= J_{yy}(K_{P\theta}(\tfrac{1}{g}[K_{Px}(x_d-x) + K_{Dx}(\dot{x}_d-\dot{x})] - \theta) + K_{D\theta}(\tfrac{1}{g}[K_{Px}(\dot{x}_d-\dot{x}) + K_{Dx}(\ddot{x}_d-\ddot{x})] - \dot{\theta})) \\
J_{xx}(PD_\phi) &= J_{xx}(K_{P\phi}(-\tfrac{1}{g}[K_{Py}(y_d-y) + K_{Dx}(\dot{y}_d-\dot{y})] - \phi) + K_{D\phi}(-\tfrac{1}{g}[K_{Py}(\dot{y}_d-\dot{y}) + K_{Dx}(\ddot{y}_d-\ddot{y})] - \dot{\phi}))
\end{aligned}
}
$$

Grouping constants, for example $J_{yy}K_{P\theta}\dfrac{1}{g}K_{Px} = P_X$ and defining zero acceleration trajectories (with constant or approximately constant velocities or smooth flight paths).

$$
\boxed{
\begin{aligned}
\ddot{x}_d &= 0 & \ddot{y}_d &= 0 \\
\ddot{x} &\rightarrow 0 & \ddot{y} &\rightarrow 0
\end{aligned}
}
$$

The expansion can be simplified as follows:

$$
\boxed{
\begin{aligned}
J_{yy}(PD_\theta) &= P_X(x_d-x) + D_{X1}(\dot{x}_d-\dot{x}) + P_\theta(0-\theta) + D_{X2}(\dot{x}_d-\dot{x}) + D_\theta(0-\dot{\theta}) \\
J_{yy}(PD_\theta) &= P_X(x_d - x) + D_X(\dot{x}_d - \dot{x}) + P_\theta(0 - \theta) + D_\theta(0 - \dot{\theta})
\end{aligned}
}
$$

In a similar way:

$$J_{xx}(PD_\phi) = -P_Y(y_d - y) - D_Y(\dot{y}_d - \dot{y}) + P_\phi(0 - \phi) + D_\phi(0 - \dot{\phi})$$

Both equations are reduced to the following:

$$J_{yy}(PD_\theta) = PD_X + PD_\theta$$
$$J_{xx}(PD_\phi) = -PD_Y + PD_\phi$$

This means that for the case of linear flight with small angles, with constant or smooth velocities (without noticeable or sudden acceleration changes and applying a linear control PD, PID, etc.), the control experiments a linear decoupling, and the angular control with respect to the planar control can be carried out independently. This happens despite the interdependence of the roll and pitch angles to the X and Y positions.

In summary, you must apply the following controls for a smooth and linear flight with constant velocities, without aggressive movements, and with yaw, pitch, and roll angles tending to zero:

$$u = mg + PD_Z$$
$$\tau_\psi = PD_\psi$$
$$\tau_\theta = PD_X + PD_\theta$$
$$\tau_\phi = -PD_Y + PD_\phi$$

Retaking the previously developed propulsion/allocation matrix for the quadcopter with X configuration, you obtain the control to be injected to the motors. We will address this briefly. Notice that the bias value over which your control oscillates among positive values is given by (mg) or the vehicle's weight. We will readdress this comment in the implementation code. Remember that each chosen configuration will result in a different propulsion matrix. You must be careful when assigning axes, angles, and names (theta, X, roll; phi, Y, pitch; theta, X, pitch; phi, Y, roll, etc).

$$\begin{bmatrix} \omega_1 \\ \omega_2 \\ \omega_3 \\ \omega_4 \end{bmatrix} = \begin{bmatrix} -\tau_x + \tau_y + \tau_z + F_z \\ \tau_x - \tau_y + \tau_z + F_z \\ \tau_x + \tau_y - \tau_z + F_z \\ -\tau_x - \tau_y - \tau_z + F_z \end{bmatrix}$$

$$F_z = u \qquad \tau_z = \tau_\psi \qquad \tau_x = \tau_\theta \qquad \tau_y = \tau_\phi$$

$$\begin{bmatrix} \omega_1 \\ \omega_2 \\ \omega_3 \\ \omega_4 \end{bmatrix} = \begin{bmatrix} -[PD_x + PD_\theta] + [-PD_y + PD_\phi] + [PD_\psi] + [mg + PD_z] \\ [PD_x + PD_\theta] - [-PD_y + PD_\phi] + [PD_\psi] + [mg + PD_z] \\ [PD_x + PD_\theta] + [-PD_y + PD_\phi] - [PD_\psi] + [mg + PD_z] \\ -[PD_x + PD_\theta] - [-PD_y + PD_\phi] - [PD_\psi] + [mg + PD_z] \end{bmatrix}$$

Implementation Tip   Although, for convenience and logic, the P gain must be greater than D, due to the noisy measurement of the positions and, consequently the even noisier measurement of the speeds, in this case, the D gain must be tuned with higher positive values with respect to the proportional gain. (This is especially true for the XYZ translational variables. In the case of the angular ones, we can follow the same standard rule.)

Important Note   This section assumes that you want to perform motor-level control. In the appendix dedicated to the SDK comparative commands, you will notice that the control loop is external in other projects because it operates directly in the center of the autopilot (which should be located in the gravity center of the drone or near it).

Implementation Tip   Nesting corresponds to the two control levels of the vehicle. The first one involves altitude and angular equations of control. The second level involves the desired angular definitions as a function of the XY planar movements. The previously seen control confers a false "independent" character to the XY planar positions concerning the angles, but allows programming synthesis for a quick way to locate codification errors.

IMPLEMENTATION TIP: BIAS

This section also assumes that you are familiar with the bias translation concept; that is, while the control can vary between positive and negative values, the propellers can only take positive values (remember that, in general, the propellers should not change their direction of rotation, only their speed). This way, the question arises: how do you associate the positive and negative values that the control can take with those of the propellers that are exclusively positive? The answer is by adding a positive value called bias, over this value your control will be performed (for this reason, the ideal thing is not to operate the full-automatic mode until you have reached an operating altitude with the remote control). The bias or positive setup value is a remote-controlled signal that will raise the vehicle to the desired height. This value is usually related to the vehicle's weight. From that height, you obtain a range so that the control does not fall into negative values. In the case of Figure 6-36, the original signal oscillated between -1 and 1, and the modified signal is such that it now oscillates between 1 and 3, having a tolerance range from 0 to 1 for the modified signal to be altered and still stay positive. See Figure 6-36.

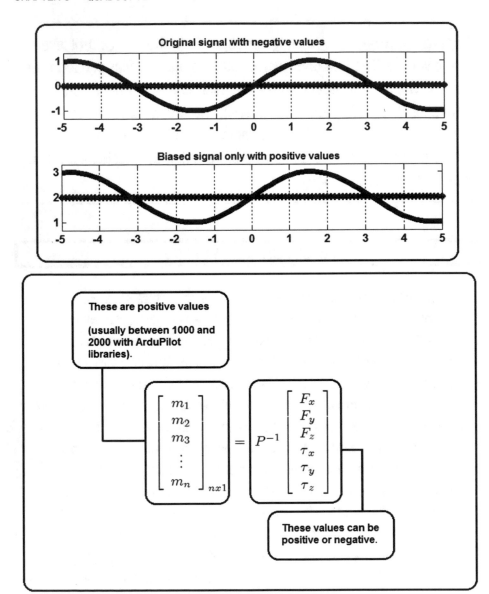

Figure 6-36. *Effects of signal biasing and range of values at motor and control levels*

This way you can see that the bias value is essential to establish a coherent relation between the values that the motors admit and those that are generated by the control. As you will see, this is done by sending a positive value to the control altitude channel (in fact, it is necessary to do it in order to overcome gravity and that the vehicle can take off).

IMPLEMENTATION TIP: SATURATION

Once you satisfy the part of moving the zero of the control values to a positive reference and allowing the motors to receive only these positive values, it is time to ensure that they always remain in a range with minimum and maximum allowed levels. For this purpose, you use the concept of a boundary, which is to saturate a signal between two limit values that have a critical behavior. This is achieved through the saturation function you previously studied. See Figure 6-37.

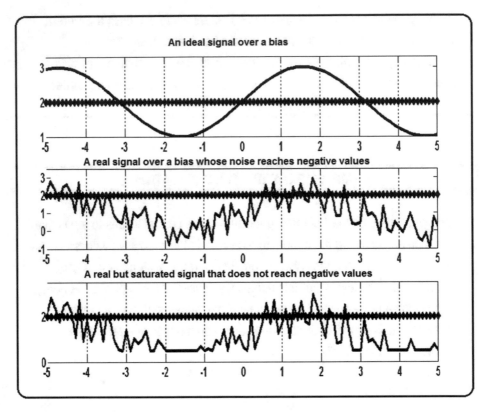

Figure 6-37. Application and effects of signal saturation

The lower critical behavior prevents the signal from becoming negative and the upper one from exceeding the limit value of each motor.

Drone Flight Implementation

Components involved: A quadcopter drone with a Pixhawk autopilot

The following illustrative code is moderately functional since the best operation is achieved in real-time mode and not sequentially, like in this case. However, it is useful for understanding the control process of an unmanned vehicle. A safe way to test this code is without propellers, just by observing the reactions of the motors and deducing if the control is successful or not before placing the props. The processes labeled as DEFINED BY THE READER depend entirely on the vehicle used by you for its correct tuning and operation, so the illustrative values will surely change. The processes without this label are generic.

1. Initializing hardware

2. Obtaining manual commands, positions, orientations, and speeds

3. Filtering (necessary if not already included in some commands)

4. Defining target values DEFINED BY THE READER

5. Defining errors

6. Defining controllers DEFINED BY THE READER

7. Defining propulsion/allocation or actuator mixer matrix DEFINED BY THE READER

8. Writing to the motors

9. Cycling or repeating steps 2-8

The following are secondary, complementary, or alternative tasks (they are not included in this code, but with the previously explained programs, you should be able to use them):

1. Analog reading (alternate mode of measuring spatial position or other data)

2. Digital reading/writing (for example, activating a paint sprayer or a mechanical sensor as an emergency stop button for avoiding contact with walls)

3. Use of visual alerts

4. Battery monitoring (this can particularly affect the control)

5. Barometric reading (alternate mode of measuring altitude)

6. Saving specific data in the SD memory (useful for publishing articles, reports, theses, etc.)

7. Wired and wireless serial communication (useful particularly for communicating with other vehicles or using coordinated processing with a Raspberry Pi development board, for example)

Listing 6-2. Quadcopter Pose Control, a Full Example in Sequential Mode

Command :   **Use: Semi-automatic hover control of an**
Various   **aerial vehicle**
Code:

```
/////////////////////////// DECLARATION //////////////////////////
//                    Paste the header code here
//                          See appendix

// verify or add this line
static AP_InertialNav_NavEKF inertial_nav(ahrs);

//////////////////////// place here your code//////////////////////

//         verify or add this lines

static Vector3f pos_gps;
static Vector3f vel_gps;
static AP_GPS  gps;
static Compass compass;
```

```
static float refx,refy,refz,ref_px,ref_py,ref_pz,errorx,errory,
errorz,posx,posy,posz;
static float roll,pitch,yaw,err_yaw,gyrox,gyroy,gyroz,velx,
vely,velz;
static float kp_roll, kd_roll,kp_pitch,kd_pitch,kp_yaw,kd_yaw;
static float p_x,d_x,p_y,d_y,p_z,d_z;

// the reader should add the rest of the necessary variables (see
// writing to engines and see radio reading)

//////////////////////////// INITIALIZATION ////////////////////////

void setup(){

//             verify or add those lines

    gps.init(NULL,serial_manager);
    ahrs.set_compass(&compass);
    hal.rcout->enable_ch(0);
    hal.rcout->enable_ch(1);
    hal.rcout->enable_ch(2);
    hal.rcout->enable_ch(3);
    hal.rcout->set_freq( 15, 490);
// reseting all the engines
    hal.rcout->write(0,0);
    hal.rcout->write(1,0);
    hal.rcout->write(2,0);
    hal.rcout->write(3,0);

}
```

```
/////////////////////////// EXECUTION ///////////////////////////
void loop(){
// the next function obtains position and velocity values posx,
// posy, posz, velx, vely, velz

    update_GPS();

// the required radio channels are read for semi-automatic
// operation
    radio[4] = hal.rcin->read(4);
    aux_1 = radio[4];

// this channel replaces the fact to add the term mg
    radio[2] = hal.rcin->read(2);
    radio_throttle = radio[2];
// altitude reference
    refalt=radio_throttle;

    ahrs.update();
    barometer.update();
// angular values of orientation and speed
    roll  = ahrs.roll;
    pitch = ahrs.pitch;
    yaw   = ahrs.yaw;

    gyro  = ins.get_gyro();

    gyrox = gyro.x;
    gyroy = gyro.y;
    gyroz = gyro.z;
// gains of the controllers CAUTION, readers are responsible
// for their own and correct tuning
```

```
kp_roll=800;
kd_roll=350;
kp_pitch=800;
kd_pitch=350;
kp_yaw=85/2;
kd_yaw=100/2;
```

```
// in this case, since the speed measurements were very noisy, the
// differential values are greater than the proportional ones,
// that's the responsibility of the user and the employed vehicles
```

```
d_x=80;
p_x=35;
d_y=80;
p_y=35;
d_z=80;
p_z=35;
```

```
// PD controllers
```

```
err_yaw=yaw-0;
c_roll  = kp_roll  * roll  + kd_roll  * gyrox;
c_pitch = kp_pitch * pitch + kd_pitch * gyroy;
c_yaw   = kp_yaw   * err_yaw   + kd_yaw   * gyroz;
```

```
// this reference holds the altitude while varying with the remote
// control or semiautomatic hover mode
refx=0;
refy=0;
refz=posz;
ref_px=0;
ref_py=0;
ref_pz=0;
```

```
errorx=posx-refx;
errory=posy-refy;
errorz=posz-refz;

error_px=velx-ref_px;
error_py=vely-ref_py;
error_pz=velz-ref_pz;

cx=satu(((p_x*(errorx)+d_x*(error_px)),50,-50);
cy=satu(((p_y*(errory)+d_y*(error_py)),50,-50);
cz=satu(((p_z*(errorz)+d_z*(error_pz)),80,-80);

// z control plus manual mg
  c_gas=refalt+cz;

    // BEWARE the signs of roll, X, pitch and Y, can vary
    // according to the sense of the remote control (the lever
    // can be reversed)

// saturated propulsion matrix so that the engines never turn off
// and at the same time do not reach the maximum value of
// operation, this also is the responsibility of the reader,
// see also the section of the propulsion matrix

    m1_c=satu(((-c_roll -cx  +c_pitch -cy  +c_yaw +cgas),1700,1100);
    m2_c=satu((( c_roll +cx  -c_pitch +cy  +c_yaw +cgas),1700,1100);
    m3_c=satu((( c_roll +cx  +c_pitch -cy  -c_yaw +cgas),1700,1100);
    m4_c=satu(((-c_roll -cx  -c_pitch +cy  -c_yaw +cgas),1700,1100);

// writing to the motors if the auxiliary lever that serves as
// emergency stop is activated, otherwise, stop the motors
```

```
if (aux_1<1500)
{
    hal.rcout->write(0,uint16_t(m1_c));
    hal.rcout->write(1,uint16_t(m2_c));
    hal.rcout->write(2,uint16_t(m3_c));
    hal.rcout->write(3,uint16_t(m4_c));
}

else
{
    hal.rcout->write(0,900);
    hal.rcout->write(1,900);
    hal.rcout->write(2,900);
    hal.rcout->write(3,900);
}

    hal.scheduler->delay(50);

}

// auxiliary functions including the AP_HAL_MAIN

// saturation function

static float satu(float nu, float ma, float mi){
    if(nu>=ma) nu=ma;
      else nu=nu;
      if(nu <= mi) nu=mi;
      else nu=nu;
    return nu;
}

// update function of x, y and z via gps
```

```
static void update_GPS(void){
      static uint32_t last_msg_ms;
      gps.update();
       if (last_msg_ms != gps.last_message_time_ms())
       {
           last_msg_ms = gps.last_message_time_ms();
           const Location &loc =gps.location();
           flag = gps.status();
       }

      uint32_t currtime = hal.scheduler->millis();
      dt = (float)(currtime - last_update) / 1000.0f;
      last_update = currtime;
// a delta t is required to internally calculate velocity
// estimations
      inertial_nav.update(dt);
// this part verifies that there are at least 3 satellites to
// operate and turn on the led if true, also changes a variable
// called flag2 to update speeds
      flag= gps.num_sats();

      if(pos.x!=0 && flag >=3 && flag2==1){
           const Location &loc = gps.location();
           ahrs.set_home(loc);
           compass.set_initial_location(loc.lat, loc.lng);
           toshiba_led.set_rgb(0,LED_DIM,0);    // green
           flag2 = 2;
       }
```

```
    pos_gps  = inertial_nav.get_position();
    vel_gps = inertial_nav.get_velocity();
// a gps of centimetric resolution is assumed
// and its value it is transformed to meters
    posx=((pos_gps.x)/100);
    posy=((pos_gps.y)/100);
    posz=((pos_gps.z)/100);
    if(flag2==2){
        velx=((vel_gps.x)/100);
        vely=((vel_gps.y)/100);
    }
    velz=((vel_gps.z)/100);
    flag2==1;

}

AP_HAL_MAIN(); // Ardupilot function call
```

Chapter Summary

In this chapter, you learned the following:

- The basis of a PD controller

- The basis for modelling a quadcopter

- How to link theory with practice by means of the
  allocation matrix, which is a really useful tool in any
  other kind of robotic vehicles

- How to test controllers without damaging the
  equipment or yourself just by deducting the operation
  of the system

- How many kinds of subcontrollers exist inside the operation of a vehicle, including automatic or manual, closed or open loops

- How to linearize a system and the conditions to do it, including control decoupling

- The difference among control methods, planning tasks, and flight modes (in general, movement modes)

- Control adequations such as biasing and saturation

- To identify the main processes for commanding a vehicle and the secondary ones

Now you have finished the second section about sequential programming of robotic vehicles. With the explained commands and the quadcopter example you are able to start to code your own robot.

In the next section, we will teach you about real time or parallel programming mode, and we will start the upcoming chapter with generalities on the ArduPilot libraries real-time working environment.

Part 2 References

Recommended website a very good introduction and summary of the minimum commands of the Ardupilot libraries necessary for the partial flight of a quadcopter, not including storage in memory or serial communications, in this case it is with the the APM autopilot (fly at your own risk)

https://blog.owenson.me/build-your-own-quadcopter-flight-controller/

Thesis of the University of Seville with a brief explanation of the Ardupilot libraries and its application to an aerial vehicle (dirigible type aircraft), in spanish

Alejandro Romero Galan, Revision y modificacion del firmware de libre acceso arducopter para su uso en el proyecto airwhale, Tesis, Universidad de Sevilla, 2015.

Mexican thesis on the design and modeling of a quadcopter, as well as the implementation of some control laws using the Ardupilot libraries, in spanish

Gerardo Arturo Ponce de Leon Zarate, Modelado dinamico y control de un cuadrotor para el seguimiento de trayectorias, Tesis, CIDETEC IPN, 2016

Formal but entertaining and very complete book about modeling, control and components of a multicopter

Quan Quan, Introduction to multicopter design and control, Springer, 2017.

Book with maker style to enter the world of quadcopters type drones, includes projects with Arduino

David McGriffy, Make: Drones: Teach an arduino to fly, Maker Media, Inc., 2016.

Book that describes brushless motors and ESCs at depth

Matthew Scarpino, Motors for makers: A guide to steppers, servos, and other electrical machines, Que Publishing, 2015.

Classical books which serve as reference for basic modeling and control of multicopters

Luis Rodolfo Garcia Carrillo, Alejandro Enrique Dzul Lopez, Rogelio Lozano, Claude Pegard, Quad rotorcraft control: vision-based hovering and navigation, Springer Science & Business Media, 2012.

Pedro Castillo, Rogelio Lozano, Alejandro E Dzul, Modelling and control of mini-flying machines, Physica-Verlag, 2006.

MOOC about modeling and basic control of quadcopters (Cartesian particle mode)

```
https://www.edx.org/course/autonomous-navigation-flying-
robots-tumx-autonavx-0
```

MOOCs about modeling and advanced control of quadcopters (three-dimensional body mode)

`https://es.coursera.org/learn/robotics-flight`

`https://www.edx.org/course/robotics-dynamics-control-pennx-robo3x`

Basic and advanced level C ++ programming courses highly recommended (in French with subtitles in English)

`https://es.coursera.org/learn/initiation-programmation-cpp`

`https://es.coursera.org/learn/programmation-orientee-objet-cpp`

Book chapter highly recommended for the complete modeling of a quadcopter, as well as its frames of reference

Jinhyun Kim, Min-Sung Kang, and Sangdeok Park, Accurate modeling and robust hovering control for a quad-rotor vtol aircraft, Selected papers from the 2nd International Symposium on UAVs, Reno, Nevada, USA June 8–10, 2009, Springer, 2009, pp. 9–26.

For the understanding of Euler's angles and their relationship with quasi-velocities in a geometric way

Anthony Bedford, Wallace Fowler, Dinamica: Mecanica para ingenieria, vol. 1, Pearson Educacion, 2000. pp 468-470

Beer, Flori and Johnston: Mechanics for engineers: dynamics, McGraw-Hill, 2007

The same in above but in a vectorial way, which by the way is a good book of quadcopters with a theoretical level in terms of modeling and automatic control also theoretical, in Spanish

Miranda, Garrido, Aguilar, Herrero, Drones: modelado y control de cuadrotores, Alfaomega, 2018

The matrix form

Fumio Hamano, Derivative of rotation matrix direct matrix derivation of well known formula, 2013

Additionally, a good course on dynamic and kinematics of rigid body is recommended for those who like to deepen in aerial or aquatic vehicles of aggressive movements, the authors recommend

`https://www.coursera.org/specializations/spacecraft-dynamics-control`

Online section with the complete codes of the Ardupilot libraries

`https://github.com/ArduPilot/ardupilot/tree/master/libraries/AP_HAL`

Descriptive webpages about the serial communication process type UART, the concepts of masking and the basic algorithms of checksum

`http://www.circuitbasics.com/basics-uart-communication/`

`https://en.wikipedia.org/wiki/Parity_bit`

PART III

Real-Time Mode

CHAPTER 7

Real-Time Working Environment

In this chapter, you will learn key concepts for using the ArduPilot real-time working environment libraries, such as the concept of a linker, the scheduler and its parameters, how to measure the current time of a task, the parts of a scheduler-mode program, and a really simple and understandable code demo for starting real time.

Linker

As you have seen, it is convenient to work with external functions called modules. In modular programming, the functions of a main program are separated into subprograms or modules.

To join all these module files with the main code, a linker is necessary. In the case of the ArduPilot libraries (and specifically in Windows via the Eclipse interface), linking is done automatically and users only need to ensure that the modules are located in the same folder as the main file.

© Julio Alberto Mendoza-Mendoza, Victor Gonzalez-Villela 2020
J. A. Mendoza-Mendoza et al., *Advanced Robotic Vehicles Programming*,
https://doi.org/10.1007/978-1-4842-5531-5_7

Scheduler Description

The scheduler operates with base time multipliers. For the version of the Pixhawk employed, they are multiplied by 2.5 milliseconds:

```
1     = 400 Hz
2     = 200 Hz
4     = 100 Hz
8     = 50 Hz
20    = 20 Hz
40    = 10 Hz
133   = 3 Hz
400   = 1 Hz
4000  = 0.1 Hz
```

The scheduler or task scheduler is the most important part of executing tasks in real time. In this section of the code, sequences of three arguments are declared: the name of the task, the estimated time of duration of said task, and the frequency or period of execution or repetition of said task. This last declaration is measured as a fraction of the maximum frequency of the autopilot. The higher the number assigned, the less frequent the task will be executed, and vice versa: the lower the number, the more frequently the task will be executed.

```
{onesecondtask,       400,   10}
```

In the example, the name of the task is onesecondtask. The second argument indicates that it will be repeated every second ($400 * 2.5$ milliseconds = 1000 ms = 1 second; remember also that 2.5 milliseconds is the inverse of 400 Hz). The last argument is 10, which indicates that this task must last 10 microseconds in its execution, which means the task is repeated every second but takes 10 microseconds to be completed.

Note that the use of real time is better than time management by the system clock previously seen, because a maximum estimated time of each task is used as a watchdog, a common concept in microcontrollers and programmable devices, and is responsible for determining if a task has been delayed or carried out successfully. In the case of a delay, it is automatically removed and the system continues with the performance of other events in the scheduler, which is not feasibly done by means of the system clock time previously seen. The use of real time is the most powerful method for time management for the Pixhawk and ArduPilot libraries.

As you will see in Listings 7-1 and 7-2, the scheduler also has a preferential or elitist mode for executing tasks, including your coding scheme. **A block called `fast loop`, which is not declared in the scheduler,** tells the Pixhawk that the priority of execution is in the fast loop cycle and if there is time (generally there is always time), execute all the other tasks declared in the scheduler. Then, in the fast loop, only the essential tasks to keep the vehicle operating must be declared (motor writing and inertial sensor reading).

The ArduPilot libraries give execution priority to the cycle called `fast loop` and allow the system to literally stop wasting time on functions not as relevant to its operation.

ArduPilot Usual Parts in Real-Time Mode/Scheduler Mode

The fast loop block and the scheduler declaration must be added to your original scheme. See Figure 7-1 and Table 7-1.

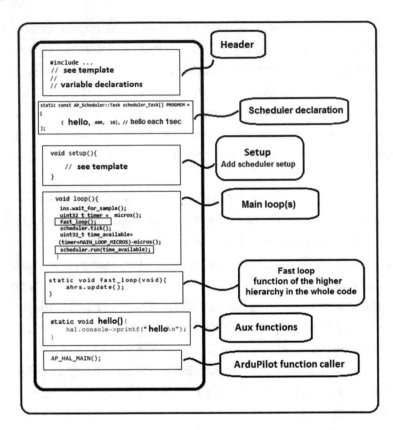

Figure 7-1. *Usual parts of an ArduPilot real-time mode program*

Table 7-1. *Usual parts of an ArduPilot real-time program*

Name	Contents	Allowed actions
Header	Definitions of libraries	Use only for ArduPilot libraries; Use and creation for the definitions of variables or classes (objects)
Schedule declaration	*All the functions that must be executed in real time other than the fast loop*	*Use, but the user only uses a template where they indicate which functions should be executed in the real-time scheduler.*
Setup	Initialization of ports or functions, only executed once	Use only for initialization methods.
Main loop	The main program of the user, it first executes the fast loop and then everything that is defined in the scheduler.	Use of the classes defined in the ArduPilot libraries, creation of own algorithms and use of auxiliary functions
Fast loop	*Higher hierarchy function, must have the essential tasks for the vehicle (for example, reading of the inertial sensor and writing to motors)*	*Use, but the user defines the contents present into this function.*
Auxiliary functions	Both internal and external, contain extensive code segments, or those that will be used in multiple segments of the loops	Creation for later use in the main loop cycles
AP_HAL_ MAIN ()	Allows the invocation of all the available classes in the ArduPilot libraries	Use

Measuring the Execution Time of a Task

One of the least intuitive parameters of the scheduler is the one related to the execution time of a task. The question is, how do you measure it? To answer this question, you'll use Listing 7-1, which does not use real time yet, but estimates the duration of one or more tasks.

Listing 7-1. System Clock Invoation

```
///////////////////////// DECLARATION //////////////////////////////
//                       Paste the header here
//                           see the appendix

/////////////////////// place your code here ///////////////////////

// Here the code of each example will be placed the respective
// defined functions, the setup cycle, the loops and fast loop
// before initializing definitions of other variables or
// libraries that are needed must be placed integers that
// contain time, these are of unsigned type because time is
// always positive and also of value 32 which equals a maximum
// of 4,294,967,296 milliseconds although a type 16 could be
// used, but that would only stores one minute or approximately
// 65536 milliseconds note that for variables that collect
// microseconds 4,294,967,296 microseconds are only 4295 seconds
// or 70 minutes

uint32_t begin=0,ending=0, timer, timemod;

///////////////////////// INICIALIZATION ///////////////////////////

void setup(){
    // copy here the basic setup
}
```

////////////////////////// EXECUTION //////////////////////////////

```
void loop(){
// a function scheme is used as required for real time
    fast_loop();
}

static void fast_loop(void){

// the current time is invoked
    timer=hal.scheduler->millis();

// you get the module between the time you want to display the
// data on the screen here every 3 seconds or equivalently 3000
// milliseconds

    timemod=timer%3000;

// if the module is exactly 3 seconds or around (2.9 seconds)

    if(timemod<=100)
    {

// displaying the value of the chronometer as at the beginning
// there are not start and end values these were initialized to 0
// in the declaration

        hal.console->printf("%d\n",ending-begin);
    }

// the fast loop must contain at least the ahrs.update

    ahrs.update();

// here starts the chronometer, we are interested in measuring
// the task a and b that we know they have about 56,000
// microseconds long
```

```
    begin=micros();
    atask();
    btask();

// here the chronometer stops
    ending=micros();
}

//              auxiliary functions

// tasks a and b last together approximately 56 milliseconds 11 + 45
// those are approximately 56,000 microseconds they are used
// like this to show the reader their usefulness, but in
// general it is unknown the duration of an specific task

static void atask(void){
    hal.scheduler->delay(11);
}

static void btask(void){
    hal.scheduler->delay(45);
}

// this function is defined to simplify writing

static uint32_t micros(){
    return hal.scheduler->micros();
}

AP_HAL_MAIN(); // Ardupilot function call
```

If you observe the result of the code in any terminal (shown in Figure 7-2), you will notice that the chronometer registers values between 56,000 and 58,000 microseconds. You can see that it is feasible to measure the execution times of a certain task. To include these times in the real-time scheduler, you can leave some gap and indicate that instead of the 56,000 it will take 60000 microseconds. In other cases, you can simply check the scheduler of the ArduCopter.pde file, search for some specific task (for example, read the GPS) and copy the times that were assigned (this time is already tested and is functional!).

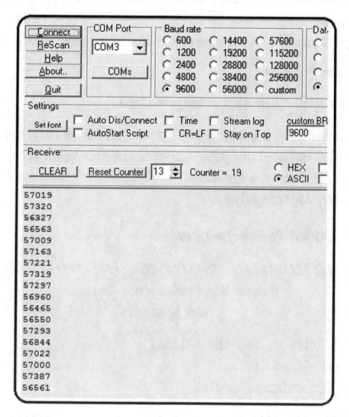

Figure 7-2. *Runtime of a task*

In other cases, since the serial terminal can interrupt the correct operation of some tasks, instead of analyzing the execution times in this serial screen, you can save them into the SD memory and visualize them offline (for example, writing to servos, wired or wireless serial transmission, etc.).

It is advisable to perform this measurement of the execution time of a task in a cyclical way and take an average for each one of the tasks whose duration does not seem clear to you; once done, you will know how much time to assign in the scheduler.

The code shown in Listing 7-2 already uses real time for the execution of three tasks.

Listing 7-2 provides an example of real time processing. Note the following:

- The syntax is:

```
void run(uint32_t time_available)
```

You can find more information at: http://ardupilot.org/dev/docs/code-overview-scheduling-your-new-code-to-run-intermittently.html
https://github.com/ArduPilot/ardupilot/blob/master/libraries/AP_Scheduler/AP_Scheduler.h

Listing 7-2. Real-Time Scheduler

```
////////////////////////// DECLARATION ///////////////////////////
//                  Paste the header code here
//                          see appendix

/////     verify or add these lines
#include <AP_Scheduler.h>
static AP_Scheduler scheduler;

//////////////////// place your code here ////////////////////

/////     this is the scheduler structure definition

static const AP_Scheduler::Task scheduler_task[] PROGMEM = {
        {onesec,      400,  10}, //400 dvided by 400 is 1 s
        {threesec,   1200,  10}, // 1200 divided by 400 are 3 s
        {fivesec,    2000,  10}, // 2000 divided by 400 are 5 s
};
```

```
///////////////////////// INICIALIZATION ///////////////////////////
void setup(){
    // add this line in the basic setup
scheduler.init(&scheduler_task[0],sizeof(scheduler_task)/
sizeof(scheduler_task[0]));
}
///////////////////////// EXECUTION ////////////////////////////////
void loop(){

    ins.wait_for_sample();
// the inertial sensor determines the use of the scheduler
    uint32_t timer =  micros();
    fast_loop();  // fast loop is ejecuted
    scheduler.tick(); // fast loop ends
    uint32_t time_available=(timer+MAIN_LOOP_MICROS)-micros();
// current time
    scheduler.run(time_available);
// execute what is defined in the scheduler
// if there is time available
}

// the fast loop is not declared in the scheduler and the tasks
// within should be only the most relevant, in this case only
// ahrs is updated but you can add the control loop and writing
// to the engines

static void fast_loop(void){
    ahrs.update();
}
```

```
//              auxiliar functions
static void onesec(){
    hal.console->printf("one \n");
}

static void threesec(){
    hal.console->printf("three \n");
}

static void fivesec(){
    hal.console->printf("five \n");
}

static uint32_t micros(){
    return hal.scheduler->micros();
}

AP_HAL_MAIN(); // Ardupilot function call
```

Chapter Summary

In this chapter, you learned the following:

- The concept of a linker, which is the way in which the ArduPilot libraries join modules of code

- The concept of the ArduPilot scheduler and its parameters

- How to measure the runtime of a task

- The parts of a real-time ArduPilot libraries program

- A basic but operative demo for understanding real-time mode

In the following chapter, you will modify your previous code for flying a quadcopter in order to include real-time modules and assign task execution priorities.

CHAPTER 8

Compendium of the Previous Chapters in Real Time with Application Code

In this chapter, the functions previously described are combined into a real-time code with their respective modules. Some other functions not added in the sequential code are included, simply to demonstrate the versatility of the real-time mode in the assignment and hierarchy of auxiliary tasks.

In the main code in Listing 8-1, note that the scheduler invokes both internal and external functions defined in the auxiliary modules of the code. Also note that only the most important functions are placed in the main code, in this case writing to the engines and reading orientations (don't try to use with propellers until you have tested without them).

© Julio Alberto Mendoza-Mendoza, Victor Gonzalez-Villela 2020
J. A. Mendoza-Mendoza et al., *Advanced Robotic Vehicles Programming*,
https://doi.org/10.1007/978-1-4842-5531-5_8

Listing 8-1. Quadcopter Pose Control, a Full Example in Real-Time
Mode

```
///////////////////////// DECLARATION //////////////////////////
//                  Paste the header code here
//                          see appendix

// verify or add this line
static AP_InertialNav_NavEKF inertial_nav(ahrs);

//////////////////////// place your code here //////////////////////

//         verify or add those lines

Vector3f gyro;
static float baro_alt;
int radio_roll, radio_pitch, radio_yaw, radio_throttle, aux_1,
aux_2, aux_3;
uint16_t radio[6];
float c_roll, c_pitch, c_yaw, volt, corriente_tot;
static Vector3f pos;
static Vector3f ref;
static Vector3f ref_p;
static Vector3f error;
static Vector3f error_p;
static Vector3f ctrl;
static Vector3f vel;
static Vector3f pos_gps;
static Vector3f vel_gps;
static Vector3f off;
static uint8_t flag=0,flag2=1;
uint8_t mode_flight=1;
bool flag_aux1=true;
```

```
// the reader should verify the necessary variables

//////////////////////// INITIALIZATION ////////////////////////

// secondary tasks defined in the scheduler

static const AP_Scheduler::Task scheduler_task[] PROGMEM = {
        {update_GPS,      8,   90}, // update GPS positions
        {update_Baro,    40,  100}, // update barometer altitude
        {Trajectory, 40,  20}, // update trajectory to follow
        {Read_radio,  4, 20}, // remote control reading
        {Flight_modes,     4,   50}, // update the flight mode
        {Read_battery, 400, 50},   // battery reading
        {Save_data, 20, 100},   // saving data into SD
};

void setup(){

//              verify or add those lines

    gps.init(NULL,serial_manager);
    ahrs.set_compass(&compass);
    hal.rcout->enable_ch(0);
    hal.rcout->enable_ch(1);
    hal.rcout->enable_ch(2);
    hal.rcout->enable_ch(3);
    hal.rcout->set_freq( 15, 490);
scheduler.init(&scheduler_task[0],sizeof(scheduler_task)/
sizeof(scheduler_task[0]));
    toshiba_led.init(); battery.set_monitoring(0,AP_
    BattMonitor::BattMonitor_TYPE_ANALOG_VOLTAGE_AND_CURRENT);
    battery.init();
    init_flash();
```

```
// setting the motors
    hal.rcout->write(0,0);
    hal.rcout->write(1,0);
    hal.rcout->write(2,0);
    hal.rcout->write(3,0);

}

/////////////////////////// EXECUTION ///////////////////////////

void loop(){

    ins.wait_for_sample();
    uint32_t timer =  micros();
    fast_loop();
    scheduler.tick();
    uint32_t time_available=(timer+MAIN_LOOP_MICROS)-micros();
    scheduler.run(time_available);
}

static void fast_loop(void){
    ahrs.update();
    compass.read();
    gyro  = ins.get_gyro();

    c_roll  = phi_p  * ahrs.roll  + phi_d  * gyro.x;
    c_pitch = th_p * ahrs.pitch + th_d * gyro.y;
    c_yaw   = psi_p * (ahrs.yaw-0)  + psi_d  * gyro.z;

    // writing to motors
    float m1_c, m2_c, m3_c, m4_c;
    float c_gas=radio_throttle+ctrl.z;

    m1_c=satu((-c_roll -ctrl.x  +c_pitch -ctrl.y  +c_yaw+radio_
    yaw  +cgas),1700,1100);
```

```
    m2_c=satu(( c_roll +ctrl.x  -c_pitch +ctrl.y  +c_yaw+radio_
    yaw  +cgas),1700,1100);
    m3_c=satu(( c_roll +ctrl.x  +c_pitch -ctrl.y  -c_yaw-radio_
    yaw  +cgas),1700,1100);
    m4_c=satu((-c_roll -ctrl.x  -c_pitch +ctrl.y  -c_yaw-radio_
    yaw  +cgas),1700,1100);

// emergency stop

    if (radio_throttle>1149)
    {
        hal.rcout->write(0,m1_c);
        hal.rcout->write(1,m2_c);
        hal.rcout->write(2,m3_c);
        hal.rcout->write(3,m4_c);
    }

    else
    {
        hal.rcout->write(0,1000);
        hal.rcout->write(1,1000);
        hal.rcout->write(2,1000);
        hal.rcout->write(3,1000);
    }

}

//          auxiliary functions

// saturation function
static float satu(float nu, float ma, float mi){
    if(nu>=ma) nu=ma;
      else nu=nu;
      if(nu <= mi) nu=mi;
```

```
      else nu=nu;
   return nu;
}

static uint32_t micros(){
    return hal.scheduler->micros();
}

static void Read_battery(){
    battery.read();
    volt=battery.voltage();
    corriente_tot=battery.current_total_mah();
}

static void Save_data(){
    Log_Write_Pose();
    Log_Write_Control();
    Log_Write_Errors();
}

AP_HAL_MAIN(); // Ardupilot function call
```

Module radio.pde

Listing 8-2 contains the Read_radio() function.

Listing 8-2. Module radio.pde for Real-Time Hovering Control of a
Quadcopter

```
static void Read_radio(){
    for (uint8_t i=0;i<=6; i++)
    {radio[i]=hal.rcin->read(i);}
    radio_roll=(radio[0]-1500)/3;
    radio_pitch=(radio[1]-1500)/3;
```

```
radio_throttle=radio[2];
if(radio_throttle>=1149 && radio_throttle<1152){
    off.z=pos.z;
}

radio_yaw=(radio[3]-1500)/2;
aux_1=radio[4];
aux_2=radio[5];
}
```

Module control.pde

This control.pde file contains the Flight_modes() function; see
Listing 8-3. This function activates different control modes depending on
which auxiliary levers are activated. Basically, these flight modes modify
the controls in the X, Y, and Z axes.

Listing 8-3. Module control.pde for Real-Time Hovering Control of
a Quadcopter

```
static void Flight_modes(){

if(aux_1<1600){
    if(flag_aux1){
        ref.x=pos.x;
        off.x=pos.x;
        ref.y=pos.y;
        off.y=pos.y;
        ref.z=pos.z;
        mode_flight =2;
    }
```

```
    if(aux_2>=1600) {
        mode_flight =3;
    } else { mode_flight =2;}

}

else{
    mode_flight =1;
    flag_aux1=false;
}

switch(mode_flight) {
case 1: // just attitude
    ctrl.x=0;
    ctrl.y=0;
    ctrl.z=0;
    ref_p.x=0;
    ref_p.y=0;
    ref_p.z=0;
    break;
case 2: // hover
    error.x=pos.x-ref.x;
    error.y=pos.y-ref.y;
// check remote control levers to coincide with the signs
    error.z=ref.z-pos.z;
    error_p.x=vel.x-ref_p.x;
    error_p.y=vel.y-ref_p.y;
    error_p.z=ref_p.z-vel.z;
    ctrl.x=satu((p_x*(error.x)+d_x*(error_p.x)),50,-50);
    ctrl.y=satu((p_y*(error.y)+d_y*(error_p.y)),50,-50);
    ctrl.z=satu((alt_p*(error.z)+alt_d*(error_p.z)),80,-80);
    break;
```

```
case 3: // trajectory following
    error.x=pos.x-ref.x;
    error.y=pos.y-ref.y;
    error.z=ref.z-pos.z;
    error_p.x=vel.x-ref_p.x;
    error_p.y=vel.y-ref_p.y;
    error_p.z=ref_p.z-vel.z;
    ctrl.x=satu((p_x*(error.x)+d_x*(error_p.x)),50,-50);
    ctrl.y=satu((p_y*(error.y)+d_y*(error_p.y)),50,-50);
    ctrl.z=satu((alt_p*(error.z)+alt_d*(error_p.z)),80,-80);
    break;
default:
    break;
}
}
```

Note the following combinations (as the remote control's signal oscillates its auxiliary OFF- position between values 1590-1580, it indicates that OFF is less than 1600):

```
Aux_1  =  0     if  signal      < 1600
Aux_1  =  1     if  signal      >= 1600
Similarly
Aux_2  =  0     if  signal      < 1600
Aux_2  =  1     if  signal      >= 1600
```

This way, you reconstruct the state machine (notice that this state machine only affects the injected control and whether a predesigned trajectory is used or not). See Table 8-1 and Figure 8-1.

Table 8-1. *States of the Flight Tasks and Associated Combination of*
Auxiliar Levers

State	Task	Combination AUX1 AUX2
A	Manual takeoff with automatic attitude	(1,0) , (1,1)
B	Automatic hover with automatic attitude	(0, 0)
C	Automatic trajectory following with automatic attitude	(0, 1)

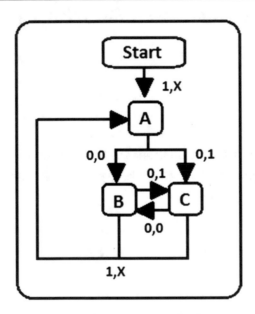

Figure 8-1. *State machine of the flight tasks*

- **State A**: Just orientation plus manual altitude (takeoff). No automatic hover or XY position.

- **State B**: Orientation plus automatic altitude and keeping current XY position (hovering).

- **State C**: Attitude, plus elevation, plus automatic XY positions (trajectory following).

Attention: While using this code for states B and C, do not move the throttle lever because the code shown does not contain stoppage for it, which, in fact, serves as a way for the drone to always maintain a positive reference. This reference is the throttle lever position at the moment when you change the AUX_1 lever. Also, always start the vehicle with the AUX_1 lever at digital value 1, because here we don't consider what happens if the vehicle is on the ground while states B or C are present. Finally, be careful when you try to turn off the motors; they will continue rotating because the attitude control is always active. Instead, try to do it on the ground without moving the quadcopter or by using a long extension with the disarming button.

Notice that there is no emergency stop or landing state. This is because the general control contains the remote control's interaction, which is always present (the user always has access to this state through the remote control). To land the vehicle, the user commands the throttle lever (remote control of hover task). Also, note that this control is risky since, if the terrain is not flat, the engines will keep rotating because attitude control, which depends on angular variations, is always present, so it is best to use the proposed code on a smooth surface without any type of slope. And, as this controller has assumed no crosswinds, it is better to try this in a closed space. Another option is to use a third aux lever, or instead of using 1,0 and 1,1 combinations of aux1 and aux2 indistinctly for state 1, maybe you could program a D state with one of those combinations for writing 0 to the motors.

Module Data.pde

The data.pde module contains the Log_Write functions of the internal Save_data() function; see Listing 8-4.

Listing 8-4. Module data.pde for Real-Time Hovering Control of a
Quadcopter

```
static uint16_t log_num;    //Dataflash

struct PACKED log_Pose{
    LOG_PACKET_HEADER;
    float    alt_barof;
    float    Roll;
    float    Pitch;
    float    Yaw;
    float    z_pos;
    float    vel_x;
    float    vel_y;
    float    vel_z;
    float    x_pos;
    float    y_pos;
    float    giroz;
    float    girox;
    float    giroy;
};

struct PACKED log_Control {
    LOG_PACKET_HEADER;
    float    time_ms;
    float    u_z;
    float    tau_theta;
    float    tau_phi;
    float    tau_psi;
    float    comodin_1;
    float    comodin_2;
```

```
    float   comodin_3; // comodines para indice de desempeño
    float   comodin_4;
};

struct PACKED log_Errors {
    LOG_PACKET_HEADER;
    uint32_t    time_ms;
    float   error_x;
    float   error_y;
    float   error_z;
    float   voltaje;
    float   corriente;
    float   comodin_5;
    float   comodin_6;
    int   comodin_7;
    float   alt_des;
    float   x_des;
    float   y_des;
};

//declaration
static const struct LogStructure log_structure[] PROGMEM = {
        LOG_COMMON_STRUCTURES,
        {LOG_POSE_MSG, sizeof(log_Pose),
        "1", "ffffffffffff", "a_bar,ROLL,PITCH,YAW,Z_POS,
        V_X,V_Y,V_Z,X_POS,Y_POS,G_Z,G_X,G_Y"},
      { LOG_CONTROL_MSG, sizeof(log_Control),
        "2", "fffffffff", "T_MS,UZ,T_TH,T_PHI,T_PSI,
        TAUX,TAUY,S_PHI,S_PSI"},
       { LOG_ERR_MSG, sizeof(log_Errors),
        "3", "IfffffffIffff", "T_MS,E_X,E_Y,E_Z,VOLT,AMP,nav_z,
        nav_zp,con_alt,ZDES,XDES,YDES"},
};
```

```
// initialization
static void init_flash() {
    DataFlash.Init(log_structure,sizeof(log_structure)/
    sizeof(log_structure[0]));
    if (DataFlash.NeedErase()) {
        DataFlash.EraseAll();
    }
    log_num=DataFlash.StartNewLog();
}

// saving data

static void Log_Write_Pose()
{

    struct log_Pose pkt = {
        LOG_PACKET_HEADER_INIT(LOG_POSE_MSG),
        alt_barof    : baro_alt,
        Roll         : ahrs.roll,
        Pitch        : ahrs.pitch,
        Yaw          : ahrs.yaw,
        z_pos        : pos.z,
        vel_x        : vel.x,
        vel_y        : vel.y,
        vel_z        : vel.z,
        x_pos        : pos.x,
        y_pos        : pos.y,
        giroz        : gyro.z,
        girox        : gyro.x,
        giroy        : gyro.y,
    };
    DataFlash.WriteBlock(&pkt, sizeof(pkt));
}
```

```
static void Log_Write_Control(){
    struct log_Control pkt = {
        LOG_PACKET_HEADER_INIT(LOG_CONTROL_MSG),
        time_ms      : (float)(hal.scheduler->millis()/1000),
        u_z          : ctrl.z,
        tau_theta    : (ctrl.x+c_pitch),
        tau_phi      : (ctrl.y+c_roll),
        tau_psi      : c_yaw,
        comodin_1        : 0,
        comodin_2        : 0,
        comodin_3    : 0,
        comodin_4    : 0,
    };

    DataFlash.WriteBlock(&pkt, sizeof(pkt));
}

static void Log_Write_Errors(){
    struct log_Errors pkt = {
        LOG_PACKET_HEADER_INIT(LOG_ERR_MSG),
        time_ms          : (hal.scheduler->millis()/100),
        error_x          : error.x,
        error_y          : error.y,
        error_z          : error.z,
        voltaje          : volt,
        corriente        : corriente_tot,
        comodin_5            : 0,
        comodin_6            : 0,
        comodin_7            : radio_throttle,
        alt_des          : ref.z,
        x_des            : ref.x,
        y_des            : ref.y,
```

```
    };
    DataFlash.WriteBlock(&pkt, sizeof(pkt));
}
```

Module Pose.pde

The pose.pde module contains the Trajectory(), update_Baro(), and update_GPS() functions. See Listing 8-5.

Listing 8-5. Module Pose.pde for Real-Time Hovering Control of a Quadcopter

```
# define LED_DIM 0x11 // LED variable definition
static float dt; // delta of time

static uint32_t last_update;     // inertial navigation variable

///////                 GPS
static void update_GPS(void){
    static uint32_t last_msg_ms;

      gps.update();

      if (last_msg_ms != gps.last_message_time_ms())
      {
          last_msg_ms = gps.last_message_time_ms();
          const Location &loc =gps.location();
          flag = gps.status();
      }

      uint32_t currtime = hal.scheduler->millis();
      dt = (float)(currtime - last_update) / 1000.0f;
      last_update = currtime;
      inertial_nav.update(dt);
```

```
      if(pos.x!=0 && flag >=3 && flag2==1){

          const Location &loc = gps.location();
          ahrs.set_home(loc);

          compass.set_initial_location(loc.lat, loc.lng);
          toshiba_led.set_rgb(0,LED_DIM,0);
          flag2 = 2;

        }

    pos_gps  = inertial_nav.get_position();
    vel_gps = inertial_nav.get_velocity();

    pos.x=((pos_gps.x)/100)-off.x;
    pos.y=((pos_gps.y)/100)-off.y;
    pos.z=((pos_gps.z)/100)-off.z;

    if(flag2==2){
        vel.x=((vel_gps.x)/100);
        vel.y=((vel_gps.y)/100);
    }
    vel.z=((vel_gps.z)/100);

}

static void update_Baro() {
    barometer.update();
    baro_alt=barometer.get_altitude();
}

static void Trajectory(){
    if(mode_flight==3 && s_time<=360){
    //posic
    ref.x=(-3*cos(s_time*(3.1416/180))+3)+off.x; // starts
    where it is currently placed
```

```
ref.y=(-3*sin(s_time*(3.1416/180)))+off.y;
ref.z=pos.z;
//veloc

ref_p.x=0; // remember the soft-flight mode but you can
           // paste here the time derivative
ref_p.y=0;
ref_p.z=0;
}
}
```

Next, the interdependence of the previous code is presented.
See Figure 8-2. Note that such interaction is simplified and more
understandable through the concept of modularity and internal and
external functions with respect to the sequential programming scheme.

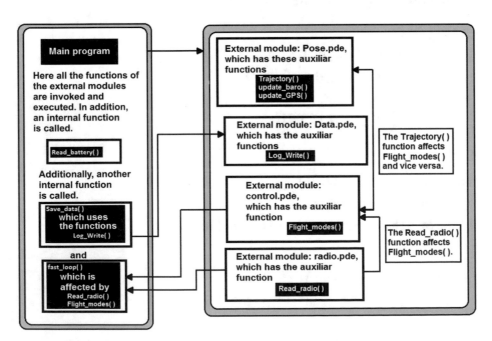

Figure 8-2. *Modules and main code relationship*

Chapter Summary

In this chapter, you learned the following:

- How to code a full program in real-time mode, divided into modules

- How to link each module with the rest of the program

- How to represent your flight tasks with state machines

It is true that you have finished, but we recommend that you read the appendices. There you can read about similar libraries and their commands in a comparative way. You will also learn about omnidirectionality and thrust vectoring if you want to design novel kinds of vehicles, about tethered vehicles for long-term operations, our libraries-version installation process, the full code of the header and the setup sections of code, how to design a quadcopter, and a useful set of keywords from this book if you want to search for more on your own.

Part 3 References

The following is an interesting article that describes in detail the Pixhawk design (useful if you want to design your own autopilot): Lorenz Meier, Petri Tanskanen, Lionel Heng, Gim Hee Lee, Friedrich Fraundorfer, Marc Pollefeys, "PIXHAWK: A micro aerial vehicle design for autonomous flight using onboard computer vision," *Autonomous Robots* 33 (2012), no. 1-2, 21–39.

The following is an interesting article complementary to the previous one for those who want to make their own autopilot. It provides an explanation of the design of tasks in real time: J. Rogelio Guadarrama-Olvera, Jose J. Corona-Sanchez, Hugo Rodriguez-Cortes, "Hard real-time implementation of a nonlinear controller for the quadrotor helicopter," *Journal of Intelligent & Robotic Systems* 73 (2014), no. 1-4, 81–97.

The following is a massive online course on real-time design:
`https://es.coursera.org/learn/real-time-systems`.

The following web page explains the use of modules and "linking" in
C++. Note that the compiler attached to the Ardupilot libraries already
automatically links as long as the working folder has the same name
as the main file. In this text, the word module is synonymous with the
independent subcomponent of a main program: `www.slothparadise.`
`com/c-libraries-linking-compiling/`.

Read the following book if you want to know more about state
machines and their robotic applications: Vojtech Spurny et al,
"Cooperative autonomous search, grasping, and delivering in a treasure
hunt scenario by a team of unmanned aerial vehicles," Wiley Online
Library, 2018.

The following web page describes the use in real time of ArduPilot
libraries: `http://ardupilot.org/dev/docs/code-overview-scheduling-`
`your-new-code-to-run-intermittently.html?highlight=scheduler`.

APPENDIX 1

Comparison of Commands with Other SDKs

Table A1-1. *Comparison with Other SDKs*

Task	ArduPilot command In C++	Dronekit command In Python	PX4 C++ messages ROS-kind logic
Screen interface: reading and writing	hal.console-> printf() hal.console-> read()	Print input() or raw_input()	PX4_INFO
Remote control reading or RC input	hal.rcin-> read()	vehicle.channels [channel]	manual_ control_ setpoint.msg

(continued)

© Julio Alberto Mendoza-Mendoza, Victor Gonzalez-Villela 2020
J. A. Mendoza-Mendoza et al., *Advanced Robotic Vehicles Programming*,
https://doi.org/10.1007/978-1-4842-5531-5

Table A1-1. (*continued*)

Task	ArduPilot command In C++	Dronekit command In Python	PX4 C++ messages ROS-kind logic
Writing to motors or RC output	`hal.rcout-> write()`	NOT TO MOTORS, ONLY TO VEHICLE: send_ned_ velocity (vx,vy,vz, duracion)	`actuator_ controls.msg` to vehicle `actuator_ direct.msg` `test_motor.msg` to motors
Analog reading	`ch=hal. analogin-> channel(channel) read=ch-> voltage_ average()`	EXTERNAL, for example, analog ports on Raspberry Pi	`adc_report.msg`
Digital reading and writing or GPIO	`hal.gpio-> read(pin) hal.gpio-> write(pin,value)`	EXTERNAL, for example, GPIO libraries on Raspberry Pi	`gpio_led start`
Wired or wireless serial UART reading/ writing	`hal.uart#- >write() hal.uart#- >read() with #=A,B,C,D`	EXTERNAL, for example, with Raspberry Pi	`modules/ mavlink`

(*continued*)

Table A1-1. (*continued*)

Task	ArduPilot command In C++	Dronekit command In Python	PX4 C++ messages ROS-kind logic
Writing to SD card	`DataFlash. WriteBlock (package,size)`	EXTERNAL by using Raspberry or another command computer with `file.write` or `mavutil. mavlink_ connection (filename)`	`https://dev. px4.io/en/log/ ulog_file_ format.html`
Time invocation or delays	`hal.scheduler-> millis() hal.scheduler-> delay()`	`time.sleep(time)`	`hrt_absolute_ time();`
Battery reading	`battery.read( )`	`vehicle.battery`	`battery_ status.msg`
GPS reading	`inertial_nav. get_ position() inertial_nav. get_velocity();`	`vehicle.gps_0`	`vehicle_gps_ position.msg vehicle_ odometry.msg`
Orientation reading	`Ahrs ins.get_gyro()`	`vehicle.attitude`	`vehicle_ odometry.msg sensor_ combined.msg`

(*continued*)

Table A1-1. (*continued*)

Task	ArduPilot command In C++	Dronekit command In Python	PX4 C++ messages ROS-kind logic
Altitude reading	`barometer.get_ altitude()`	`vehicle.location`	`vehicle_gps_ position.msg vehicle_ odometry.msg`
LED lightning	`toshiba_led.set_ rgb(R,G,B);`	EXTERNAL	`led_control. msg`
Signal filtering	`LowPassFilter2p float filtername (parameters) filtername.apply (signal);`	EXTERNAL, additional Python apps	`https://dev. px4.ii/en/ middleware/ modules_ estimesti.html`
Observations	Very complete libraries to fully use the autopilot, widely documented, and easy to use	Libraries for limited use, easy to implement, good documentation	The most complete libraries, difficult to use and with ROS style, not well documented
Webpage	`http://ardupilot. org/dev/docs/ apmcopter- programming- libraries.html`	`http://python. dronekit.io`	`https://dev. px4.io/en/`

Setup Extended Code

The following lines must be placed in each new program. It is advisable not to omit any of them in order to avoid incurring errors due to omission of data. In the best case, it is only advisable to add more lines of code as needed or to encapsulate certain specific lines in a function, as previously illustrated in the case of SD memory writing.

```
void setup()
{
    ins.init(AP_InertialSensor::COLD_START,AP_InertialSensor::
    RATE_400HZ);
    serial_manager.init_console();
    serial_manager.init();
    compass.init();
    compass.read();
    ahrs.set_compass(&compass);
    gps.init(NULL,serial_manager);
    barometer.init();
    barometer.calibrate();
    DataFlash.Init(log_structure, sizeof(log_structure)/
    sizeof(log_structure[0]));
        if (DataFlash.NeedErase()) {
            DataFlash.EraseAll();
            }
```

© Julio Alberto Mendoza-Mendoza, Victor Gonzalez-Villela 2020
J. A. Mendoza-Mendoza et al., *Advanced Robotic Vehicles Programming*,
https://doi.org/10.1007/978-1-4842-5531-5

```
log_num = DataFlash.StartNewLog();
hal.scheduler->delay(100);
}
```

As you can see, the basic setup consists of starting the serial console (to at least send messages to a terminal), and then initializing the compass, the inertial sensor, the GPS, the barometer, and the combined module AHRS (so that the autopilot has a notion of its position and spatial orientation), and finally the storage module to the SD card. This initializer is the base mode and sometimes, as illustrated in the pertinent sections, it will be necessary to add lines (for items such as motors, LEDs, batteries, UART serial communication, and analog and digital ports).

APPENDIX 3

Extended Header

This header information must be placed in each code file so that the programs can be executed.

The following header lines must be added to each new code file. They contain the invocation of all the necessary functions of the ArduPilot libraries. It is suggested to not modify them and in the best case, only add the necessary library. Do not remove any line of code if you are not sure about the library or command to be removed. Note that they have been taken almost completely from the `ardupilot.pde` file. Just copy and paste the following:

```
// place the header here //

// c libraries
#include <math.h>
#include <stdio.h>
#include <stdlib.h>
#include <stdarg.h>

// Common dependencies
#include <AP_Common.h>
#include <AP_Progmem.h>
#include <AP_Menu.h>
#include <AP_Param.h>
#include <StorageManager.h>
// AP_HAL
```

© Julio Alberto Mendoza-Mendoza, Victor Gonzalez-Villela 2020
J. A. Mendoza-Mendoza et al., *Advanced Robotic Vehicles Programming*,
https://doi.org/10.1007/978-1-4842-5531-5

```
#include <AP_HAL.h>
#include <AP_HAL_AVR.h>
#include <AP_HAL_SITL.h>
#include <AP_HAL_PX4.h>
#include <AP_HAL_VRBRAIN.h>
#include <AP_HAL_FLYMAPLE.h>
#include <AP_HAL_Linux.h>
#include <AP_HAL_Empty.h>
#include <AP_Math.h>

// Application dependencies
#include <GCS.h>
#include <GCS_MAVLink.h>        // MAVLink GCS definitions
#include <AP_SerialManager.h>   // Serial manager library
#include <AP_GPS.h>             // ArduPilot GPS library
#include <DataFlash.h>          // ArduPilot Mega Flash Memory
                                // Library
#include <AP_ADC.h>             // ArduPilot Mega Analog to
                                // Digital Converter Library
#include <AP_ADC_AnalogSource.h>
#include <AP_Baro.h>
#include <AP_Compass.h>         // ArduPilot Mega Magnetometer
                                // Library
#include <AP_Math.h>            // ArduPilot Mega Vector/Matrix
                                // math Library
#include <AP_Curve.h>           // Curve used to linearlise
                                // throttle pwm to thrust
#include <AP_InertialSensor.h>  // ArduPilot Mega Inertial
                                // Sensor (accel & gyro) Library
#include <AP_AHRS.h>
#include <AP_NavEKF.h>
#include <AP_Mission.h>         // Mission command library
```

```
#include <AP_Rally.h>             // Rally point library
#include <AC_PID.h>               // PID library
#include <AC_PI_2D.h>             // PID library (2-axis)
#include <AC_HELI_PID.h>          // Heli specific Rate PID
                                  // library
#include <AC_P.h>                 // P library
#include <AC_AttitudeControl.h>   // Attitude control library
#include <AC_AttitudeControl_Heli.h> // Attitude control
                                  // library for traditional
                                  // helicopter
#include <AC_PosControl.h>        // Position control library
#include <RC_Channel.h>           // RC Channel Library
#include <AP_Motors.h>            // AP Motors library
#include <AP_RangeFinder.h>       // Range finder library
#include <AP_OpticalFlow.h>       // Optical Flow library
#include <Filter.h>               // Filter library
#include <AP_Buffer.h>            // APM FIFO Buffer
#include <AP_Relay.h>             // APM relay
#include <AP_ServoRelayEvents.h>
#include <AP_Camera.h>            // Photo or video camera
#include <AP_Mount.h>             // Camera/Antenna mount
#include <AP_Airspeed.h>          // needed for AHRS build
#include <AP_Vehicle.h>           // needed for AHRS build
#include <AP_InertialNav.h>       // ArduPilot Mega inertial
                                  // navigation library
#include <AC_WPNav.h>             // ArduCopter waypoint
                                  // navigation library
#include <AC_Circle.h>            // circle navigation library
#include <AP_Declination.h>       // ArduPilot Mega Declination
                                  // Helper Library
#include <AC_Fence.h>             // Arducopter Fence library
#include <SITL.h>                 // software in the loop support
```

```
#include <AP_Scheduler.h>          // main loop scheduler
#include <AP_RCMapper.h>           // RC input mapping library
#include <AP_Notify.h>             // Notify library
#include <AP_BattMonitor.h>        // Battery monitor library
#include <AP_BoardConfig.h>        // board configuration library
#include <AP_Frsky_Telem.h>
#if SPRAYER == ENABLED
#include <AC_Sprayer.h>            // crop sprayer library
#endif
#if EPM_ENABLED == ENABLED
#include <AP_EPM.h>               // EPM cargo gripper stuff
#endif
#if PARACHUTE == ENABLED
#include <AP_Parachute.h>         // Parachute release library
#endif
#include <AP_LandingGear.h>       // Landing Gear library
#include <AP_Terrain.h>
#include <LowPassFilter2p.h>
// AP_HAL to Arduino compatibility layer
#include "compat.h"
// Configuration
#include "defines.h"
#include "config.h"
#include "config_channels.h"

// lines referring to the times of the pixhawk autopilot, which
// works at 400mhz or 0.0025seconds or 2500 microseconds

# define MAIN_LOOP_RATE     400
# define MAIN_LOOP_SECONDS  0.0025f
# define MAIN_LOOP_MICROS   2500
```

```
// statements referring to the autopilot objects, for example,
// gps-type objects barometer, compass, DataFlash, etc., all of
// them will subsequently be invoked in the corresponding code

const AP_HAL::HAL& hal = AP_HAL_BOARD_DRIVER;
static AP_Scheduler scheduler;

static AP_GPS  gps;
static AP_Baro barometer;
static AP_InertialSensor ins;
static RangeFinder sonar;
static Compass compass;
static AP_SerialManager serial_manager;
static ToshibaLED_PX4 toshiba_led;
static AP_BattMonitor battery;

//Data, BE CAREFUL, WHEN YOU READ THE SD SECTION DELETE THIS
//BLOCK THERE
// you will learn how to use and external module and deep
// details about these declarations
#define  LOG_MSG          0x01
#if CONFIG_HAL_BOARD == HAL_BOARD_PX4
static DataFlash_File DataFlash("/fs/microsd/APM/LOGS");
#endif

struct PACKED log_Datos{
    LOG_PACKET_HEADER;
    uint32_t  time_ms;
    float  a_roll;
    float  a_pitch;
    float  a_yaw;
```

```
    float  pos_x;
    float  pos_y;
    float  pos_z;
};

static const struct LogStructure log_structure[] PROGMEM = {
        LOG_COMMON_STRUCTURES,
        {LOG_MSG, sizeof(log_Datos),
        "1", "Iffffff", "T_MS,ROLL,PITCH,YAW,X_POS,Y_POS,Z_
        POS"},
};

static uint16_t log_num;    //Dataflash

// Inertial Navigation EKF

#if AP_AHRS_NAVEKF_AVAILABLE
AP_AHRS_NavEKF ahrs(ins, barometer, gps, sonar);
#else
AP_AHRS_DCM ahrs(ins, barometer, gps);
#endif

static AP_InertialNav_NavEKF inertial_nav(ahrs);

// place your code here //
```

Previously an abbreviated description of these libraries was made. For a more complete reference, consult the following documentation:

Alejandro Romero Galan, "Revision y modificacion del firmware de libre acceso arducopter para su uso en el proyecto airwhale," Thesis, Universidad de Sevilla, 2015 (in Spanish).

```
http://ardupilot.org/dev/docs/apmcopter-programming-
libraries.html
```

```
https://github.com/ArduPilot/ardupilot/tree/master/libraries
```

APPENDIX 4

The Fully Functional Code

Here is the complete code, including the header and setup information:

```
// paste the header here //

// c libraries
#include <math.h>
#include <stdio.h>
#include <stdlib.h>
#include <stdarg.h>

// Common dependencies
#include <AP_Common.h>
#include <AP_Progmem.h>
#include <AP_Menu.h>
#include <AP_Param.h>
#include <StorageManager.h>
// AP_HAL
#include <AP_HAL.h>
#include <AP_HAL_AVR.h>
#include <AP_HAL_SITL.h>
#include <AP_HAL_PX4.h>
#include <AP_HAL_VRBRAIN.h>
```

© Julio Alberto Mendoza-Mendoza, Victor Gonzalez-Villela 2020
J. A. Mendoza-Mendoza et al., *Advanced Robotic Vehicles Programming*,
https://doi.org/10.1007/978-1-4842-5531-5

```
#include <AP_HAL_FLYMAPLE.h>
#include <AP_HAL_Linux.h>
#include <AP_HAL_Empty.h>
#include <AP_Math.h>

// Application dependencies
#include <GCS.h>
#include <GCS_MAVLink.h>              // MAVLink GCS definitions
#include <AP_SerialManager.h>        // Serial manager library
#include <AP_GPS.h>                  // ArduPilot GPS library
#include <DataFlash.h>               // ArduPilot Mega Flash Memory
                                     // Library
#include <AP_ADC.h>                  // ArduPilot Mega Analog to
                                     // Digital Converter Library
#include <AP_ADC_AnalogSource.h>
#include <AP_Baro.h>
#include <AP_Compass.h>              // ArduPilot Mega Magnetometer
                                     // Library
#include <AP_Math.h>                 // ArduPilot Mega Vector/Matrix
                                     // math Library
#include <AP_Curve.h>                // Curve used to linearlise
                                     // throttle pwm to thrust
#include <AP_InertialSensor.h>       // ArduPilot Mega Inertial
                                     // Sensor (accel & gyro) Library
#include <AP_AHRS.h>
#include <AP_NavEKF.h>
#include <AP_Mission.h>              // Mission command library
#include <AP_Rally.h>                // Rally point library
#include <AC_PID.h>                  // PID library
#include <AC_PI_2D.h>                // PID library (2-axis)
#include <AC_HELI_PID.h>             // Heli specific Rate PID
                                     // library
```

```
#include <AC_P.h>                    // P library
#include <AC_AttitudeControl.h> // Attitude control library
#include <AC_AttitudeControl_Heli.h> // Attitude control
                                     // library for traditional
                                     // helicopter
#include <AC_PosControl.h>          // Position control library
#include <RC_Channel.h>             // RC Channel Library
#include <AP_Motors.h>              // AP Motors library
#include <AP_RangeFinder.h>         // Range finder library
#include <AP_OpticalFlow.h>         // Optical Flow library
#include <Filter.h>                 // Filter library
#include <AP_Buffer.h>              // APM FIFO Buffer
#include <AP_Relay.h>               // APM relay
#include <AP_ServoRelayEvents.h>
#include <AP_Camera.h>              // Photo or video camera
#include <AP_Mount.h>               // Camera/Antenna mount
#include <AP_Airspeed.h>            // needed for AHRS build
#include <AP_Vehicle.h>             // needed for AHRS build
#include <AP_InertialNav.h>         // ArduPilot Mega inertial
                                     // navigation library
#include <AC_WPNav.h>               // ArduCopter waypoint
                                     // navigation library
#include <AC_Circle.h>              // circle navigation library
#include <AP_Declination.h>         // ArduPilot Mega Declination
                                     // Helper Library
#include <AC_Fence.h>               // Arducopter Fence library
#include <SITL.h>                   // software in the loop support
#include <AP_Scheduler.h>           // main loop scheduler
#include <AP_RCMapper.h>            // RC input mapping library
#include <AP_Notify.h>              // Notify library
#include <AP_BattMonitor.h>         // Battery monitor library
#include <AP_BoardConfig.h>         // board configuration library
```

```
#include <AP_Frsky_Telem.h>
#if SPRAYER == ENABLED
#include <AC_Sprayer.h>              // crop sprayer library
#endif
#if EPM_ENABLED == ENABLED
#include <AP_EPM.h>                  // EPM cargo gripper stuff
#endif
#if PARACHUTE == ENABLED
#include <AP_Parachute.h>            // Parachute release library
#endif
#include <AP_LandingGear.h>          // Landing Gear library
#include <AP_Terrain.h>
#include <LowPassFilter2p.h>
// AP_HAL to Arduino compatibility layer
#include "compat.h"
// Configuration
#include "defines.h"
#include "config.h"
#include "config_channels.h"

// lines referring to the times of the pixhawk autopilot, which
// works at 400mhz or 0.0025seconds or 2500 microseconds

# define MAIN_LOOP_RATE    400
# define MAIN_LOOP_SECONDS 0.0025f
# define MAIN_LOOP_MICROS  2500

// statements referring to the autopilot objects, for example,
// gps-type objects barometer, compass, DataFlash, etc., all of
// them will subsequently be invoked in the corresponding code
```

```
const AP_HAL::HAL& hal = AP_HAL_BOARD_DRIVER;
static AP_Scheduler scheduler;

static AP_GPS  gps;
static AP_Baro barometer;
static AP_InertialSensor ins;
static RangeFinder sonar;
static Compass compass;
static AP_SerialManager serial_manager;
static ToshibaLED_PX4 toshiba_led;
static AP_BattMonitor battery;

//Data, BE CAREFUL, WHEN YOU READ THE SD SECTION DELETE THIS
//BLOCK THERE
// you will learn how to use and external module and deep
// details about these declarations

#define  LOG_MSG          0x01
#if CONFIG_HAL_BOARD == HAL_BOARD_PX4
static DataFlash_File DataFlash("/fs/microsd/APM/LOGS");
#endif

struct PACKED log_Datos{
    LOG_PACKET_HEADER;
    uint32_t  time_ms;
    float  a_roll;
    float  a_pitch;
    float  a_yaw;
    float  pos_x;
    float  pos_y;
    float  pos_z;
};
```

```
static const struct LogStructure log_structure[] PROGMEM = {
        LOG_COMMON_STRUCTURES,
        {LOG_MSG, sizeof(log_Datos),
        "1", "Iffffff", "T_MS,ROLL,PITCH,YAW,X_POS,Y_POS,
        Z_POS"},
};

static uint16_t log_num;    //Dataflash

// Inertial Navigation EKF

#if AP_AHRS_NAVEKF_AVAILABLE
AP_AHRS_NavEKF ahrs(ins, barometer, gps, sonar);
#else
AP_AHRS_DCM ahrs(ins, barometer, gps);
#endif

static AP_InertialNav_NavEKF inertial_nav(ahrs);

// place your code here //

// paste the setup here //
void setup()
{
    ins.init(AP_InertialSensor::COLD_START,AP_InertialSensor::
    RATE_400HZ);
    serial_manager.init_console();
    serial_manager.init();
    compass.init();
    compass.read();
    ahrs.set_compass(&compass);
    gps.init(NULL,serial_manager);
    barometer.init();
    barometer.calibrate();
```

```
    DataFlash.Init(log_structure, sizeof(log_structure)/
    sizeof(log_structure[0]));
        if (DataFlash.NeedErase()) {
            DataFlash.EraseAll();
            }
    log_num = DataFlash.StartNewLog();
    hal.scheduler->delay(100);
}

void loop(void)
{

    hal.console->printf("Hello %d\n",hal.scheduler->micros());
    hal.scheduler->delay(50);
}

AP_HAL_MAIN();
```

APPENDIX 5

Helpful Keywords

The following is a list of thematic keywords. Feel free to use them in order to search for more information in your web browser.

- Quadrotor, quadcopter, aircraft
- Hover-altitude, attitude-orientation, steering
- Real time, OOP, modular programming, scheduler
- Euler angles, roll, pitch, yaw, quasi-velocities
- Linear systems, linearization, non-linear systems
- Autopilot, companion computer/development board
- SDK/software development kit, GUI/graphic user interface
- Data types
- PWM/pulse width modulation, PPM/pulse position modulation, RC
- Duty cycle
- BLDC/brushless DC, BDC/brushed DC, DC
- ESC/electronic speed control, BEC/battery elimination circuit, power module

© Julio Alberto Mendoza-Mendoza, Victor Gonzalez-Villela 2020
J. A. Mendoza-Mendoza et al., *Advanced Robotic Vehicles Programming*,
https://doi.org/10.1007/978-1-4842-5531-5

- Propeller, frame

- Checksum, buffer, GPIO/general purpose input output

- Allocation matrix, thrust vectoring, tethered drone

APPENDIX 6

Installing ArduPilot Libraries

There are various ways to install the libraries depending on the operating system, the computer platform, and the code editor used. However, this appendix presents a brief installation description based on Windows 7, Vista, and 10 32/64-bit operating systems using the preloaded Eclipse interface (if this interface is already available on your computer, additional changes may be necessary).

Since we are working with open source technologies, it is very common to deal with changes without prior notice, which may even affect the installation mode. Although a set of all the necessary programs is provided with this book (all of them are open source and free), it is advisable to be aware of the important changes if you want to update versions. You should also visit the corresponding forums.

We remind you that the maximum scope of this book is to disseminate knowledge related to these technologies and it is not intended to go beyond any personal project. Any doubt in this regard, refer to web forums.

"Generic" Procedure

1. Install the driver.

2. Download the libraries.

© Julio Alberto Mendoza-Mendoza, Victor Gonzalez-Villela 2020
J. A. Mendoza-Mendoza et al., *Advanced Robotic Vehicles Programming*,
https://doi.org/10.1007/978-1-4842-5531-5

3. Download the compiler.

4. Compile the libraries.

5. Customize the code editing interface.

6. Program custom code.

7. Compile and test it.

Installation requirements: Windows Vista or superior operating system at 32- or 64-bit, 4GB of RAM for the execution of the development interface, and USB 2.0 ports for using the Pixhawk.

Installation Procedure

1. Download all the software: libraries, drivers, compiler, Mission Planner, and instructions. See Figure A6-1.

Figure A6-1. *Provided software*

2. Without modifying anything, place the `GitH` folder inside the following address, verifying that there are no accents, spaces, or special characters in the name of the folder: `C:\Users\UserName\Documents`

   For example, this will work:

   `C:\Users\Fonseca\Documents`

And this will not work because of the accent:

`C:\Users\León\Documents`

3. Once the `GitH` folder has been copied, make sure that the directory's name is made up of 50 characters counting from "C:" to the "ardupilot" folder.

    For example, this will work because it has 41 characters:

    `C:\Users\Fonseca\Documents\GitH\ardupilot`

    And this will not work because it has 51:

    `C:\Users\FonsecaMendezMend\Documents\GitH\`
    `ardupilot`

    To make it functional, it is possible to reduce the GitHub folder's name (it is only possible to modify this folder; altering the others will affect the user's computer):

    `C:\Users\FonsecaMendezMend\Documents\Gi\`
    `ardupilot`

    Now it has 49 characters and therefore it is useful.

    Note that if you have more than 50 characters or spaces, or if you have accents or symbols, you can still install these libraries by creating a new administrator user account which will comply with the above requirements. Before this, you must ensure that you have removed all of the installation folders from your actual user account.

4. Install the Pixhawk drivers; see Figure A6-2.

Figure A6-2. *Autopilot drivers*

5. Click the OK, Next, Accept, or Install buttons in the auxiliary windows that appear; see Figure A6-3.

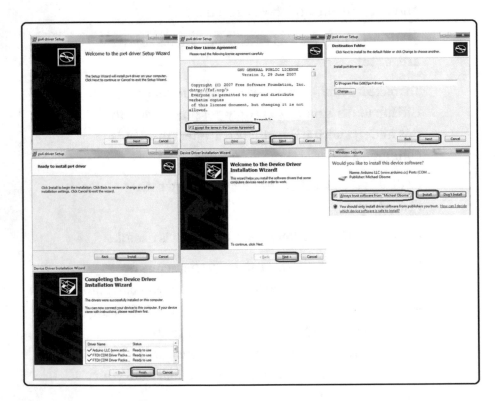

Figure A6-3. *Driver installation, step 1*

6. When this window appears, it's an indicator that the drivers were correctly installed. Click Finish and close it; see Figure A6-4.

Figure A6-4. *Driver installation, step 2*

7. Install the toolchain, which is the software that contains the libraries' compiler and the development interface (an Eclipse version).

8. Before installing it, verify that the ardupilot folder created in step 1 exists; see Figure A6-5.

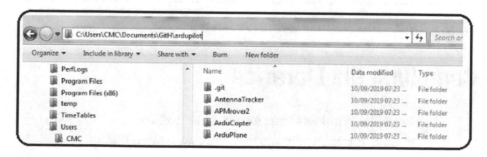

Figure A6-5. *Toolchain installation, step 1*

9.   Run the toolchain; see Figure A6-6.

Figure A6-6.   *Toolchain installation, step 2*

10.   Click the OK, Next, Accept, and Install buttons in the windows that appear; see Figure A6-7.

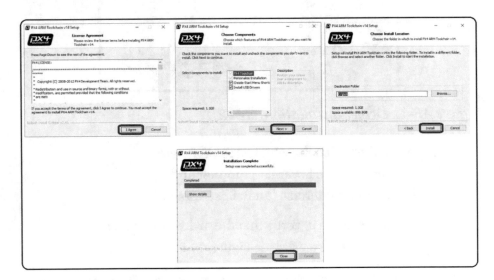

Figure A6-7.   *Toolchain installation, step 3*

Compiling the Libraries

1.   From the Windows Start menu, type "px". You should automatically see the program named PX4 Console. Run it. See Figure A6-8.

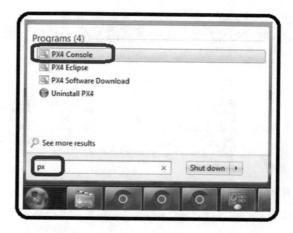

Figure A6-8. *Compilation process, step 1*

2.   When executing it, the auxiliary screen shown in
     Figure A6-9 should appear (note that the colors were
     inverted for presentation purposes of this book).

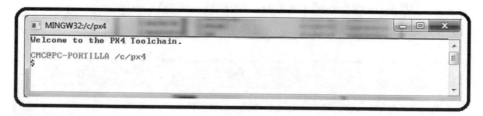

Figure A6-9. *Compilation process, step 2*

3.   Move to your ArduCopter folder using the linux-kind
     commands cd and ls; see Figure A6-10.

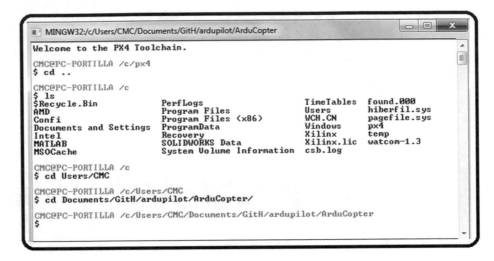

Figure A6-10. *Compilation process, step 3*

4.   Once there, execute the make px4-v2 command, which will compile the libraries to be used in the Pixhawk's fmuv2 family including cloned versions; see Figure A6-11.

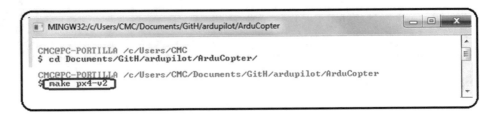

Figure A6-11. *Compilation process, step 4*

5.   With some time and patience, if the compilation was successful, the following message should automatically appear: "PX4 ArduCopter firmware is in ArduCopter-v2.px4." Close the window with the exit command or by pressing the X button; see Figure A6-12.

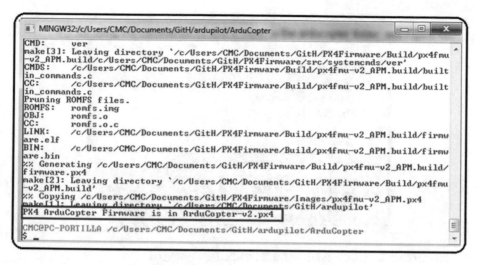

Figure A6-12. Compilation process, step 5

A frequent error during this procedure is the message indicating that the Arducopter.pde file is not found. The way to solve it is to search via Windows Explorer in the directory where it is compiling for a file with a similar name, such as arducopter.pde. Rename it so that it matches in upper and lower cases with the name the error indicates and repeat the process from the make px4-v2 command.

Interface Customization and Recompilation from the Preloaded Version of the Eclipse Editor

1.   From the Windows Start menu, type "px". The program named PX4 Eclipse should automatically appear. Run it. See Figure A6-13.

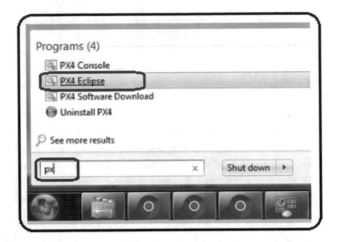

Figure A6-13. *Code editor customization, step 1*

2.   Click the OK button in the next window. It may take a while to appear. See Figure A6-14.

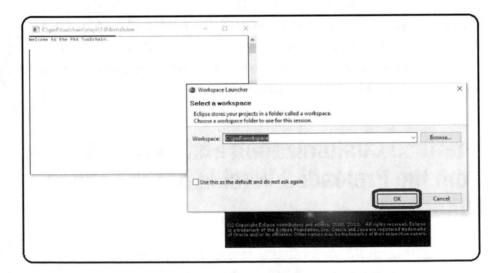

Figure A6-14. *Code editor customization, step 2*

A second frequent problem that occurs during this procedure appears when the OK button is pressed. If a warning message is displayed or the window is closed automatically, it means that a JAVA development package update is necessary. It is called `jdk-8u111-windows-i586.exe`. In this case, we must be careful given that it is a third-party dependency, so we only provide the full name of the file as a reference.

Once the update is installed, repeat the process from step 1 (this update's download address and its license type is in the section "Licenses" at the beginning of this book).

3. If there is no error, the screen in Figure A6-15 will appear. Close it by clicking the X in the Welcome tab.

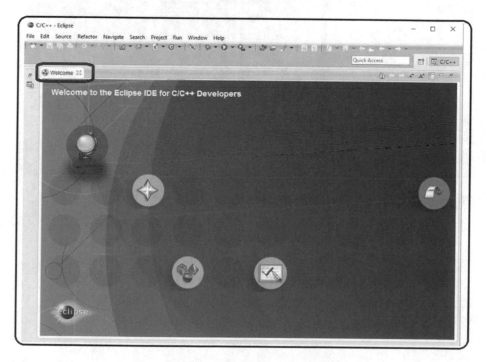

Figure A6-15. *Code editor customization, step 3*

4. Modify the preferences to have spaces instead of tabulations. Some programming languages use tabulations, but the ArduPilot libraries use spaces, so see Figure A6-16. Here is the path: Window ➤ Preferences ➤ General ➤ Editors ➤ Text Editors ➤ Insert spaces for tabs ➤ Apply ➤ OK.

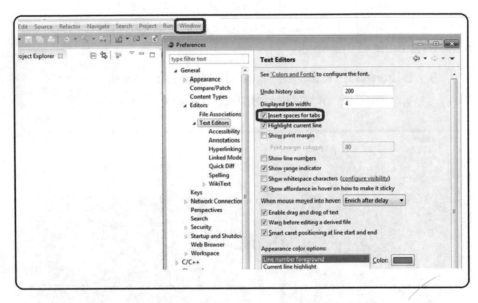

Figure A6-16. *Code editor customization, step 4*

5. Modify the preferences so that the code style uses spaces instead of indentation. See Figure A6-17. Here is the path: Window ➤ Preferences ➤ C/C++ ➤ Code Style ➤ Formatter ➤ New ➤ Write "K&R Tab" ➤ Change "Indentation" set to "Spaces only" ➤ Apply ➤ OK.

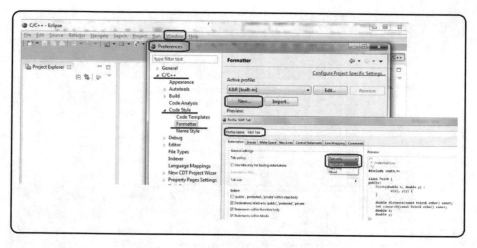

Figure A6-17. *Code editor customization, step 5*

6. Associate files with a `.pde` extension to C++ source
   code (many of the source files of ArduPilot libraries
   have a `.pde` extension). See Figure A6-18. Here is the
   path: Windows ➤ Preferences ➤ C/C++ ➤ File Types
   ➤ New ➤ Write "*.pde" ➤ Change the Type to C++
   Source File ➤ OK ➤ OK.

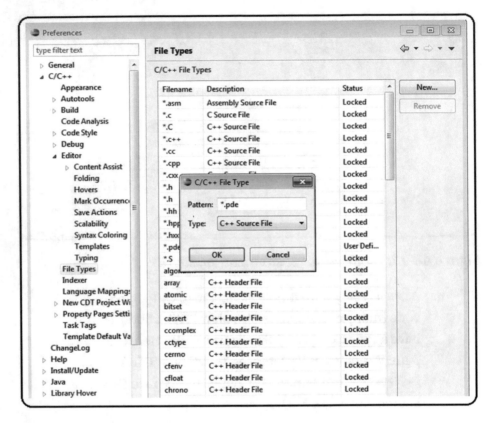

Figure A6-18. *Code editor customization, step 6*

7. Load the ArduCopter project. See Figure A6-19. Here is the path: File ➤ New ➤ Makefile Project with Existing Code.

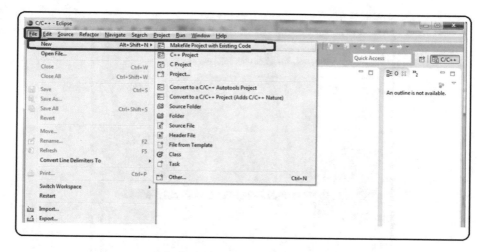

Figure A6-19. *Code editor customization, step 7*

8. In the auxiliary window that appears next, select the C and C ++ language checkboxes. Search for the ArduCopter folder; if you select correctly, the ArduCopter project will appear automatically (note that the main project shares the name with the folder). Select the Cross GCC option and click the Finish button. See Figure A6-20.

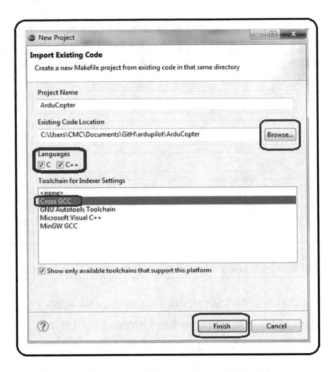

Figure A6-20. *Code editor customization, step 8*

9. In the project explorer, the ArduCopter project and all
    the auxiliary files will be loaded. Search for the main
    file called ArduCopter.pde. Open it and look for a
    green button on the right side named Make (under a
    sign that reads Quick Access); see Figure A6-21.

Figure A6-21. *Code editor customization, step 9*

10. When pressing the green button called Make, it should show the ArduCopter project folder. Right-click that folder. You should see another green button that says New. Click it. See Figure A6-22.

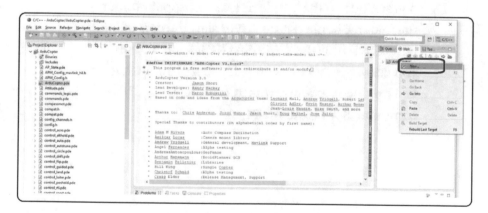

Figure A6-22. *Code editor customization, step 10*

11. An auxiliary window will appear. Type "px4-v2" and then click the OK button. See Figure A6-23.

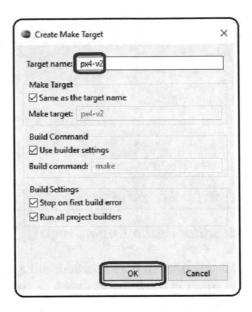

Figure A6-23. *Code editor customization, step 11*

12. A green button that reads px4-v2 will appear under
    the folder. Double left-click it to start the compilation.
    NEVER STOP THE COMPILATION. Even though
    you know the code is wrong, if you try to stop it, it
    will produce general errors in the operation of the
    computer. See Figure A6-24.

Figure A6-24. *Code editor customization, step 12*

13.   In the lower menu, change to the Console section
      and ignore the problems section. If everything was
      done correctly, after a considerable compilation
      time, the message "Firmware is in ArduCopter-v2.
      px4" should appear in the Console menu followed
      by the exact date and time of completion and the
      message "Build Finished." See Figure A6-25.

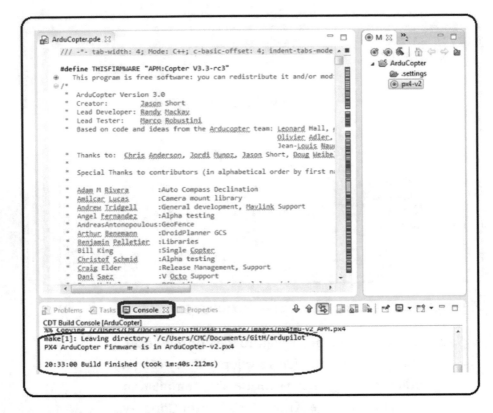

Figure A6-25. *Code editor customization, step 13*

14. Check in the ArduCopter folder that the
ArduCopter-v2.px4 file exists and that its
modification date is exactly as indicated in the
previous point. The files with the .px4 extension are
the ones that will be uploaded into the autopilot.
See Figure A6-26.

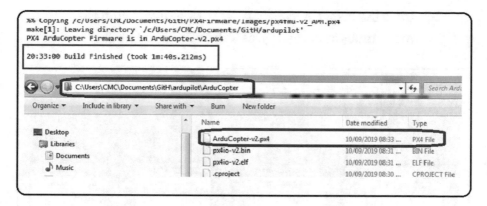

Figure A6-26. *Code editor customization, step 14*

15. In the ardupilot folder is a directory called hellodrone. Load the project and try to compile it. Then repeat the process of creating a new project as stated in the "Making New Projects by Using Eclipse" section. Try this with one of the examples of code previously shown (the projects about terminal writing or reading are a good starting point).

Uploading * .px4 Files to the Autopilot

1. Install Mission Planner. See Figure A6-27.

Name	Date modified	Type
GitH	10/09/2019 07:08 ...	File folder
install_toolchain_eclipse	10/09/2019 07:20 ...	File folder
MissionPlanner-latest	06/03/2016 12:14 a...	Windows Installer ...
px4_toolchain_installer_v14_win...	22/06/2016 04:37 ...	Application
px4driver	17/06/2016 09:32 a...	Windows Installer ...

Figure A6-27. *Uploading code to the autopilot, step 1*

2. Click the Install, Accept, Ok, Next, or Finish buttons as
    many times as necessary, as shown in Figure A6-28.

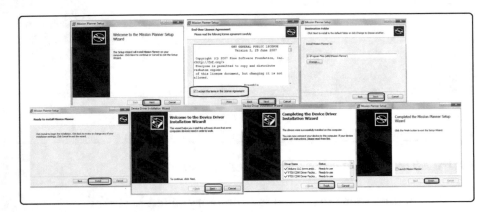

Figure A6-28. *Uploading code to the autopilot, step 2*

From this moment on, NEVER PRESS THE CONNECT BUTTON during
sequence of steps. See Figure A6-29.

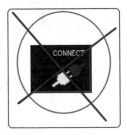

Figure A6-29. *Uploading code to the autopilot warning*

3. Open Mission Planner, discard all messages about
    new updates, and go to the Initial Setup tab. Search
    for the Install Firmware tab. If an unexpected error
    message appears, just ignore it. See Figure A6-30.

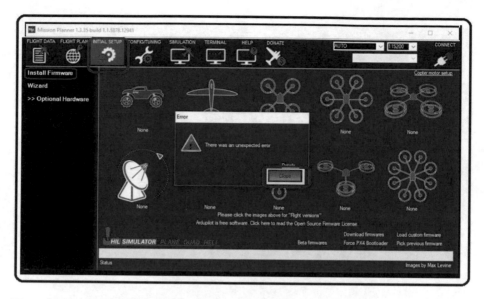

Figure A6-30. *Uploading code to the autopilot, step 3*

4. Connect the autopilot to the computer and look
    for it in the drop-down list where the AUTO tag
    is labeled; it usually comes up as a COM PX4
    FMU. Once you have found it, select your device.
    Remember: NEVER PRESS THE CONNECT
    BUTTON. Now, look for the Load custom firmware
    button. If it does not appear, try to install previous
    or recent Mission Planner versions until this button
    is enabled. This button is essential to load custom
    software. See Figure A6-31.

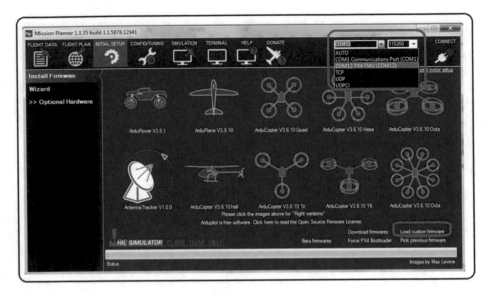

Figure A6-31. *Uploading code to the autopilot, step 4*

5. When the Load custom firmware button is there, click
    it. An auxiliary box will appear; in it you must indicate
    the location of the *.px4 file to be uploaded into the
    autopilot. Select it, click the Open button, and follow
    the instructions on the screen. See Figure A6-32.

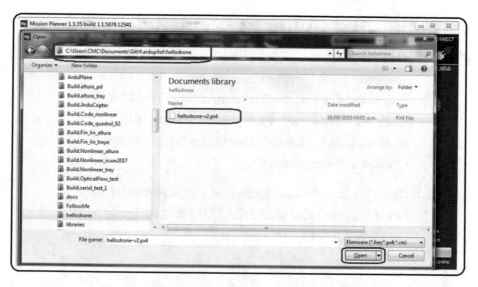

Figure A6-32. *Uploading code to the autopilot, step 5*

6. If the upload was successful, a message indicating not to disconnect until you hear the buzzer will be displayed. Click the OK button. Now the autopilot can be disconnected and used. Mission Planner can be closed also. See Figure A6-33.

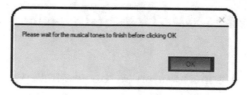

Figure A6-33. *Uploading code to the autopilot, step 6*

Terminal Test of the Previously Loaded Program

1. Reconnect the Pixhawk, remembering the address assigned in step 4 above. If you don't know this address, look for it in devices and printers, or in the Windows device manager.

2. Open the terminal program that you prefer (we use Terminal.exe) and select the COM port assigned to the Pixhawk autopilot. See Figure A6-34.

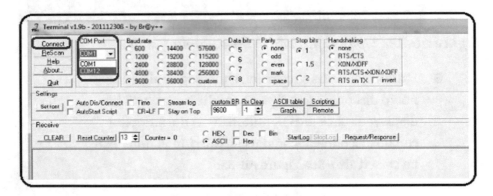

Figure A6-34. *Testing code with a serial terminal, generic procedure Step 2*

3. Press the Connect button on the terminal. As you can see, all the information displayed in your program by using the command hal. console-> printf () is shown. NEVER UNPLUG THE PIXHAWK WITHOUT PRESSING THE DISCONNECT BUTTON. See Figure A6-35.

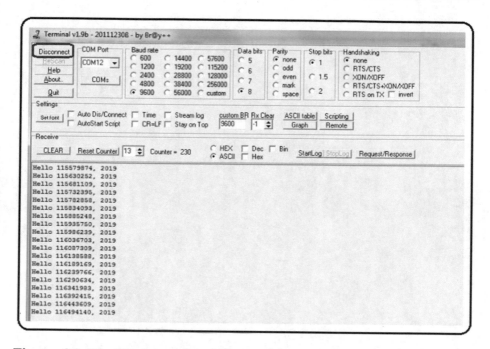

Figure A6-35. *Testing code with a serial terminal, generic procedure step 3*

References and Suggested Websites

Website about the different types of installation of the ArduPilot libraries:
http://ardupilot.org/dev/docs/building-the-code.html

Websites about the type of installation seen specifically in this appendix:

http://ardupilot.org/dev/docs/building-setup-windows.
html#building-setup-windows

http://ardupilot.org/dev/docs/building-px4-with-make.
html#building-px4-with-make

http://ardupilot.org/dev/docs/editing-the-code-with-eclipse.
html#editing-the-code-with-eclipse

APPENDIX 7

Thrust Vectoring

By controlling each one of the vehicle engines including the auxiliary servos, the ArduPilot libraries and Pixhawk autopilot become a team of great features. One of these features is the feasibility of designing unusual or non-existent systems. For this, two concepts are presented: thrust vectoring and omnidirectionality.

Thrust vectoring is the ability to regulate a motor's main thrust direction. This is achieved through several methods; see Figure A7-1.

1. **With flaps**: This method has been used for decades by airplanes, ships, and cars. It uses one or more fixed main engines, and flaps are used to deflect the airflow (they are usually placed on the wings or the tail). Once the main flow has been redirected, the aircraft can change its flight direction.

2. **With direct movement of the motor**: This method is feasible in toy airplanes since it involves directly moving a full motor, which is already rotating at high speeds, and moving an object that is rotating at high speeds entails a lot of force by the servos that move this engine (due to gyroscopic effects). It has also been used in boats for several decades, where the pilot moves a helm or rudder that deflects the direction where the main engine pushes the boat.

© Julio Alberto Mendoza-Mendoza, Victor Gonzalez-Villela 2020
J. A. Mendoza-Mendoza et al., *Advanced Robotic Vehicles Programming*,
https://doi.org/10.1007/978-1-4842-5531-5

3. **With direct movement of the propeller's blades**: This is a very useful method in large aircraft such as helicopters. It allows deflecting the aircraft without moving the main rotor—just by moving the blade's orientation by means of cyclic or collective plates or swashplates.

4. **With pneumatic and vacuum methods**: This is a similar idea to the use of flaps, but instead uses tubes that blow air, liquid, or generate a vacuum to divert the main airflow thrusted by the propellers.

5. **With variations on the effect of multiple engines**: This is how quadcopter drones work. All engines have a fixed position and direction of rotation in a rigid body, and the movement of the body in different directions is achieved by selectively varying each engine's speed.

6. **With movement of a built-in mass**: In this case, a "massive" object placed in the vehicle's center of gravity is used. If a direction change is wanted, that mass is moved, and the vehicle is forced to move in the direction where this mass has been placed. This example has been employed for decades with roller skates, kayaks, and motorcycles, where the drivers, in order to change vehicle's direction, must tilt their body toward the side where they want to move.

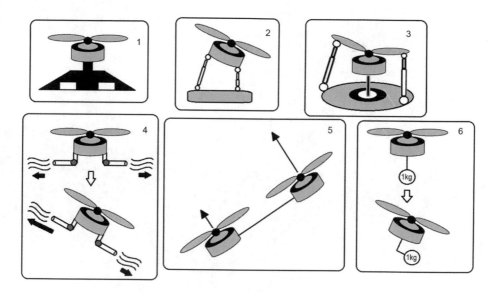

Figure A7-1. *Thrust vectoring methods*

APPENDIX 8

Omnidirectionality

It is possible to introduce the concept of omnidirectionality by using one of the vectorization methods previously explained. It basically provides a vehicle with total mobility or the ability to achieve the reached position regardless of orientation.

For example, a standard quadcopter cannot tilt and stay floating at the same time because when it tilts, it tends to move in the direction it has been tilted.

But if a standard quadcopter (or underwater vehicle) is fitted with extra motors different to its planar configuration (like individual vectorizers for each motor), you can get a system that floats at any point in space with variable and independent orientation (maybe full movement, maybe restricted). See Figure A8-1.

© Julio Alberto Mendoza-Mendoza, Victor Gonzalez-Villela 2020
J. A. Mendoza-Mendoza et al., *Advanced Robotic Vehicles Programming*,
https://doi.org/10.1007/978-1-4842-5531-5

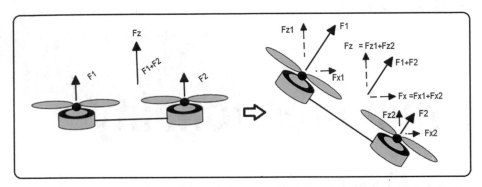

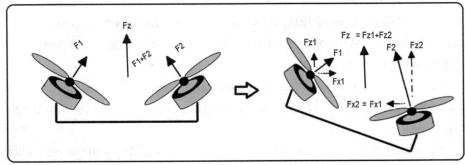

Figure A8-1. _How to obtain omnidirectionality_

Note that the control of this kind of vehicle is no longer as trivial as the one presented here for the quadcopter, and you must read about geometric methods of acrobatic or aggressive maneuvers.

In summary, the omnidirectionality is highly feasible with the ArduPilot libraries and Pixhawk autopilot, but it requires greater immersion in mathematical theory.

References and Suggested Websites

Articles on the different types of vectorization:

J. Pascoa, A. Dumas, M. Trancossi, P. Stewart, D. Vucinic. "A review of thrust-vectoring in support of a v/stol non-moving mechanical propulsion system." _Open Engineering_, 3(3):374–388, 2013.

C. Bermes, S. Leutenegger, S. Bouabdallah, D. Schafroth, R. Siegwart. "New design of the steering mechanism for a mini coaxial helicopter." In *Intelligent Robots and Systems, 2008. IROS 2008. IEEE/RSJ International Conference on*, pages 1236–1241. IEEE, 2008.

J. Paulos, M. Yim. "Cyclic blade pitch control for small uav without a swashplate." In *AIAA Atmospheric Flight Mechanics Conference*, page 1186, 2017.

X. Yuan, J. Zhu. "Inverse dynamic modeling and analysis of a coaxial helicopters swashplate mechanism." *Mechanism and Machine Theory*, 113:208–230, 2017.

Articles on omnidirectional aircraft:

D. Brescianini, R. D'Andrea. "Design, modeling and control of an omni-directional aerial vehicle." In *Robotics and Automation (ICRA), 2016 IEEE International Conference on*, pages 3261–3266. IEEE, 2016.

M. Tognon, A. Franchi. "Omnidirectional aerial vehicles with unidirectional thrusters: Theory, optimal design, and control." *IEEE Robotics and Automation Letters*, 3(3):2277–2282, 2018.

A. Nikou, G. C. Gavridis, K. J. Kyriakopoulos. "Mechanical design, modelling and control of a novel aerial manipulator." In *Robotics and Automation (ICRA), 2015 IEEE International Conference on*, pages 4698–4703. IEEE, 2015.

Application of vectorization and omnidirectionality in aerial robotic manipulators:

J. Mendoza-Mendoza, G. Sepulveda-Cervantes, C. Aguilar-Ibanez, M. Mendez, M. Reyes-Larios, P. Matabuena, J. Gonzalez-Avila. "Air-arm: A new kind of flying manipulator." In *Research, Education and Development of Unmanned Aerial Systems (RED-UAS), 2015 Workshop on*, pages 278–287. IEEE, 2015.

www.inrol.snu.ac.kr/

S. Park, J. Her, J. Kim, D. Lee. "Design, modeling and control of omni-directional aerial robot." In *Intelligent Robots and Systems (IROS), 2016 IEEE/RSJ International Conference on*, pages 1570–1575. IEEE, 2016.

413

M. Zhao, T. Anzai, F. Shi, X. Chen, K. Okada, M. Inaba. "Design, modeling, and control of an aerial robot dragon: A dual-rotor-embedded multilink robot with the ability of multi-degreeof-freedom aerial transformation." *IEEE Robotics and Automation Letters*, 3(2):1176–1183, 2018.

www.jsk.t.u-tokyo.ac.jp/~chou/

D. Mellinger, M. Shomin, N. Michael, V. Kumar. "Cooperative grasping and transport using multiple quadrotors." In *Distributed autonomous robotic systems*, pages 545–558. Springer, 2013.

Control methods employed with omnidirectional vehicles:

T. Lee. "Geometric controls for a tethered quadrotor uav." In *Decision and Control (CDC), 2015 IEEE 54th Annual Conference on*, pages 2749–2754. IEEE, 2015.

D. Lee, C. Ha, Z. Zuo. "Backstepping control of quadrotor-type uavs and its application to teleoperation over the internet." In *Intelligent Autonomous Systems 12*, pages 217–225. Springer, 2013.

D. Mellinger, N. Michael, V. Kumar. "Trajectory generation and control for precise aggressive maneuvers with quadrotors." *The International Journal of Robotics Research*, 31(5):664–674, 2012.

H. Abaunza, P. Castillo, A. Victorino, R. Lozano. "Dual quaternion modeling and control of a quad-rotor aerial manipulator." *Journal of Intelligent & Robotic Systems*, pages 1–17, 2017.

APPENDIX 9

Extended Power Methods

As a curious reader, you will have already realized that these vehicles consume a large amount of energy. A single basic brushless motor consumes 12V and 10A on average. This implies using high current energy sources and a power of at least 500 watts. Although LIPO batteries provide these characteristics and portability, they only last between 10 and 30 minutes of flight in average vehicles. In order to satisfy this level of power consumption, there are only three extended energy methods available in the market:

- **Internal combustion**: In this case, motors called glow-engines are used in aeromodelling. However, their application in multicopters is hard and it is only a matter of recent research.

- **Solar energy**: The area that a solar cell must occupy is only viable in fixed-wing aircraft. Research into small size, rotating-wing aircraft and multicopter vehicles is just being developed.

- **Direct electrical connection**: This is a viable way as long as you have the drone operating with an umbilical cord anchored to the ground or to a car. In this case, a ground source provides the necessary power to

© Julio Alberto Mendoza-Mendoza, Victor Gonzalez-Villela 2020
J. A. Mendoza-Mendoza et al., *Advanced Robotic Vehicles Programming*,
https://doi.org/10.1007/978-1-4842-5531-5

the vehicle through a series of transformers. It is an interesting option because the operating power allows for a very thin cable operating with high voltage and low current to be then converted to low voltage and high current, thus achieving mobility independence up to 500 meters. This method is widespread and you can find more about it by Googling "tethered drone" or "tethered vehicle." See Figure A9-1.

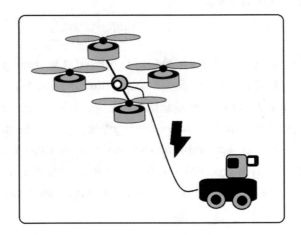

Figure A9-1. *Tethered vehicle*

References and Suggested Websites

Morus project NATO: `www.fer.unizg.hr/morus`

A small discussion of the known energy sources for a drone: `www.techinasia.com/talk/6-known-ways-power-a-drone`

Thesis and articles about the control of internal combustion engines applied to unmanned aerial vehicles: Paul D. Fjare. "Feedback speed control of a small two-stroke internal combustion engine that propels an unmanned aerial vehicle." Master's thesis, University of Nevada, 2014.

Tomislav Haus, Marko Car, Matko Orsag, Stjepan Bogdan. "Identification results of an internal combustion engine as a quadrotor propulsion system, Control and Automation (MED)." *2017 25th Mediterranean Conference on, IEEE, 2017*, pp. 713–718.

Solar drone article: M. Hasan Shaheed, Aly Abidali, Jibran Ahmed, Shakir Ahmed, Irmantas Burba, Pourshid Jan Fani, George Kwofie, Kazimierz Wojewoda, Antonio Munjiza. "Flying by the sun only: The solarcopter prototype." *Aerospace Science and Technology 45* (2015), 209–214.

Articles on "tethered" drones or drones with specialized electrical extensions:

Beom W. Gu, Su Y. Choi, Young Soo Choi, Guowei Cai, Lakmal Seneviratne, Chun T. Rim. "Novel roaming and stationary tethered aerial robots for continuous mobile missions in nuclear power plants." *Nuclear Engineering and Technology 48* (2016), no. 4, 982–996.

Christos Papachristos, Anthony Tzes. "The power-tethered uav-ugv team: A collaborative strategy for navigation in partially-mapped environments, Control and Automation (MED)." *2014 22nd Mediterranean Conference of, IEEE, 2014*, pp. 1153–1158.

Tethered units for sale: search keywords "tethered drone"
http://sph-engineering.com/airmast
http://elistair.com

Future wireless power of drones and other vehicles as well as a state of the art on current energy technologies: Chun T. Rim, Chris Mi. *Wireless Power Transfer for Electric Vehicles and Mobile Devices*, John Wiley & Sons, 2017.

Compact and robust converters useful for tethered vehicles design:
www.vicorpower.com/

APPENDIX 10

Summary of the Design of a Quadcopter

The design process of a multicopter is illustrated as a flow diagram. This contemplates three aspects that are considered standard and frequent in the design process: the body or vehicle, the brain or autopilot, and the external control or radio control selection. Notice that the selection of sensors has been omitted as it is a very variable task among end users. For example, some users will want cameras, some will prefer LIDARs, ultrasounds, etc. For more information in this regard, consult this appendix's bibliography.

Vehicle Design

The vehicle design is shown in Figure A10-1.

J. A. Mendoza-Mendoza et al., *Advanced Robotic Vehicles Programming*,
https://doi.org/10.1007/978-1-4842-5531-5

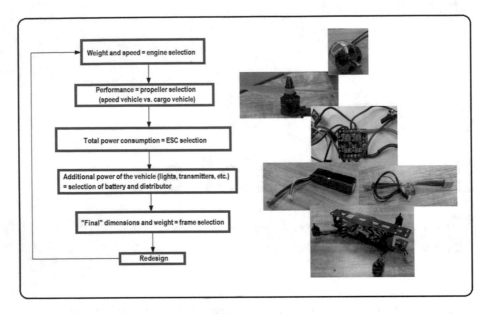

Figure A10-1. *Multicopter vehicle design*

1. **Weight to move + maximum flight speed**: This point concerns motor selection.

2. **Performance of flight (Is it more of an agile, a cargo, or mixed type of vehicle?)**: The answer indicates the selection of propellers.

3. **Motor and propellers power consumption**: This implies a selection of ESCs and BECs.

4. **Total power consumption = ESCs consumption + the rest of the drone (radios, stabilizers, cameras etc)**: This concerns battery selection.

5. **Total dimensions based on the selection of the previous equipment**: This is related to frame selection.

6. A full design means you're ready to build.

Otherwise, a redesign means going back to step 1.

Autopilot Selection

The autopilot selection is shown in Figure A10-2.

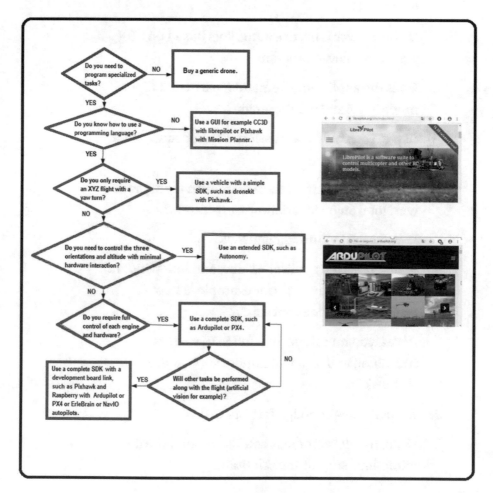

Figure A10-2. *Multicopter autopilot selection*

1. Can the required application be done with manual operations? Remember that the GUI has a very robust control, while the SDK allows the reader to operate with the least detail possible but the control and its robustness will be designed by the user.

   IF the answer is yes, use autopilots based on GUI type CC3D.

   IF the answer is no, use autopilots based on SDKs, if you know how to program.

2. Does the application demand a particular flight mode X Y Z and turning angle?

   IF yes, you could use Mission Planner scripts or a simplified SDK.

3. IF no, does the application demand a flight mode with total angular variation and altitude?

   IF yes, look for an extended SDK.

4. IF not, does the application demand independent control of each engine (for example, a new prototype that does not exist)?

   IF yes, you must look for a full SDK such as ArduPilot, and a good autopilot such as the Pixhawk.

5. Is the Pixhawk enough for your task?

   IF no, use development boards combined with autopilots, such as the ErleBrain.

Selection of the Remote Control

Figure A10-3 shows the selection of the remote control.

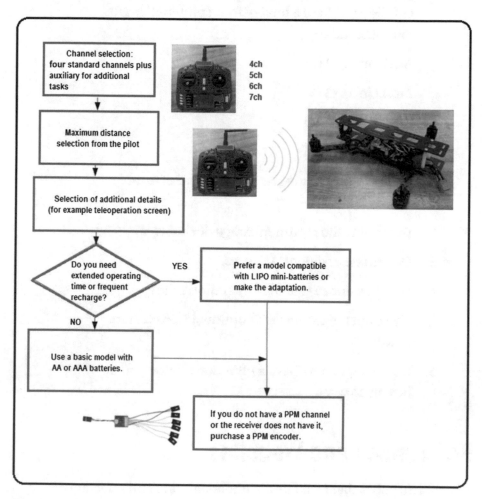

Figure A10-3. *Remote control selection*

1. How many tasks are required in addition to the four basic movements? For example, a six-channel radio where the two additional channels are levers of type ON/OFF will have a total of four combinations for four other tasks:

   Aux1 On Aux2 On

   Aux1 On Aux2 Off

   Aux1 Off Aux2 On

   Aux1 Off Aux2 Off

   Result = four-channel radio + number of extra channels

2. Determine the maximum range distance.

3. Determine additional features.

4. Do you want an extended operation time?

   If yes, opt for a model with optional LIPO battery power.

5. Does your control have a PPM port? If not, you must buy an adapter.

References and Websites

Maker-style books that facilitate the understanding and selection of various components of a multicopter:

II Davis, Robert James. *Arduino Flying Projects: How to Build Multicopters, from 100mm to 550mm*, CreateSpace Independent Publishing Platform, 2017.

Terry Kilby, Belinda Kilby. *Getting Started with Drones: Build and Customize Your Own Quadcopter,* Maker Media, Inc., 2015.

Vasilis Tzivaras. *Building a Quadcopter with Arduino,* Packt Publishing Ltd, 2016.

A very complete article that deals with the process of designing, modeling, and controlling a multicopter from the scientific point of view: Hyunsoo Yang, Yongseok Lee, Sang-Yun Jeon, Dongjun Lee. "Multi-rotor drone tutorial: systems, mechanics, control and state estimation." *Intelligent Service Robotics 10,* 2017, no. 2, 79–93.

On the use of Python scripts in Mission Planner:

`http://ardupilot.org/planner/docs/using-python-scripts-in-mission-planner.html`

`https://github.com/ArduPilot/MissionPlanner/tree/master/Scripts`

About the SDK autonomy for the Parrot Bebop: `https://bebop-autonomy.readthedocs.io/en/latest/`

On the different platforms, prebuilt drones, and navigation cards supported by the ArduPilot libraries: `http://ardupilot.org/dev/docs/building-the-code.htm`

Alternative project Crazyflie: `www.bitcraze.io/getting-started-with-development/`

APPENDIX 11

Working with Header Files

You probably want to work with additional header files beyond those already included in the extended header (`defines.h`, `configs.h`, and `compat.h`). This is possible under the following restrictions. The distribution of ArduPilot libraries included with this book is limited for use with internal libraries (internal with respect to the project). This way, it is only possible to use internal header files (which are defined in the project folder). Also, these header files must contain declarations and definitions in a single file with the extension `.h` (not as in the common way found in many software projects where the declaration is indicated in an `.h` file and the definition in a `.c` or `.cpp` file).

Having said that, we recommend generating header files that contain very simple definitions, constants, or functions (port registers, control constants, communication speeds, etc.).

Any other way to use header files, such as using commands from external libraries other than ArduPilot, is left as your responsibility. This way, you can search in forums or verify through them if an improvement is available with recent versions or alternative versions of the ArduPilot libraries.

© Julio Alberto Mendoza-Mendoza, Victor Gonzalez-Villela 2020
J. A. Mendoza-Mendoza et al., *Advanced Robotic Vehicles Programming*,
https://doi.org/10.1007/978-1-4842-5531-5

ATTENTION: Do not attempt to invoke the extended header within a header file. For reasons of compilation with the distribution included with this book, Eclipse does not detect the extended header encoded within the header file. You must copy the extended header to the main file for each one of your projects.

Having indicated the characteristics and restrictions of these header files, the procedure to create them is as follows:

1.   In Eclipse, right-click the project folder, look for the New tab, and then search for and click the Header File. See Figure A11-1.

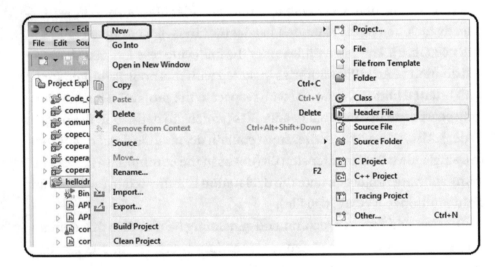

Figure A11-1. *Making header files, step 1*

2.   Next, you must assign a name with the extension .h; in this example, it's aloh.h. Then click the Finish button. See Figure A11-2.

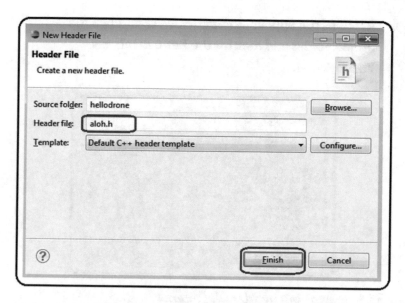

Figure A11-2. *Making header files, step 2*

3. Once created, it will appear automatically.
    Now open the file and edit it. See Figure A11-3.

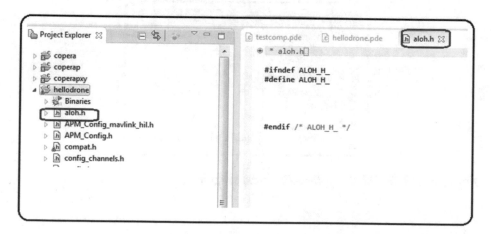

Figure A11-3. *Making header files, step 3*

4. If it does not appear automatically, right-click the project folder and look for the Refresh tab. See Figure A11-4.

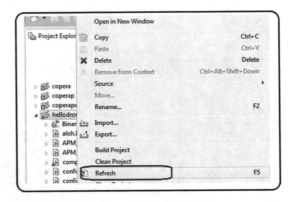

Figure A11-4. *Making header files, step 4*

5. Edit your header file with simple definitions or functions. See Figure A11-5.

```
#ifndef ALOH_H_
#define ALOH_H_

int addd(int a, int b)
{
    return a+b;
}

#endif /* ALOH_H_ */
```

Figure A11-5. *Making header files, step 5*

6. To use the definitions or functions coded in the
   header file, you must first indicate the header's
   name between quotation marks in the includes-
   section of the extended header. After that, the
   content of these definitions or functions can be used
   within the main code or in secondary modules. See
   Figure A11-6.

```
#include "config.h"
#include "config_channels.h"
#include "aloh.h"


void loop(void)
{
    int xx=addd(2,5);
    hal.console->printf("Hello %d, %d\n",xx,hal.scheduler->micros());
    hal.scheduler->delay(50);
}
```

Figure A11-6. *Making header files, step 6*

Index

A

ArduPilot elementary code,
    parts, 81, 82
Allocation matrix, 247, 249
    arm affects, components, 270
    control components, 269
    factors, 251
    geometrical explanation, 266
    yaw-dependant, 271
Antivibration mount, 65
Arduino's serial plotter, 199
Arduino's transmitter code, 173
ArduPilot-compatible motors, 212
ArduPilot libraries, 15
    coding and compiling, 23
    compatibilities and projects, 16
    display, 24
    error checking
        compilation process, 37–39
        error line, 42
        explicit error message, 42
        intentional error, 40, 41
        project, secondary
            files, 43, 44
    feedback, 24
    file extensions, 19, 20
    interface, 23

physical execution, 24
problems, 45
Program flow, 23
projects, 16
ArduPilot libraries employ
    objects, 75
ArduPilot libraries installation
    code editor customization
        ArduCopter.pde.
            file, 394, 395
        ArduCopter project, 392,
            393, 395
        ArduCopter-v2.px4
            file, 398, 399
        auxiliary window, 393, 394
        Console section, 397, 398
        C++ source file, 391, 392
        hellodrone, 399
        jdk-8u111-windows-i586.
            exe., 388, 389
        PX4 Eclipse, 387, 388
        spaces, 390, 391
        Welcome tab, 389
    compiling libraries
        auxiliary screen, 385
        Linux-kind commands cd
            and ls, 385, 386

© Julio Alberto Mendoza-Mendoza, Victor Gonzalez-Villela 2020
J. A. Mendoza-Mendoza et al., *Advanced Robotic Vehicles Programming*,
https://doi.org/10.1007/978-1-4842-5531-5

Printed in the United States
By Bookmasters